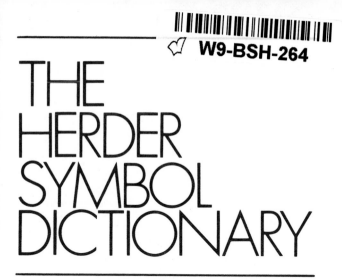

W9-BSH-264

THE HERDER SYMBOL DICTIONARY

Symbols from Art, Archaeology, Mythology, Literature, and Religion

Translated by
Boris Matthews

with over 1,000 entries
and 450 illustrations

CHIRON PUBLICATIONS • Wilmette, Illinois

First printing 1986
Second printing 1987
Third printing 1988

**Originally published in 1978 as *Herder
Lexikon: Symbole***
Copyright 1978, Herder Freiburg

Translation © 1986 by Chiron Publications
Library of Congress Catalog Card Number: 85-30872

Book design by Elaine M. Hill

Library of Congress Cataloging in Publication Data

Herder Lexikon. Symbole. English.
The Herder symbol dictionary.

Translation of: Herder Lexikon. Symbole.
1. Symbolism—Dictionaries.   I. Title.
CB475.H4713 1986   001.51   85-30872
ISBN 0-933029-03-9

Acknowledgments

This English translation of the Herder Lexikon *Symbole* was prepared by Boris Matthews, Ph.D.

For imposing editorial consistency on the dictionary and for researching seemingly endless minutiae, we are indebted to editors Deborah Farrell and Carole Presser.

Chiron Publications

Introduction

Every language functions as vehicle for and mediator of meanings. So, too, the language of symbols lives from the tension between reference and referent. But while linguistic units, as, for example, the word, are *assigned* to the object meant in each instance, the symbol *binds together* designator and designated as tightly as possible. At times—especially in the mythico-magical view of the world—this bond is so intense that it often approaches an identity. Consequently, numerous meanings that we experience only as symbols were originally understood immediately as statements about realities. The sun was not the symbol of divine sight but rather was itself a god; the snake was not an image of evil but was evil itself; the color red was not merely a symbol of life but was itself vital energy. The boundary between mythical or magical ideas and symbolic thought is, consequently, seldom to be drawn sharply.

A further peculiarity of the symbol as a vehicle of meaning is its strongly marked polyvalence, which can often go so far that explicitly antithetical meanings come together in one image. While we can often resolve or diminish the ambiguity of spoken or written linguistic signs by the addition of further signs and the observation of grammatical rules, sometimes we can translate the polyvalence of a symbol only very incompletely or only vaguely into a coherent description: The richness of the symbolic image remains ultimately untranslatable, reserved for inner contemplation.

These two difficulties confront whoever attempts to come to terms with symbols. Above and beyond this, the editors of the present volume found themselves faced in a special way with the problem of *selection*, since they had undertaken the challenge of presenting in a small space information on symbols from numerous cultures. By preference, symbols were included that are still familiar or close to Western European consciousness. In this, the concept of "symbol" was taken quite broadly; but, for reasons of space, it was not possible to discuss allegories and signs. Above all, it was the "old" symbolic ideas that were taken into account, those that have lived for peoples for thousands of years or are still alive. (Hence as a rule, the source is not mentioned each time as *ancient* China or *ancient* Egypt, but rather China, Egypt, etc.). Moreover, sometimes symbol-like, imagistic representations were included which, for example, live on in our consciousness as proverbs or colloquial expressions; also various superstitious speculations that are often indebted to symbolic thought were taken into account. Furthermore, imaginal interpretations of the world (e.g., cosmogonic or alchemical) make up a relatively wide area. On the other hand, mythological figures, such as figures of gods and heroes, were not included; exceptions are the various monsters or animal-human hybrids of antiquity (e.g., centaurs, chimerae, furies), which frequently play the role of symbol-like pictures in contemporary linguistic usage. With a few exceptions (e.g., the seasons) groups of symbols such as those referring to Mary, law, sexuality, and death were not included because of the abundance of material that would have had to have been dealt with and which would have exceeded the space available. Psychoanalytic interpretations of symbols were expressly mentioned only when their reference to depth-psychological thought is especially clear. It is, of course, fundamentally true that every symbolic meaning has psychoanalytic relevance.

With the aid of examples the reader will find in the present volume a survey of the abudance of types of human symbolic thinking and will simultaneously be stimulated to further exploration. We hope this book will help those of us who often may too easily dismiss symbols as preconceptually imprecise not only to consume the flood of images from the mass media but also to reactivate the remnants of our imagistic thinking which have atrophied in the course of development. For, indeed, while the symbol may never be as precise as the abstract word, it always directs us to ponder the great complexity of reality.

Abracadabra It is a magical word that appeared in late Greek writings and was probably related to ABRAXAS. It was used as an AMULET inscription, primarily to vanquish illness.

Abraham The biblical patriarch who was often thought of as a symbolic figure for the new race of humanity, he represents the man chosen by God and blessed with fulfilled promises (riches, progeny). He also symbolizes unconditional, obedient faith and unquestioning readiness to sacrifice. The "sacrifice" of his son Isaac has been interpreted as the symbolic precursor of Christ's passion. —Representations of *Abraham's bosom* symbolize the security of the faithful in God. Abraham, who in the New Testament is seen as one privileged in paradise, is depicted as holding a group of the elect in a cloth on his lap. Lazarus occasionally appears in Abraham's lap (in reference to the parable).

Abraham's Bosom See ABRAHAM.

Abraxas It is a magical word, which in Greek gnosis is the name of the God of the Year. The word probably comprises the initial letters of the Hebrew name of God. The seven letters of the name have the numerical value of 365 (a = 1, b = 2, r = 100, x = 60, s = 200). In Hellenistic magical papyri, the word occurs as a magical sign and totality symbol (probably with reference to the number SEVEN). It also appears in that context on antique and medieval AMULET stones, usually in conjunction with a human torso with a rooster's head, human arms, and snakes as legs.

Abyss It is a symbol of conditions that have not yet achieved form and shape, or which from the standpoint of average consciousness are irrepresentable. The abyss therefore represents the origin and the end of the world, which lie in darkness; the indefiniteness of early childhood and the dissolution of the individual in death; and the union with the absolute in the *unio mystica*. — Jung sees the image of the abyss in connection with the forces of the unconscious, and with the archetype (see ARCHETYPES) of the loving yet terrifying mother.

```
A B R A C A D A B R A
 A B R A C A D A B R
  A B R A C A D A B
   A B R A C A D A
    A B R A C A D
     A B R A C A
      A B R A C
       A B R A
        A B R
         A B
          A
```

Abracadabra:
Written in the usual inverted schema.

Abraham:
Abraham's bosom. Miniature from the 12th century.

Abraxas:
Abraxas cameo.

Acanthus:
Above: Blossom and leaf. *Below*: Acanthus on a capital.

Acacia It is a tree frequently equated with the locust or the mimosa. The wood of the acacia is very durable; hence it symbolizes constancy and unchangeability. Among the Freemasons it is a symbol of purity, immortality, and consecration.

Acanthus It is a thistlelike plant found in warmer climes. The sinuate, notched leaves of two kinds of acanthus in the Mediterranean region provided the pattern for a leaflike ornamentation, used particularly on Corinthian capitals; it was also used as a festoon. The symbolic significance of the acanthus probably derives from its thorns, signifying that a difficult task has been fully accomplished.

Acedia The female personification of *sloth*, one of the seven mortal sins, she rides on an ass. The OSTRICH with its head in the sand is also a symbol of sloth.

Adam In the biblical account of creation, he represents the first man (i.e., original humanity). In art he is represented relatively seldom without Eve (see ADAM AND EVE). According to legend Adam was buried on Golgotha ("the place of the skull"), often depicted in crucifixion scenes by showing Adam's skull under the cross (occasionally also with the rib, out of which Eve was made, or with the entire skeleton); this depiction refers to Christ as the new Adam. —In alchemy Adam frequently represents the *prima materia*. —In Jung's view, Adam symbolizes the "cosmic human," the original totality of all psychic energies. In dreams Adam sometimes appears in the form of the old wise man.

Adam and Eve:
Eve hands Adam the apple. Reims Cathedral, 13th century.

Adam and Eve According to the biblical story of creation, they embody the first (i.e., typical) human couple. The most frequent representation of them is the temptation by the SERPENT in paradise, often in connection with the first appearance of shame and expulsion from paradise. Adam and Eve are also represented standing on either side of Christ's cross, thus symbolizing all human beings who, by following Christ, will find salvation. Not infrequently other symbolic references appear with Adam and Eve. A LAMB at Eve's feet suggests Christ, one of her descendants; sheep, sheaves, and implements refer to the labor that must be done following the expulsion from paradise.

Aegis It is the shield of Zeus, made by Hephaestus; in the middle it bears the Gorgon's head (see GORGONS). On the basis of etymological misinterpretation in post-Homeric tales, the shield was thought to be covered with the skin of the GOAT Amalthea. Zeus loaned it to Athena, among others. It is a sign of the protection of the gods, hence the expression "to stand under someone's aegis." The interpretation of the aegis as a symbol of storm and storm clouds is contested.

Agate Since antiquity, it has been a highly valued gemstone that was thought to have healing and aphrodisiacal properties and to be a source of protection against bad weather, snake bites, and the evil eye.

Agave See ALOE.

Age A temporal category embracing long periods in the early history of humanity, it is frequently thought of as the sequence of symbolic images typifying the time embraced. The idea of (usually) four or five succeeding ages, particularly of an original Golden Age, is found in many cultures (e.g., in antiquity) and has been attested since Hesiod. In the antique Greek depiction of the Golden Age, humankind lived long, free of cares, without suffering, work, or laws. The people of the Silver Age were godless and destroyed by Zeus. In the succeeding Bronze Age, humans killed each other and after death ceased to live. The Heroic Age, in which the wars in Troy and in Thebes took place, brought with it a new ascendancy of human virtues, but led to the Iron Age, which lasted into the days of the ancient authors and was thought to bring total decline and ruin.

Agrimony It is a common herb of the rose family having upright yellow flower clusters. It was an ancient medicinal and magical plant. When dug up on Good Friday with nonferrous (see IRON) tools, agrimony is supposed to secure the favor and love of women. —Sometimes on

Agrimony

3

medieval murals it is pictured beside Mary as a salvation symbol.

Air Along with EARTH, WATER, and FIRE, it is one of the four ELEMENTS in the cosmogonic ideas of many peoples. Like fire, it is thought to be movable, active, and masculine, in contrast to the feminine, passive elements of water and earth. Air stands in close symbolic relation to breath (see SKY) and WIND. It is thought to be a subtle material realm between the earthy and the spiritual realms and is sometimes taken as a symbol of the invisible spirit whose effects are palpable. —In astrology, air is linked with three signs of the ZODIAC: GEMINI, LIBRA, and AQUARIUS. —In alchemy, air is often designated with the sign △.

Alchemy Probably originating in Egypt and practiced from the Middle Ages until the late seventeenth century, it was a theoretical and experimental approach to chemical substances. Alchemy was a high point in symbolic thinking and reveals an intense interpenetration of early natural scientific, religious, and psychological ideas; moreover, it stood in close association with the astrology and medicine of its time. The alchemists aimed at an ennobling of substances, a mystical union of microcosm and macrocosm, and a purification of the soul. —In addition to recognizing the four ELEMENTS of Greek natural philosophy (AIR, EARTH, FIRE, AND WATER), the alchemists also recognized the "philosophical elements" of SALT, SULFUR, and Mercury (See MERCURIUS). See also METALS.

Alcohol Also called *firewater*, it symbolizes the union of the opposed elements of FIRE and WATER; hence it is also a symbol of vital energy.

Almond As a sweet fruit in a hard shell, it symbolizes the essential, the spiritual, and that which is concealed behind the external. It also represents Christ (because his human nature conceals his divine nature) and his incarnation. In antiquity the almond, like the nut, symbolized pregnancy (because of its protected kernel) and fertility, and hence was scattered at weddings. Since the edible kernel had first to be removed from the shell, it was also a symbol of patience. —For the Greeks the oil extracted from the almond had phallic significance and was symbolic of the seed of Zeus.

Almond Tree Because it blossoms in January in Mediterranean lands, it became a symbol of alertness (because it "awakes" so early) and rebirth.

Aloe The aloe mentioned in the Bible is a tall tree from the wood of which a very precious, bitter, fragrant oil is extracted. It was often used in combination with MYRRH. The aloe and its oil represent repentance and abstinence. Because it is mentioned in connection with Christ's burial, it is also associated symbolically with Christ's death. —The frequently very tall *agave* (also called *century plant* or *century aloe*) grows a single stalk bearing many flowers and then dies. In the Middle Ages it was a symbol of Mary's virginity.

Alpha The first letter of the Greek alphabet and of the word *arche* (beginning). In the Bible as well as in Christian art and literature, alpha symbolizes the primal origin. See ALPHA AND OMEGA.

Alpha and Omega The first and last letters of the Greek alphabet. Because they "embrace" all other letters, they are a symbol of the all-embracing, the totality, as well as of God and particularly Christ as the first and last (frequently associated with the Christ monogram). Teilhard de Chardin used the two letters as illustrative of his theory of evolution. See ALPHA, OMEGA.

Alpha and Omega: A and O with the Christ monogram.

Alphabet See LETTERS.

Altar It is a raised place (from Latin *altus*, high) within a cult precinct that serves the purpose of sacrifice and other sacred acts in almost all religions. The raised location represents the elevation of the sacrifical gifts to the gods or to God. Occasionally the altar is considered the spiritual center of the world. —In Christianity it represents the holy table of the Last Supper with Christ or the body of Christ itself (the white altar cloth thus symbolizes the shroud). Since the fourth century the altar has been understood to be a place of protection and refuge; even the grossest criminals may not be arrested in the church, and above all not at the altar.

Altar: Slaughtering the calf on the sacrificial altar. After a miniature in the Auersbach Gospel, 12th century.

5

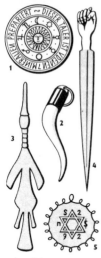

Amulet:

1. Astrological health amulet. 2. "Evil eye" amulet of buffalo horn. 3. Bird amulet of the Tungus peoples (Siberia). 4. Finger amulet (expressing envy or obscenity), found particularly in Mediterranean lands. 5. Medallion with "drude's foot."

Anastasius Cross: From a sarcophagus, 4th century.

Ambrosia Mentioned frequently in antiquity along with nectar as food of the gods, it grants immortality. —In Christian literature the Word of God and the Eucharist are sometimes symbolically called ambrosia.

Amen It is a word that occurs in the Jewish synagogue services, in the New Testament, in all Christian liturgies, and in the Islamic liturgical acclamation and confirmation formulas. In the Apocalypse, Christ is symbolically called "the Amen." See NINETY-NINE.

Amethyst It is a precious stone that was thought in antiquity to be a remedy for poison and drunkenness (from Greek *amethystos*, remedy for drunkenness). —In Christian symbolic usage, it is an image of humility because it has the color of the modest violet as well as the symbolic reference to Christ's passion (see VIOLET). In addition, amethyst was said to be one of the foundation stones of the Heavenly Jerusalem (see JERUSALEM, HEAVENLY).

Amulet It is a small object usually worn on the body. It was thought to serve humankind as magic protection (against spirits, the evil eye, misfortune, illness) and as a bringer of luck. The specific form of the object was probably considered to be a symbolic expression of the coercion of particular powers of fate. Predominant types of amulets are the HORN, reptiles, spiders, CLOVER leaves (see LEAF), indecent gestures (see FINGER), semiprecious and precious stones, names or letters, striking natural substances and forms (see MANDRAKE), and pictures of saints. Wearing jewelry as adornment probably evolved from the use of amulets. — Amulets were common in prehistoric times, especially in the ancient Orient and in China; in Egypt mummies were protected from "death" with amulets. Wearing of amulets is still not uncommon. See ABRACADABRA; PENTAGRAM; SATOR AREPO FORMULA.

Anastasius, Cross of In sarcophagus art it is the symbolic representation of the death (a cross without Christ but with the Christ monogram) and resurrection (sleeping guards, cross of victory) of Christ.

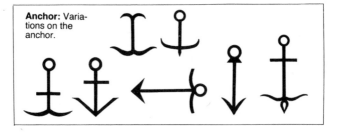

Anchor: Variations on the anchor.

Anchor It is an attribute of various sea deities. Because the anchor is the ship's only source of stability during storms, it is a symbol of hope, especially in Christian usage (it is frequently depicted on grave markers and sarcophagi), and a sign of steadfastness and fidelity. In early Christian times it was used as a disguised symbol of the cross (through the addition of the stock).

Anemone A short-lived flower (from Greek *anemos*, wind), it is a symbol in antiquity of the transitory. It is the flower of Adonis, whom Venus transformed into a reddish-purple anemone. —In Christian symbolism anemones (as well as roses and marguerites) signify the blood shed by the saints.

Anemone

Angelica It is a plant of the northern hemisphere, and one of the oldest symbolic plants in Christianity. It is a symbol of the Trinity and the Holy Ghost because the stem grows out of two skins that enclose it on either side. It was considered to be the main remedy for pestilence; according to legend, an angel brought the plant to a monk.

Anger See IRA.

Animals They often symbolically represent overpowering divine and cosmic forces, as well as the powers of the unconscious and of instinct. The ROCK PAINTINGS of animals may be closely associated with mythic and religious ideas and ceremonies. —Many peoples depict gods in the shape or as the heads (or as other parts) of animals (e.g., in Egypt and India), and in Christianity the Holy Spirit is represented by an animal, the DOVE. Among primitive peoples the animal frequently represents a person's al-

Angelica

7

Animal:
The Egyptian
falcon-headed
god, Horus.

ter ego. In the symbolic language of many cultures, the animal, including the fabulous animal, also symbolizes human characteristics. Animal-human hybrids can signify the twofold corporeal-spiritual nature of humans. See CENTAUR; EVANGELISTS, SYMBOLS OF; MINOTAUR; SACRIFICE; ZODIAC.

Ankh An Egyptian T-shaped cross surmounted by a loop, which symbolizes life as well as the sun's fructification of the earth, the ankh is common in Egyptian art and is often depicted in the hands of gods or kings. In funereal pictures it is held erect on the side of the loop (perhaps symbolizing the key that opens the realm of the dead). —The Egyptian Christians (the Copts) borrowed the image as a symbol of the life-giving power of the cross of Christ.

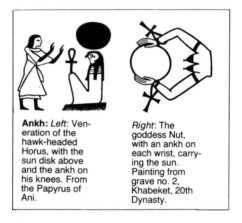

Ankh: *Left*: Veneration of the hawk-headed Horus, with the sun disk above and the ankh on his knees. From the Papyrus of Ani.

Right: The goddess Nut, with an ankh on each wrist, carrying the sun. Painting from grave no. 2, Khabeket, 20th Dynasty.

Anointing See CHRISM, OILS.

Ant Like the BEE, the ant is a symbol of diligence and organized communal life; because of its extensive winter foodstores, it also represents foresight. —In India ants are symbols of the nullity of all worldly actions because of their unceasing activity. —Among African peoples the *anthill* is sometimes related to cosmogonic ideas; occasionally it is associated with female fertility because it supposedly imparts fertility to women who sit on it.

Anthill See ANT.

Anvil It is an object frequently interpreted as the feminine counterpart to the HAMMER, which is conceived of as symbolically active and masculine. Occasionally the anvil appears as an attribute of the cardinal virtue of bravery.

Ape It is a common symbolic animal because of its mobility and intelligence, but also because of its cunning, strong sexual drive, ability to imitate, and its quarrelsome greediness. —In the Far East, the ape is often a symbol of wisdom. The three apes from the "Holy Stall" in Nikko are famous in this regard: one covers its eyes, another its ears, and the third its mouth ("see no evil, hear no evil, speak no evil"). Today the ape is popularly interpreted as symbolizing a life full of wisdom (and thereby of good fortune), especially in human relationships. Originally they played a role as messengers who were supposed to report to the gods on the affairs of people and were consequently depicted (as a kind of defensive magic) as blind, deaf, and dumb. —In Egypt the *baboon* was revered as divine; large, white, squatting, with erect phallus, and often with the moon sickle on its head, it is the incarnation of the moon god Thoth, the patron of scholars and scribes, who also often appears as a messenger of the gods and a guide of souls. In the world of the dead, not only good but also demonic apes meet the soul of the deceased and, for example, threaten it with entrapment in a net. —In India apes are still often thought of as holy and untouchable. —In Christian art and literature, the ape is usually viewed negatively. Often represented with a MIRROR in its hand, it symbolizes (through the physical similarity between people and apes) humankind sunk to the animal level because of their vices, particularly the mortal sins of greed, lust, and vanity. Tethered with a chain, the ape usually represents Satan conquered. —Psychoanalytic dream interpretation often sees in the ape a symbol of shamelessness, of inner tumult, or (because of its humanlike appearance) the animal caricature of personality. —The ape is the ninth sign in the Chinese ZODIAC and corresponds to SAGITTARIUS.

Ape: Baboon from an underworld scene. From the grave of Tutankhamen, 18th Dynasty.

Ape: Capital in the Church of Saint Jouin-de-Marnes.

Apocalypse Written by St. John on Patmos, it is the last canonical and the only prophetic book of the New Testament. It contains seven epistles to Christian communities in Asia Minor and accounts of the imminently expected end of the world. These accounts, parts of which are difficult to interpret, depict the approaching terror, the dominion of the Antichrist, and his defeat.

Apophis See SERPENT.

Apostles, Attributes of In Christian art since the thirteenth century, the apostles have been differentiated by means of symbols of their attributes.

Andrew: cross in the form of an X.

Bartholomew: three flaying knives (or one); flayed skin.

James the Elder: three scallops; pilgrim's staff; pilgrim's cloak and hat.

James the Younger: fuller's club; pennant; sword.

John: serpent issuing from common cup; eagle rising from caldron.

Judas Thaddaeus: sailboat with mast in shape of a cross; staff with cross at end; book.

Matthew: ax; pouch or purse; sword.

Paul: sword; scrolls; open Bible with sword behind it.

Peter: cross; two keys in form of X.

Phillip: staff surmounted by a cross (in shape of T), usually with a loaf of bread on each side.

Simon: fish on a book; cross.

Thomas: lance; T-square.

Matthias: ax; stone; open Bible.

Apotropaic Figures They are grotesque heads or faces whose horrific expressions have served since ancient times to ward off hostile influences (e.g., the GORGONEION). Their repulsive appearance symbolizes the gesture of rejection and banishment. The Egyptian BES, when depicted with a grotesque appearance rather than with a smiling face, fulfilled the same function.

Apple An ancient fertility symbol (particularly the red apple), it is also a widespread symbol of love. Because of its spherical form, it can be a sign of eternity and a symbol of spiritual knowledge (e.g., in the Celtic tradition). —The golden

apples of the Hesperides represent immortality.
—In Christian symbology (among others), the
spherical form of the apple is an image of the
earth; its beautiful color and sweetness correspondingly represent the temptations of this
world. The apple consequently symbolizes the
Fall. An apple in Christ's hand thus symbolizes
the redemption from original sin; apples on the
CHRISTMAS TREE signify humanity's return to paradise brought about by Christ. In this context, the
apple is an attribute of Mary, the new Eve.
—The *Imperial Apple*, emblem of the world,
symbolizes dominion over the world; it is represented variously in antiquity with Nike, goddess
of victory, and is shown with Christian rulers
usually crowned with the cross.

Apron A ritual garment of the Freemasons, it is
usually WHITE and symbolizes work and
innocence.

Aquarius The water bearer is the 11th sign of
the ZODIAC; its element is AIR.

Aquarius: The
astrological sign.

Arbor Philosophica Also called *Arbor Dianae,
Philosophers' Tree*, and *silver tree*, it is a tree-
like, branched product of crystallization from a
solution of silver nitrate treated with mercury.
—For the alchemists it is a symbol and proof of
the "plantlike, sprouting nature" of the metals. In
addition, the concept designates the (usually)
twelve "alchemical operations" (i.e., *calcinatio,
solutio, elementorum separatio, coniunctio, putrefactio, coagulatio, cibatio, sublimatio, fermentatio, exaltatio, augmentatio, proiectio*),
whose interrelationships are graphically represented in the form of a branched tree.

Arborvitae It is any of various evergreen trees,
especially the genus Thuja of the pine family.
Like all evergreen plants, it is an immortality
symbol. Arborvitae literally means "the tree of
life." See CROSS, TREE.

Archer See BOW.

Archetypes They are the primordial images
which, according to the philosophy of late antiquity, exist in the unmanifest realm as proto-
types or "ideas." —Jung used the term to designate the symbolic patterns and images common

Ark: Noah's Ark. After a drawing in Queen Mary's Psalter, 14th century.

Arm: Trinity symbol comprising the Arm of God with the Lamb (Christ) and the Dove (Holy Ghost). After a drawing by R. Seewald.

Arm: Shiva with four arms, dancing. Bronze, ca. 1400.

to all humanity that occur in dreams as well as in myths, fairy tales, etc. Called the "collective unconscious" or "objective psyche," these symbols and images inform the ever-recurring fundamental structures in the development of the individual and are also manifested in imaginal form.

Architectural Symbolism It refers to the symbolic meaning of a building or its parts, often through later attribution (e.g., ritual usages, but also through interpretations according to theory). In ancient oriental architecture, it played a significant role (e.g., the ZIGGURAT as a representation of ascent through the planetary spheres, the grave cupola as a maternal earthy shell). It also fundamentally determined medieval Christian church architecture (e.g., the Byzantine domed church as the replica of the cosmos, the basilica form as a SHIP).

Ariadne's Thread See THREAD.

Aries See RAM.

Ark In the Bible the ark of Noah is the SHIP on which Noah, his family, and selected animals escaped the flood. Noah's ark has been seen as the prototype of salvation through baptism. It is also a symbol of the church; moreover, it represents the sum of holy knowledge that cannot be destroyed. —Jung speaks of Noah's ark as a symbol of the maternal womb. —The *Ark of the Covenant* is the name given by the Israelites to the chest containing the two tablets of stone on which the Ten Commandments were written; the Mother of God, as the intermediary of salvation, is also addressed thus.

Arm It is a symbol of strength. The extended arm is frequently a symbol of the power of justice. —Various Indian deities possess more than two arms, thus expressing their omnipotence. —In Christian liturgy the raised arms signify the soul's opening and plea for grace. In medieval Christian paintings, the arm (or the HAND) that reaches out of heaven is a symbol of God. —Raised arms as a gesture of subordinates signify the renunciation of all self-defense.

Arnica It is any of a variety of herbs (genus *Arnica*) of the aster family, including some with yellow, spicy flowers. Used among the ancient Germans as medicinal plants, they were originally sacred to the Germanic mother goddess Freya, and later to Mary. They were also valued as protection against lightning, witches, and magicians.

Arrow See BOW.

Arum The arum may be any of several related plants, such as the jack-in-the-pulpit, with whitish, lilylike flowers in a fleshy spike subtended by a leafy bract. In the Middle Ages, the plant was an attribute of Mary. Because the plant is reminiscent of the sprouting staff of Aaron, it is related to resurrection symbolism (as is the staff of Aaron).

Ascension The representation of a figure ascending to heaven, frequently with extended or raised arms, symbolizes the soul after death (see EAGLE) or a consecration, a spiritual calling, or a union with God.

Asclepius, Staff of The staff of Asclepius, the ancient god of the art of healing, is entwined by a SERPENT and is a symbol of the medical profession. In conjunction with the basin, the staff is the sign of the apothecary. The snake, which sheds its skin annually, appears in connection with the staff as symbolic of the renewal of life; it also conveys the beneficial uses of its poison. See CADUCEUS.

Ashes The symbolic meaning of ashes is related to their similarity to dust and to the fact that ashes are the cold as well as the purified residue left after fire has burned down. In many cultures ashes thus symbolize death, transitoriness, remorse, and penance, but also purification and resurrection. —Covering the head or the body with ashes expressed mourning among the Greeks, Egyptians, Jews, Arabs, and—occasionally today—some primitive peoples. —The Indian yogis cover their bodies with ashes as a sign of their renunciation of the world. —The Jews and others believed the holy ashes of animals sacrificed to fire were cleansing. —Christians regard ashes as symbolic of penance and purification in certain ritual acts

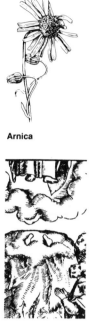

Arnica

Ascension: Christ's ascension (note the footprints). Detail from a woodcut by H. L. Schaeufelein.

Ascension: Christ's resurrection depicted as ascension. After Mathias Grunewald's painting in the Isenheim Altar.

Ash Tree

Asclepius:
Asclepius with staff and serpent.

Ash Tree

Aspis: After an English miniature.

(e.g., on Ash Wednesday and for church dedications).

Ash Tree It plays a significant role in Norse mythology as Yggdrasil, the eternally green ash TREE that holds together earth, heaven, and hell. —For the Greeks the ash, and particularly its wood, signified mighty solidity and stability; occasionally the ability to frighten away SERPENTS was ascribed to it.

Aspen See POPLAR.

Asphodel It is a variety of lily indigenous to the Mediterranean region and having white, loosely branched flower clusters and a fleshy, sweet root (e.g., the daffodil, narcissus). Among the Greeks and Romans, asphodels were considered to be death plants (and were thus sacred to Hades and Persephone); the roots were thought to be food for the dead, who occasionally (e.g., in Homer) wandered in fields of asphodels. In addition, the asphodel was thought to protect against evil spirits. —In the Middle Ages the asphodel was associated with the planet Saturn.

Aspis The aspic viper (*Vipera aspis*), a SERPENT or DRAGON (occasionally also a quadruped), is a symbol of evil and stubborness. It is often depicted in medieval architectural ornamentation or book illustration with the BASILISK, LION, or DRAGON, sometimes with one ear to the ground, the other stopped with its tail.

Ass An animal with extremely mixed symbolic meanings. In Egypt the red ass signified a dangerous being that met the soul after death. —In India the ass appeared as the mount of deities that bring harm. —It was generally viewed in antiquity as a dumb, obstinate animal; however, it was also offered as a sacrifice at Delphi, Dionysus and his followers rode on asses, and the Romans associated it with the fertility god Priapus. —In the Bible the ass often appears as a sign of impurity, but it is also mentioned in various positive contexts. For example, Bileam's talking she-ass represents the creature that can understand more of God's will than people can. Asses and oxen at the manger possibly refer to the fulfillment of the prophecy of Isaiah: "The ox knoweth its owner, and the ass, his master's crib"(Isa. 1:3). Christ's mount on entering Jerusalem is the foal of a she-ass, which usually symbolizes gentleness and humility (but at that time the she-ass's foal—especially a white one—could be seen as a sign of high rank and distinction). —Especially in Romanesque art the ass often symbolizes fornication, laziness, and stupidity. Asses reading the mass refer to the famous "asses feast" of the Middle Ages. See ONAGER.

Ass: Human-animal hybrid, with ass's head, symbolizing coarseness and narrowness. From U. Aldrovandi's *Monstrorum Historiae*, 1642.

Astral Dances Ritual dances depicting the movements of the stars, they are found in many cultures and are usually an expression of the attempt to conjure the cosmic powers.

Athanor The alchemical furnace, in which the physical, mystical, and moral transformations took place, it is occasionally compared with the WOMB and the world EGG.

Atlantis According to Plato, a fabled realm in the Atlantic Ocean that was swallowed by the sea. In an extended sense it is a symbol of paradise lost and of the Golden Age.

Atman In Hinduism, it is the innermost essence of each individual or the supreme universal self (from Sanskrit *atman*, breath, soul). See WIND.

Attributes See APOSTLES, ATTRIBUTES OF; SAINTS, ATTRIBUTES OF.

Aum See OM.

Aureole Particularly in Christian art, it is a luminescence or wreath of light rays surrounding the entire figure, symbolizing divine light. The HALO, in contrast, is reserved in Christian art for Christ and Mary. In an oval shape it is known as the MANDORLA.

Avarice See AVARITIA.

Avaritia The female personification of avarice, one of the seven mortal sins, she rides on a BADGER, TOAD, or WOLF.

Avens A common member of the rose family, it has yellow blossoms and roots that smell like carnations. It was used as a medicinal plant and hence was an attribute of Mary. In connection

Ass: Christ on a she-ass entering Jerusalem. After Master Bertram.

Aureole: Resurrection of Christ. Detail from a mural by A. da Firenze, 1366.

Avens

Ax: Ancient Cretan double-ax image with loop.

with Christ, it points to him as the salvation (or "healing") of the world.

Ax It is a symbol (especially among North American Indians) of war and destruction. —As an instrument for sacrificing animals, it is also a cult symbol; additionally, it is a symbol of power and an emblem of rank (e.g., the *double ax*, particularly in the Near East, the Minoan culture, and Northern Europe). —It is occasionally interpreted in connection with LIGHTNING. —In the Bible the ax, struck at the base of a tree, is a sign of the Last Judgment. —An ax at the apex of a pyramid or a cube standing on one corner sometimes appears in older Freemasonry documents; it may have to do with an initiation symbol that points to the courageous act of liberating the hidden secret.

Axis See WORLD AXIS.

Babel, Tower of Babel, the Hebrew name for Babylon, is a symbol of proud, unrestrained humanity, which nevertheless fails to raise itself above the limits set by God. God's punishment of the confusion of tongues finds its correlation in the New Testament in the descent of the Holy Ghost at Pentecost and the speaking in tongues that resulted.

Baboon See APE.

Babel, Tower of: after an etching by C. Anthonisz, 1547.

Babylon An ancient city on the Euphrates, Babylon means "the portal of God." In the Bible, however, it is associated with the idea of confusion. Nebuchadnezzar II deprived the Jews of their national sovereignty to the city and enslaved a large number of them; thus Babylon is often depicted by the Jews as the antithesis of the Heavenly Jerusalem (see JERUSALEM, HEAVENLY). —In Revelation, Babylon is the seat of all anti-Christian powers, a place of godless life and fornication. John describes the vision of the "whore of Babylon," a woman dressed in scarlet and purple who holds a golden goblet of filth in her hand. In the New Testament, however, Babylon is a code name for the anti-Christian power of Rome. See BABEL, TOWER OF.

Badger In Japan it is a symbol of cunning in the positive sense; the thick-bellied badger is also a symbol of self-satisfaction. —In Christian art it is the steed of personified avarice (see AVARITIA).

Balance See SCALES.

Baldachin A fabric or structure representing a canopy that is fixed or carried over an important person or sacred object. Particularly in the Orient, it symbolizes the dignity of the ruler (thus it was usually made of silk). —In Christian architecture it is typically placed over the altar, chancel, tombs, and statues; symbolically it increases the spiritual significance or power of whomever sits or stands beneath it.

Babylon: The whore of Babylon on the apocalyptic animal. After Durer's *Apocalypse.*

Bamboo In the Far East the bamboo plant is thought to bring good fortune. It is frequently the object of meditative painting; the joints, individual segments, and straight growth of the bamboo symbolize in Buddhism and Taoism the path and individual steps of spiritual development.

Banana tree It is a giant shrub with a soft stem and usually with wind-torn leaves. To Buddha the tree was a sign of the transience of all earthly life. It is often depicted in Chinese painting with a wise man sitting under it, meditating on the vanity of the world.

Baptism A ritual washing by submersion in or sprinkling with WATER to achieve spiritual cleansing, it is common in many cultures, primarily in connection with the rites of birth, death, or INITIATION. In oriental religions spiritual cleansing is often practiced by bathing in holy rivers (e.g., the Euphrates, the Ganges). —In the cults of Attis and Mithras, baptism with the blood of a STEER was customary. —In contrast to repeated washings and cleansing rites, Christian baptism, originally a kind of bath, is an act performed only once that seals one's acceptance in the Christian church. The baptism in Christ signifies both spiritual cleansing and the descent of the Holy Spirit. According to St. Paul, Christian baptism by immersion is a symbol of death and resurrection in Christ. See HAND AND FOOT WASHING.

Baldachin: Baldachin above a Gothic statue in the vestibule of the Freiburg Cathedral.

Baptism: The baptism of Jesus. Relief from the font in the Hildesheim Cathedral, ca. 1220.

Basilisk: Engraving on the Shrine of St. Elizabeth, Marburg.

Bat: St. Anthony, tempted and carried aloft by devils with bat wings. Detail after M. Schongauer.

Barque See BOAT.

Basilisk It is a fabulous creature that is supposedly hatched from a misshapen chicken's egg by a snake or by a TOAD on a bed of manure. In the symbolism of late antiquity, it is depicted as a SERPENT; in the Middle Ages, it is depicted as a fantastic hybrid (i.e., as a rooster with a serpent's tail or a combination of rooster, toad, serpent, and the like). Its breath or look was said to be fatal; thus it signifies death, the Devil, the Antichrist, or sin. It is often represented under the feet of the victorious Christ.

Basket It is a symbol of the maternal WOMB. When filled with fruits it is sometimes an attribute of the fertility goddesses (e.g., Artemis of Ephesus).

Bat A symbolic animal with a wide range of meanings, in the Far East it is a symbol of good fortune because the words for *bat* and *good luck* (*fu*) are homonymns. Because it lives in the HEIGHTS, which represent the portal to the world beyond, it was thought to be immortal and hence became an immortality symbol. —Awaking only at night, the bat, like the vampire, is associated with sexual symbolism; in Europe people imagined demons and spirits, which supposedly cohabit at night with women, as bats. As a nocturnal animal, the bat is also an emblem of melancholia. —Their ability to orient themselves accurately in the dark caused black African peoples, for example, to view the bat as symbolic of intelligence; however, as nocturnal animals they are seen in other contexts as enemies of LIGHT. As an animal that sleeps "upside down," it can also appear as an enemy of the natural order. —The Bible counts the bat among the impure animals. —In the Middle Ages it was considered to be a malevolent animal (e.g., it would suck the blood out of sleeping children); the Devil was frequently represented with a bat's wings. —Sometimes a bat's wings allude to death. —Since the bat flies under the protection of twilight or darkness, it is, especially in German art, a sign of envy, which does not reveal itself openly. —In alchemy the bat, seen as a sort of mongrel creature between mammal and bird, plays a role as a symbol of ambivalent phenomena (e.g., of the HERMAPHRODITE).

Bath In a positive sense, it is a place of cleansing, renewal, and rebirth, as well as—in alchemy—a place of mystical union. In a negative sense, the bath—especially a warm bath—is the sign of growing soft, of luxury, and a place of unchaste pleasures of the flesh. In many cultures the bath is closely connected with rituals (i.e., washing away all sins; see BAPTISM). In antiquity even statues of the gods were ceremoniously bathed as a sign of the renewal of the relationship between gods and humans. See HAND AND FOOT WASHING.

Bath: The union of Sol and Luna in the bath. From Mylius's *Philosophia Reformata*, 1622.

Battle Various peoples practiced ritual battles of symbolic meaning (e.g., the battle between order and chaos, and ultimately the victory of the former over the latter). In many places in the spring, battles between the sexes were fought according to specific rules; these battles were magically supposed to bring about, as well as to symbolize, the victory of fertility and life over death and the numbness of winter.

Beans As seeds of a prolific cultivated plant, they promise (especially in Japan) happiness, good fortune, and fertility. They also offer protection against evil spirits, illness, and lightning.

Bear It is an animal that played an important ritual role as early as prehistoric times, as evidenced by ROCK PAINTINGS and excavations of

Bear: The Celtic goddess Artio with her symbolic animal.

Bear: The black bear as steed of a horned demonic being. After a picture in Jean Wier's *Pseudomonarchia Daemonum*.

1

2

Beard:

1. Zeus. Marble sculpture, Greece. **2.** Chons. Granite statue, Egypt.

bones. Particularly among peoples of the North, it was revered as a creature resembling humans and was seen as a mediator between heaven (see SKY) and EARTH. The bear was thought by many peoples to be an ancestor of humans. —According to Northern European traditions, the bear, not the lion, was the king of animals. Among the Celts the bear was closely connected to warriors and the military. —In Siberia and Alaska the bear, because of its hibernation, was associated with the MOON, since they both periodically "come and go." In medieval art the bear's hibernation symbolizes old age and death. Hibernation suggests reawakening and rebirth in the spring; thus the bear has special significance in initiation symbolism. —In so-called primitive cultures, the bear was a savior figure. American Indian medicine men have been portrayed as riding a bear to indicate their power. —In China the bear is associated with the "masculine" principle, yang (see YIN AND YANG). —The alchemists see in the bear an image of the obscurity and mystery of the *prima materia*. —In Greek mythology the bear accompanies, or is the incarnation of, Artemis. In ancient Greece the bear skin was used to protect against early sexual involvement; young girls therefore wore bear skins during the period of their intellectual training. —In Christian symbolism it usually appears as a dangerous animal that sometimes represents the Devil; occasionally it also symbolizes the mortal sin of gluttony. A female bear, however, often represents the virgin birth, since she supposedly gives shape to her young only as she licks them. —In both Greek and Latin the word for bear is of feminine gender, reflecting the bear's positive motherly qualities (especially the ethical and caring aspects).

Beard A symbol of masculinity and strength, a long beard is often a symbol of wisdom. Gods, rulers, and heroes are usually represented with beards (e.g., Indra, Zeus, Hephaestus, Poseidon, the God of the Jews and the Christians). Even female Egyptian rulers were provided with beards as a symbol of their power. In antiquity philosophers and rhetoricians wore beards as a sign of their dignity. Christ, on the other hand, was usually depicted without a beard (i.e., as a youth) until the sixth century. —In many cultures it was a severe insult to cut off one's enemy's beard; as a sign of mourning, on the other hand, one sometimes cut off one's own beard.

Bee It is an insect that primarily symbolizes diligence, social organization, and cleanliness (since it avoids everything dirty and lives from the fragrance of flowers). —In Chaldea and imperial France, the bee was a regal symbol (for a long time the queen bee was thought to be a king); it is possible that the fleur-de-lis of the House of Bourbon developed from the bee symbol. —In Egypt the bee and the sun were associated, and the bee was considered to be a symbol of the soul. —In Greece it was considered a priestly creature (the priestesses of Eleusis and Ephesus were called bees, probably with reference to the virginity of the worker bees). —The bee, which appears to die in winter and return in spring, is sometimes a symbol of death and rebirth (e.g., of Persephone, Christ). Because of its untiring work, the bee is a Christian symbol of hope. For Bernard of Clairvaux the bee signifies the Holy Ghost. The bee is a Christ symbol as well. Its HONEY represents Christ's gentleness and compassion; its stinger symbolizes Christ as judge of the world. —Since according to ancient tradition bees do not hatch their own young but collect them from blossoms, bees were symbols in the Middle Ages of the Immaculate Conception. —The bee is also symbolic of honey-sweet eloquence, intelligence, and poetry.

Bee: Two bees with a honeycomb. Minoan jewelry pendant.

Bee: The rush and the bee, hieroglyphs from the royal title signifying King of Upper and Lower Egypt.

Beehive In Christian art of the Middle Ages, it is a symbol of Mary, who in her womb carried Jesus in all sweetness. See BEE.

Beech Tree In antiquity it was sacred to Hades and Cybele; today it is still considered to be a plant of the dead and also a symbol of immortality, since it always remains green. As a leathery, hard plant, it also denotes endurance and steadfastness; hence its wood was used as the symbolic hammer of the Freemasons.

Beech Tree

Beelzebub See FLY.

Bell A symbol of the connection between heaven (see SKY) and EARTH, the bell calls people to prayer and calls to mind obedience to divine laws. The ringing of the bell often symbolizes (e.g., in China) the cosmic harmonies. In Islam as in Christianity, the sound of bells is considered to be an echo of divine omnipotence (the voice of God), the hearing of which carries the soul beyond the limits of the mundane. —It is a widespread belief that bells ward off misfortune.

Bellows It is a word that is closely associated symbolically with breath (see WIND). In Taoism it represents the relationship between heaven (see SKY) and EARTH: the upper side of the bellows represents heaven; the lower, the earth.

Belly It is a symbol of maternal warmth and protection (see WOMB), but also of being devoured. —Emphasis on the belly as the location of the stomach is also a symbolic reference to gluttony and materialistic approaches to life. —In Buddhist plastic art, particularly in Japan, a nude, protruding belly on male figures (e.g., of gods of good fortune) symbolizes friendliness, peace, and well-being.

Bes A grimacing, dwarflike protective spirit of the Egyptians, usually depicted with the tongue sticking out, it was supposed to protect from evil influences and bring cheerfulness. See APOTROPAIC FIGURES.

Billows See WAVES.

Bind and loose It was a frequent symbolic practice in magical rites that was intended either to restrict (through binding) or to set free (through loosing) specific energies or forces. See KNOT, RIBBON.

Birch It is a symbol, particularly in Russia, of spring and of the young girl.

Birch

Birds Because of their connection to the SKY, birds have been regarded since ancient times as mediators between heaven and EARTH and as embodiments of immaterial things, particularly the soul. In Taoism, for example, the immortals are represented in the form of birds. —A common belief was that after physical death, the soul departs the body as a bird. —Many religions speak of heavenly beings with *wings* or in the form of birds (e.g., angels or cupids; see CHERUB, SERAPH). —The Koran speaks of birds as symbolically related to fate and immortality. —In various occidental and (east) Indian mythologies, birds populate the world TREE as spiritual and emotional intermediate beings or as the souls of the deceased. The Upanishads, for example, speak in this context of two birds: one that eats the fruits of the world tree (symbolizing the active individual soul) and the other that does not eat but merely observes (symbolizing the absolute spirit and pure cognition). —The idea of a close relationship between birds and divine powers also underlies the prophetic significance ascribed to the flight of birds (e.g., in Rome). —In Africa birds often occur as symbols of vital power, sometimes battling with the SERPENT, which symbolizes death or powers that bring destruction and decay. —In early Christian art, birds appear as symbols of saved souls. See COCK, DOVE, DUCK, EAGLE, HAWK, KINGFISHER, KITE, MAGPIE, NIGHTINGALE, ORIOLE, PEACOCK, PELICAN, PHEASANT, PHOENIX, QUAIL, RAVEN, SPARROW-HAWK, STORK, SWALLOW, SWAN, WOODPECKER.

Birds: A winged Eros. Myrina, Hellenistic epoch.

Birds: The soul of the deceased departing the body in the form of a bird with human head. After an Egyptian funereal papyrus.

Black A color symbolically analogous to WHITE and that similarly corresponds to the absolute; hence it can express both the abundance of life and its total emptiness. In the sense of the undifferentiated and abysmal, it often appears as the designation of darkness, primal chaos, and death. As the color of mourning, it is closely associated with resigned pain (thus differing from the light color white, which signals hope). —As the color of the night, it shares in the symbolic complex of mother-fertility-mystery-death; black is thus also the color of fertility, mother goddesses, and their priestesses (in this context it is sometimes related symbolically to RED, the color of blood). In China, black is the color of the feminine principle, yin (see YIN AND YANG) and contrasts with its opposite, YELLOW (or sometimes also RED), rather than with white, as in the West. —As the color of evil, black occurs, for example, in the term *black magic*. —In the Spanish court, black was for a long time the color of great dignity.

Black Sun See SUN.

Blessing It is a transfer of energy or an invocation of divine grace associated with symbolic gestures (e.g., laying on of hands, making the sign of the cross). It is understood to be empirically effective. See HAND, RIGHT AND LEFT.

Blindfold A symbol of "not seeing," in a positive sense it refers to the blindfold of JUSTICE, who judges without respect to person. In a negative sense it refers to the blindfold of FORTUNA, who gives her blessings indiscriminately. Occasionally hollow eye sockets replace the blindfold.

Blindness Blind old men often symbolize wisdom, the inner light, the visionary view; thus seers (e.g., Tiresias) are often blind. At the same time, blindness (even in seers) can be divine punishment for having seen something divinely forbidden. In the Bible, blindness and madness are punishments for disobedience to God. —Christ's healings of the blind are sometimes understood to be acts that symbolize illumination in spiritual darkness; thus they can also represent illumination through baptism.

Blond As a light hair color, it shares the symbolism of GOLD. The Greeks thus depicted their gods as blond-haired.

Blood Since ancient times, it has been symbolic of the seat of the soul and the life force; it is closely associated with FIRE and the SUN. —The Greeks let blood flow into the graves of the deceased to give vitality to the soul in the beyond. —In various cultures the seers drank blood to put themselves into ecstasy. —In the cults of Cybele and Mithras, the initiates were baptized with the purifying and vivifying blood of sacrificed bulls (see SACRIFICE, STEER). —Particularly among primitive peoples, blood is believed to contaminate; hence menstruating women, or women who have just given birth, are subjected to specific rites of seclusion and purification. —In Christianity the blood of Christ has the power of penance and salvation.

Blindfold:
Sculpture on the Strasbourg Cathedral, ca. 1230.

Blindness:
Christ healing the blind. Bernward Column, Hildesheim, ca. 1020.

Blossom An image of the essential and of victorious conclusion, it is above all a symbol of feminine beauty. The blossom's receptive relationship with SUN and RAIN also makes it an image of passive surrender and modesty; because of its usually radial arrangement of petals, it can also symbolize the sun. Since it quickly blooms and withers, it represents inconstancy and transience. Occasionally blossoms—as well as the butterflies (see BUTTERFLY) that visit them—are associated symbolically with the souls of the deceased. Differentiated according to color, yellow blossoms are associated symbolically with the SUN, white with death or innocence, red with BLOOD, and blue with dreams and secrets (see BLUE FLOWER). Golden blossoms occur in various contexts (e.g., as Taoist symbols of the highest spiritual life). —In Japan the art of flower arrangement (*ikebana*) developed into an expressive form that found various manifestations in diverse schools; frequently occurring basic positions of flowers include heaven (above), the human (midpoint), earth (below).

Blue The color of heaven (see SKY), distance, and WATER, it is usually experienced as transparent, pure, immaterial, and cool. In addition, blue is the color of the divine, of truth, and of fidelity (in the sense of clinging to truth, as well as with reference to the fixed firmament of heaven). —Blue is the color of the unreal and fantastic (see BLUE FLOWER). Occasionally it is used in a negative sense (e.g., in German "to be blue" means to be too drunk to think straight; in American usage "blue" means sad or morose). —Egyptian gods and kings are often depicted with blue beards and wigs. —The Hindu divinities Shiva and Krishna are usually shown as blue or bluish-white. —Jesus and Yahweh are enthroned above the azure sky. —In Christian painting the battle between heaven and EARTH was frequently imaged in the opposition of blue and WHITE against RED and GREEN (e.g., the battle of St. George and the dragon). As the color of Mary's robe, blue is also a purity symbol. —In the Orient, blue is still thought to protect against the evil eye.

25

Boat:
The Egyptian boat of the dead. After a mural in the grave of Sen-nufer, Thebes, 18th Dynasty.

Boat: Egyptian representation of the sun boat (with serpent heads) in which Ra sails daily across the heavens.

Book: Lion with inscribed tablet; Salzburg; 1st third of the 13th century.

Book: St. John, depicted with a book; Cathedral in Meissen.

Blue Flower A symbol of poetry in Novalis's novel *Heinrich von Ofterdingen*, it is usually a symbol of the romantic yearning for the infinite and of romantic literature in general.

Boar See SWINE.

Boat In the mythologies of many peoples, it frequently symbolizes the crossing from the realm of the living to the realm of the dead or vice versa. — In Greek mythology the ferryman Charon transports the dead in his boat over the boundary river (Styx or Acheron) into the underworld. — According to Egyptian myth, the sun god Ra sails in a sun boat across the heavens during the day and in a night boat through the underworld. — The comparison of the CRESCENT MOON to a boat is common. — Because of its form, which permits navigating in both directions, the boat is also a symbolic embodiment of the double-faced Roman god JANUS.

Bodhi Tree See FIG TREE.

Bone As a relatively hard and durable component of higher life forms, bone was believed (especially among hunting peoples) to be the seat of the essence or life force. It was a widespread custom after eating the flesh of an animal to return the bones to nature (i.e., to the earth, water, or fire) to ensure the continuation of the species.

Book It is a symbol of wisdom, knowledge, and the totality of the universe (as a unity composed of many individual letters and pages). Sometimes it also appears as the ideal of the *Liber Mundi* (*Book of the World*) containing all the laws that divine intelligence used at the creation of the world. — Islam occasionally distinguishes between macro- and microcosmic aspects of book symbolism: in juxtaposition to the *Liber Mundi*, there is the book of the totality of each individual person. — The belief in a book in which the history of humankind is recorded goes back to the oriental belief in the divine tablets on which individual fates were inscribed. — In the Bible the expression *Book of Life* occurs as a designation for the totality of the elect. In Revelation, the book with seven seals is a symbol of esoteric secret knowledge. Eating a book or a scroll signifies taking the divine word into one's heart. —A closed book refers in the plastic arts to potentialities not yet actualized or to secrets. In Christian art, a closed book refers to Mary's virginity; an open book in connection with Mary points to the fulfillment of the prophecy that she would bear the Christ. —As an attribute, the book appears with evangelists, apostles, and church fathers (among others). —The power of knowledge or of written laws is sometimes symbolized by LIONS holding books or inscribed tablets.

Borage

Borage It is an herb that had the reputation of driving off evil thoughts. Because it is coarse and has little bristles but is also a tasty seasoning, it is a symbol of excellent qualities disguised by a simple appearance. In particular, it signifies the external plainness of the Virgin Mary.

Bouquet It is a symbol of unity in diversity, since it is the joining of many, often different, flowers.

Bow (Bow and Arrow) It is a symbol of war and power. —The bow often refers to vigor and vital energy; the arrow is a symbol of swiftness and the quick appearance of death (e.g., it is sometimes symbolic of pestilence). The arrow frequently symbolizes a movement that reaches beyond set boundaries. It sometimes represents the rays of the sun (e.g., Apollo's arrows); as a light symbol it is also a sign of knowledge and learning. —It can have phallic significance. The archer in medieval (particularly Romanesque) art is often associated with sensuality and lust (also, but infrequently, with God's punishment). A similar significance is ascribed to the archer in the form of the bow-bearing CENTAUR. Amor (Cupid) is often represented with bow, arrow, and quiver, shooting arrows of love. —In Hinduism and Buddhism, the sacred sound OM signifies an arrow (shot by a human, representing the bow) that penetrates ignorance and reaches the true and highest state of being; conversely, *Om* can also signify the bow from which the arrow of the ego flies toward the absolute (Brahma), with whom the ego wants to unite. —Aiming an arrow at a target with one's

Bow and Arrow: Eros with bow and arrow. Detail after a painting by Franceschini.

Bow and Arrow: Death as horseman with bow and arrow. Detail from a woodcut in *Der Akkermann aus Bohmen* by Johann von Tepl, 1461.

eyes blindfolded is a Japanese meditation technique, *kyudo*, the purpose of which is to let go of one's own ego-directed will. Similar practices are found in Islam.

Box It is a symbol of protection, the female womb, or a secret. Closed boxes and chests (often three in number) that contain good and evil sometimes occur in fairy tales in which decisions must be made. Boxes are also symbols for truths that do not lie open to view.

Branch Green branches or boughs (and, less often, golden boughs) symbolize honor, fame, and immortality. In folk custom, the branches of some trees and shrubs were regarded as granting good fortune and protection. See CHERRY BLOSSOM, OLIVE TREE, PALM, WILLOW.

Branch: The Archangel Gabriel appearing to Mary carrying a branch. After the *Annunciation* by Simone Martini, 1333.

Bravery See FORTITUDO.

Bread As one of the most important physical foods, it is also a symbol of spiritual nourishment. Among the sacrifices of the Old Testament belong the twelve showbreads, symbolic of the bread of life. In the New Testament Christ is "the living bread, which came from heaven." Through the Eucharistic transformation, the bread and the WINE receive their most sacred meaning in Christianity. See SALT.

Bread cabinet In medieval symbolism it represents Mary, Mother of God, who carried the BREAD of life in her womb.

Breath See WIND.

Breath: God the Creator inspiring Adam with the breath of life. After a mosaic, Cathedral of Monreale, 12th century.

Bridge As a uniting link between spatially separated things, it is a common symbol of joining and mediation. Among many peoples there is the idea of a bridge uniting heaven (see SKY) and EARTH; such a bridge is often depicted as a RAINBOW. Frequently a bridge must be traversed by souls after death. In Islam, for example, the bridge is narrower than a hair and smoother than a knife blade so that the damned fall into hell while the elect reach paradise, quickly or slowly, according to their merits. This conception graphically documents the double symbolic meaning of the bridge: it not only unites but also "bridges over" (i.e., overcomes).

Broad Bean It is an edible seed that has long been recognized as useful. The black-flecked blossom is sometimes considered a death symbol. The seed is symbolically associated with fertility and embryos (especially male embryos); it is also associated with the souls of the deceased and subterranean realms, and thus with death. Because of its dual symbolism, sacrifices of broad beans were made at the time of tilling and harvest and at weddings and burials. See BEANS.

Bronze Age See AGE.

1 Broom It is not only a profane but also a ritual implement, used for symbolic cleansing of the temple. In a negative sense it is the instrument on which witches were thought to ride. (It may be a phallic symbol or a symbol of the powers that the broom could not banish and that have taken possession of it.)

Broom: The witch's journey on the broom. Woodcut from *The History of Mother Shipton*, 18th century.

2 Broom A shrublike, papilionaceous flower with yellow or white blossoms, the thorny broom is a symbol of human sins, to atone for which the sinner must till fields full of thorns and thistles. Additionally, it is a symbol of Christ's sufferings for humankind (it is sometimes represented among the instruments of martyrdom), but it is also a symbol of salvation, as is the THISTLE.

Brown It is the color of the earth and of autumn. In antiquity and in the Middle Ages, it was a color of mourning. In folk song and lyric poetry since the late Middle Ages, brown has also had erotic significance.

Broom: Thorny broom.

Bubble It is a symbol of vacuous, unrealistic plans and wishes. In moral and religious contexts, particularly in Buddhism and Taoism, it signifies the vanity and transitoriness of the world.

Buffalo See OX.

Bull See OX, STEER.

Bull-Roarer A ritual instrument (especially in Australia, Africa, and among the North American Indians and the Eskimos) used only by men. Women are usually forbidden even to see it. It is a lance-shaped piece of wood with a single hole at one end through which a string is drawn; the bull-roarer is swung in a circle and thus produces a whirring sound which is usually understood to be the voice of spirits, of the THUNDER, or an expression of masculine generative power. It is used in rain and fertility rites; in Greece it was sometimes associated with explicitly sexual rites.

Bundle of Faggots A symbol in China of the becoming and passing away of humankind. Just as a bundle of faggots is tied and untied, the entire history of humankind consists of perpetually new formations that death again dissolves. —As a favorite form of fuel, the bundle of faggots also has a symbolic relationship to FIRE (e.g., as an attribute of witches).

Bustard It is a sort of crane that often runs rather than flies. The male is usually accompanied by several females; hence the bustard is regarded by black African peoples as a symbol of polygamous marriage. Because it does not fly, this bird also symbolizes children who do not want to leave their mothers.

Butter: Krishna as a child playing with a ball of butter. Bronze miniature.

Butter Valued especially in India as the bearer of cosmic energies, it was ritually sacrificed (e.g., poured in the fire). See MILK, WHIP.

Butterfly Because of its lightness and beautiful colors, in Japan it is a symbol of women; two butterflies symbolize marital happiness. —The essential symbolic meaning of the butterfly lies in its metamorphosis from EGG to larva, or CATERPILLAR, whose skin hardens to form the deathlike case of the pupa, or chrysalis, from which emerges the radiantly colorful winged insect attracted to the sunlight. Since antiquity it has thus been a symbol of the soul that physical death does not destroy (its Greek name is *psyche*); in later times the butterfly's pleasing, fluttering flight and its association with Eros, the god of love, were emphasized. —In Christian symbolism the butterfly is a symbol of resurrection and immortality, but also of empty vanity and futility because of its short life span and its transient beauty. See MOTH.

Butterfly: Eros with a plow drawn by butterflies. 18th century cameo.

30

Caduceus The Latin modification of the Greek *kerykeion*, meaning herald's staff, it was originally a magical instrument, around the top of which two SERPENTS are entwined, their heads facing each other. It is the attribute of Hermes (Mercury), and symbolizes fertility (two snakes mate on an erect phallus), as well as balance and equilibrium. In alchemy it is a symbol of the union of opposing forces. See ASCLEPIUS, STAFF OF.

Calamus It is the sweet flag, a variety of arum growing next to water in Asia and Europe, from which is extracted oil for anointing and for medicines. In the Middle Ages it was sometimes associated with Mary.

Caldron In fairy tales and for the alchemists and practitioners of rituals (particularly in the Indo-European linguistic area), it is the vessel wherein magical and mystical transformations take place; hence it symbolizes change, renewal, initiation, and resurrection. As a container with bubbling, boiling contents, it can also symbolize fullness and abundance. —In China it is often a symbol of good fortune and well-being.

Caduceus: Hermes with the kerykeion (caduceus).

Calf As an animal to be slaughtered, it is a symbol of sacrifice; as such it occasionally replaces the STEER as an attribute of St. Luke the evangelist. See EVANGELISTS, SYMBOLS OF, GOLDEN CALF.

Camel It is a symbol in North Africa of sobriety, obstinacy, and pride. It is sometimes mentioned in the Old Testament as an unclean animal. —As a beast of burden it symbolizes modesty and obedience in Christian writings and art; however, it is also a symbol of anger, lethargy, and narrow-mindedness.

Cancer See CRAB.

Candle It is a symbol of light, the individual soul, and the relationship between spirit and matter (the FLAME consumes the wax). In fairy tales death has power over burning candles, which represent human lives. —The Romans used candles ritually. —In Christianity, especially in the Roman Catholic liturgy, candles are symbolic of faith and light during the Mass, funerals,

Caldron: Two witches attending a magical transformation in a witch's caldron. Woodcut from the *Tractatus on the Evil Women, Whom One Calls Witches,* Ulm, ca. 1490.

Candlestick:
The seven-armed candlestick as a symbol of the Old Testament. After an Alsatian miniature, 12th century.

Capricorn: The astrological sign.

Cat: The Egyptian goddess Bastet. Bronze statuette from the late period.

processions, and on special feasts. See LAMP, TORCH.

Candlestick It is a symbol of spiritual light and salvation. The seven-armed gold candlestick in Judaism probably corresponds in part to the Babylonian tree of lights; it is also associated with cosmic symbolism (seven planets, seven heavens; see GOLD, SEVEN). —In Christian art of the Middle Ages, the seven-armed candlestick often symbolizes Judaism.

Capricorn The goat is the tenth sign of the ZO-DIAC; its element is EARTH.

Cardinal Virtues These are bravery (personified by *Fortitudo*), justice (*Justitia*), prudence (*Prudentia*), and temperance (*Temperantia*).

Carnation It is a perennial plant with pointed, grasslike leaves. Germanic-speaking peoples likened the form of the leaf and the petal to nails (hence the German name *Naeglein*, *Nagerl*, meaning "nail"); it thus symbolizes Christ's passion. The plant often appears in pictures of the Madonna with child. —It also appears in numerous betrothal pictures of the late Middle Ages and Renaissance, probably as a symbol of love and fertility. —Later the carnation (especially the red variety) came to represent the socialist holiday, the first day of May.

Carp A symbol of good fortune in Japan and China, particularly because of its longevity, it is seen as the steed of the immortals. Because it supposedly swims against the current, it also represents courage and perseverance.

Castle A frequent fairy-tale motif, it often stands in a bewitched forest or on an enchanted mountain and usually symbolizes the fulfillment of all positive wishes (especially when it is depicted as bright and resplendent). A black and empty castle can also symbolize loss and hopelessness.

Cat It is an ambivalent symbolic animal. —In Japan, seeing a cat is a bad omen. —In the Cabala and in Buddhism, the cat is closely associated with the symbolism of the SERPENT. —In Egypt the domestic, agile, and useful cat was honored as a sacred animal of the goddess Bastet, the protectress of home, mothers, and children. —In the Middle Ages cats were thought to be witches' animals, and black cats were seen as signs of the devil; according to superstition, the black cat brings misfortune. —The cat is the fourth sign of the Chinese ZODIAC, corresponding to CANCER (the CRAB).

Caterpillar As a creeping larva (corresponding to the WORM), it is sometimes a symbol of lowliness and ugliness. —Because it transforms into a pupa and then a butterfly, in India it symbolizes the transmigration of souls.

Cave Since prehistoric times the cave has served sacred purposes (see ROCK PAINTINGS). The cave is associated symbolically with the realm of death (the dark realm) as well as with that of birth (the maternal WOMB). Caves were therefore revered as the birth places or dwellings of gods, heroes, spirits, demons, the dead, etc.; often they were viewed as the portal to the realm of the dead. —The Sumerians imagined the realm of the dead to be in a cave in the world MOUNTAIN. —The Egyptians believed that the living water of the Nile arose from a cave. —Caves played an important role in initiation rites (*regressus ad uterum*?) such as the Eleusinian mysteries and the oracle rites of the fertility god Trophonius. —Plato's *Allegory of the Cave* is a symbolic depiction of the human epistemological condition in a world of mere likenesses and illusion; it is a person's task to escape this cave and ultimately attain a vision of the ideal world. —In the art of the Eastern church, the birth of Christ is almost always depicted in a cave. The representation of the cave as a cleft in the earth may possibly symbolize a maternal womb (with reference to the symbolism of the fertilization of the EARTH by the SKY).

Cave Paintings See ROCK PAINTINGS.

Cedar The cedar of Lebanon is often mentioned in the Bible; because of its height is is regarded as a symbol of lofty and sublime things, and since its wood is durable, it symbolizes strength and endurance. Like all conifers, it is a symbol

Cedar

33

of immortality. —In the Middle Ages it was associated with Mary.

Celandine

Celandine A variety of poppy with a yellowish, milky sap, it was used as a versatile healing plant. The alchemists attempted to make gold from the golden-yellow sap. The name of the plant is derived from the Greek word for SWALLOW, *kelidon*, since according to ancient and medieval folk belief, sparrows used the sap of the plant to impart sight to their young. Celandine thus has the symbolic significance of "imparting sight," "healing one from the spirit of blindness," and "light-bringer"; in medieval art it often points to Christ. —In folk belief the plant, which supposedly imparted to its bearer the power of settling conflicts, represents contentment.

Cellar In the symbolic language of mysticism, it is an image of the hidden treasures of the self and of self-knowledge; in other contexts it is a sign of dark drives.

Centaur: Centaur and warrior. Metope from the Parthenon in the Acropolis, Athens.

Centaur It is a wild, fabulous creature of Greek myth, with a human torso and a horse's body. The centaurs (except Chiron) were thought to be coarse and irrational and thus usually symbolize the animal side of humans (in contrast to the RIDER, who controls the animal's powers). It is also a symbol of the body/mind double nature of humans. —In medieval art centaurs are often depicted with BOW and arrow, especially on friezes and capitals; they are usually symbols of vice and sin, heretics, or the Devil. However, the fleeing centaur shooting arrows behind himself can be an image of the human conflict with evil. —In the art of the nineteenth and twentieth centuries, the centaur often has erotic significance. See MINOTAUR.

Center As the point from which everything proceeds, it is a symbol of God (sometimes also as the central position in the organization of a picture). The center of the world (see WORLD AXIS) was often imagined to be a sacred MOUNTAIN, TREE, or NAVEL.

Cerberus: Heracles fetching Cerberus from the underworld. Painting on an Attic amphora.

Cerberus In Greek mythology, he is the hound of hell who guards the entrance to the underworld. With writhing tail he meets each deceased person; however, he usually lets neither a living person enter nor a dead person leave. He is generally represented as having two or three heads and a tail of snakes; he symbolizes the horrors of death and the fact that life cannot be regained.

Chain Generally an image depicting binding and the state of being bound, it often symbolizes the relationship between heaven (see SKY) and EARTH. For the Neoplatonists the chain symbolized the unbroken emanation of the One into individual creatures and things. Similarly, in Christianity each person is pictured bound to God with a golden chain; prayer is also compared to a golden chain. — In Christian art the defeated Devil (sometimes in the form of an APE) appears on the Day of Judgment bound with a chain. See CORD.

Chain: Satan bound in chains. After an Alsatian miniature, 17th century.

Chalice See CUP.

Chamber See ROOM.

Chameleon

Chameleon Because of its capacity to change its colors, it stood for inconstancy and falsehood. — In Africa, it is a divine, solar animal.

Chamomile A species of flower with a spicy aroma that has been used since ancient times as an effective healing plant, in the Middle Ages it was particularly used to treat women's ills (hence its genus name *Matricaria*); it symbolizes Mary. The inconspicuous, useful plant also represents strength paired with modesty (according to proverb, "no virgin may pass it by without a curtsy").

Chamomile

Chaos In antiquity and in the biblical story of creation (Tohu wa bohu), it was an image of the condition of the world before anything was created. — According to ancient Egyptian ideas, chaos existed in the form of the primeval ocean Nun prior to the creation of the world, and after creation it surrounded the world as a perpetual source of strength and renewal. — For the alchemists, it designates the *prima materia*. See ABYSS.

Chaos: Chaos of the elements. From Robert Fludd's *Utriusque Cosmi Historia*, Oppenheim, 1619.

Chariot Closely associated with the symbolic meaning of the WHEEL and consequently with the

Chariot: Elijah's ascension on the chariot of fire. After an early Christian mural in the cemetery of Lucina, Rome.

symbolism of the SUN, it is also associated with the cult of the sun and with vegetation deities (e.g., Apollo, Attis, Cybele, Mithras). —Good and evil gods are imagined in many religions as coming to earth in chariots or *wagons*. The chariot rumbling across the sky is a symbol of Zeus, the "lord of the lightning." The animals pulling the chariots of the various gods modify the symbolic content of the chariot (e.g., EAGLES pull Zeus's chariot, SWANS or DOVES pull Aphrodite's chariot). The fiery chariot ascending to heaven sometimes symbolizes the spiritual elevation of an individual (e.g., Elijah, St. Francis of Assisi). —The chariot also represents the various components of the human personality that are controlled by the CHARIOTEER.

Charioteer: Greek racing chariot with charioteer and warrior. Consecrated relief for an Olympic victory, end of the 5th century.

Charioteer A symbol in antiquity of control or mastery of passions and drives, it is thus also a symbol of reason. See CHARIOT.

Cherry A symbol in Japan of self-discovery and self-sacrifice, especially in relation to the samurai's sacrifice of blood and life in war (likened to the removal of the red flesh of the cherry in order to get to the hard stone). —In Christian art of the Middle Ages, the cherry, like the apple, sometimes signifies the forbidden fruit.

Cherry Blossom A symbol in Japan of purity, beauty, and good fortune. The cherry blossom carried far away by the wind represents the ideal death. —In central Europe, cut cherry branches that blossom in the nights before Christmas (particularly before the feast of St. Barbara on 4 December and the feast of St. Lucia on 13 December, or on Christmas itself) are seen as symbols of good fortune and as pointing to early marriage.

Cherry blossom

Cherub A half-animal, half-human creature of the higher spiritual hierarchies, it is often found in the graphic symbol language of the Near East. —In the Old Testament the Cherubim are spirit creatures that accompany Yahweh. —In Christian art they are usually represented as having many wings and as covered with eyes; they symbolize the omnipresence and omniscience of higher spiritual beings. They are often depicted as TETRAMORPHS or with one head and four or six wings. Their attribute is the WHEEL (or wheels).

Chess A symbol of the battle of two opposed parties, it is usually associated with fundamental pairs of opposites: male-female, life-death, light-dark, good-evil, heaven-earth/hell. As a realm in which the planning intellect moves, the game of chess is also regarded (e.g., in India) as a symbol of cosmic order and reason.

Chestnut In China the edible chestnut was associated with the East and autumn. Since its fruit was gathered in the fall and served as food for winter, it is a symbol of wise foresight.

Chicken The psychopomp (guide of souls) in initiation rites and the sacred animal in ecstatic, magico-religious celebrations in Africa, in some places in South America (the Makumba cult), and in the Caribbean (the Voodoo cult). The belief in a relationship between the (frequently black) chicken and the dead is associated with chicken sacrifices, which were made in order to get in touch with the deceased. —The chicken is the tenth sign in the Chinese ZODIAC and corresponds to CAPRICORN. See COCK, HEN.

Child A symbol of spontaneity and innocence, qualities alluded to in the New Testament ("Except ye be converted and become as little children, ye shall not enter into the kingdom of heaven." Matt. 18:3). Children are also symbolic of the beginning and of abundant possibilities.

Chimera It is a fire-breathing monster of Greek mythology, often represented with a lion's head, a goat's body, and a dragon's or a serpent's tail (each of these parts could also have a head of its own). It was a hybrid that gave rise to various

Chimera: Etruscan bronze figurine. 5th century B.C.

37

symbolic interpretations, all of which had to do with the realm of the dark, of the uncontrolled, and of the instinctive drives. Mounted on the winged horse PEGASUS, Bellerophon slew the Chimera (just as St. George slew the dragon). —In modern usage it often denotes a vague phantasm.

Chimney In fairy tales, communication with spirits and demons often takes place via the chimney. Witches were thought to enter and exit through the chimney and the spirits of the deceased to leave the house through the chimney. The reason for these associations with the spirit realm probably have to do with the chimney's CAVElike form, which is open above and below, the FIRE, the black soot (see BLACK), and the ascending SMOKE. —In other connections the chimney is part of the symbolism of the HEARTH.

Chisel Analogous to the PLOW, it is a symbol of the active, masculine principle that works and forms the receptive, feminine principle.

Chrism A compound of olive oil and spices used in the Catholic church for anointing, it symbolizes the unity of the double nature (human and divine) of Christ.

Christ Monogram:
Two forms of the Christ monogram. After mosaics in the catacombs.

Christ Monogram A sign in various forms composed of the initial Greek letters of the name *Christ*: *X* (chi) and *P* (rho), or—earlier—from the initial letters of *Jesus Christus*: (*J* and *X*). It is used symbolically for Christ or for Christendom in general (since the time of Constantine the Great). Frequently the two letters were surrounded by a CIRCLE, thus suggesting a WHEEL; hence they became both a cosmic and a solar symbol. Often the letters *A* and *O* (see ALPHA AND OMEGA) were added, or the sun and moon, which point to the crucifixion (during which the sun darkened and the moon appeared). See ANASTASIUS, CROSS OF.

Christmas Tree It is a conifer that nearly everywhere in the Christian world is decorated and lighted at Christmas time. It became customary in the nineteenth century (but probably goes back to heathen practices) for people to hang green branches and lighted candles in their houses as protection during the nights of 25 December to 6 January (the so-called *Rauchnachte*, when spirits were supposed to be abroad). In Christendom the Christmas tree is a symbol of Christ as the true TREE of life. The lights symbolize the "Light of the World" born in Bethlehem; the apples (often used as decoration) refer symbolically to the APPLE of knowledge in the Garden of Eden. The apple denotes original sin, from which Christ's act redeemed humanity, thereby giving humans access once again to paradise, symbolized by the Christmas tree.

Chrysalis The chrysalis, or pupa, of insects, specifically of the butterfly, is in various cultures a symbol of transformation, of the human need for protection, and of solitude on the threshold of a new developmental level.

Chrysanthemum It is a symbol in China and Japan of good fortune and long life. Because of its radial arrangement of petals, it is also a sun symbol. It is the emblem of the Japanese imperial house.

Church As a personification (*Ecclesia*), it is often depicted with eyes, a crown, and a banner of victory. —The church itself points symbolically toward the Heavenly Jerusalem (see JERUSALEM, HEAVENLY), the realm of the elect.

Church: *Left*: Ecclesia.

Right: Synagogue. From the Strassburg Cathedral.

Circle: Magic
circle with
hexagram
and cross.

Circle: Magic
circle. From
Francis Barrett's
The Magus,
London, 1901.

Cinnabar Because of its RED color, it is a symbol of life and sometimes of immortality.

Circle One of the most frequent symbolic figures, it is often seen in relationship with and in contrast to the SQUARE. The circle leads back into itself and is consequently a symbol of unity, the absolute, and perfection; it therefore also represents heaven (see SKY) in contrast to EARTH, or the spiritual in contrast to the material. There is a close connection between the symbolism of the circle and that of the WHEEL. As an endless line, it symbolizes time and infinity, often in the form of a SERPENT that bites its own tail (see UROBOROS). — In magical practices, the circle is valued as an effective symbol of protection against evil spirits, demons, etc.; the protective function ascribed to such items as the belt (see GIRDLE), RING, hoop, and circular AMULET) probably derives from the symbolic value of the circle. — In Zen Buddhism concentric circles symbolize the highest level of enlightenment, the harmony of all spiritual powers. — In Christianity concentric circles represent various spiritual hierarchies or the various levels of creation. Three interlocked circles symbolize the Trinity. — The circle inscribed in a square is a common cabalistic symbol of the divine spark hidden in matter.

Circumambulation The circumambulation of holy precincts (e.g., the altar in Judaism, the Kaaba in Islam, the stupa in Buddhism, the church in Christianity [in processions]) is widely practiced in religious ceremonies. As an imitation of the movements of sun and stars, it may be related to cosmic symbolism as well as to the symbolic significance of the CIRCLE. The number of circumambulations is usually in accord with sacred symbolic numbers.

Circumcision A practice common among many peoples, it is often part of the initiation rites that accompany the transition to sexual maturity. It is also possibly a symbolic sacrifice to the gods of fertility. — Among some African peoples (some of whom practice female circumcision) the circumcision of the foreskin, which represents the female element of the man, or the clitoris, which is the locus of the male element in the woman, signifies a definitive assignment to one sex and therewith, sexual maturity. —For the Jews, circumcision signifies the covenant with God.

Citadel Generally a symbol of protection and safety, it is also a sign of renunciation of the world and of inner dialogue with God or with oneself. See FORTRESS.

City A secured place of dwelling arranged in an orderly fashion, it is a symbol of divine order. —Because the city protects and defends its citizens as a mother does her children, the city is often personified as a maternal goddess wearing a crown in the form of a stone wall. —In the Christian art of the Middle Ages, the city appears as the Heavenly Jerusalem (see JERUSALEM, HEAVENLY) or as the juxtaposition of two cities: Jerusalem (representing the Temple of the Jews) and Bethlehem (representing the Christian church). In the later Middle Ages, the city, as an enclosed area, also represents the Virgin Mary.

City: Personification of Roma as the goddess of the city. After a miniature in the *Book of Pericopes of Henry II*.

Clay See CONTAINER.

Cloak It is a symbol of protection (e.g., the cloak of Mary, protectress in medieval Christian art) or of dignity or rank (e.g., the king's cloak).

Clothing According to biblical tradition, garments have been worn since the Fall. In contrast to NAKEDNESS, they are the consequence and expression of human modesty. They exist in a variety of forms and colors and reflect social adaptation and social rank; they often signify a calling or profession. As an ethnic costume, clothing is also an expression of membership in a specific ethnic group. White, shining garments frequently point to the victory over the body and earthly things (e.g., the garments of angels, the BLESSED, the deceased). Changing clothing symbolizes the passage into a new phase of life or a new community; donning monastic clothing, for example, symbolizes a second baptism and the renunciation of the world.

Cloak: Madonna with protective cloak. From the *Speculum Humanae Salvationis*, ca. 1350.

Clouds Because of their mysterious, veiling character and because they are part of the SKY, they have been interpreted as the dwelling places of the gods, especially those clouds surrounding high mountain peaks (e.g., Olympus).

Clover

Club: Hercules with club riding in the sun caldron on his night sea journey. Bottom of an Attic vase, 5th century B.C.

Cock: Weather cock on the cocktower of the Freiburg Cathedral.

—Epiphanies are sometimes also accompanied by clouds (e.g., in the Bible). —In Islam, clouds are regarded as a symbol of the complete unrecognizability and inscrutability of Allah prior to creation. —In China the cloud that dissolves in the sky is a symbol of the necessary transformation to which wise persons must submit in order to extinguish their earthly personalities and enter eternity. —As a bringer of rain, the cloud is sometimes a fertility symbol.

Clover It is a widely distributed papilionaceous flower. Because of its vigorous growth, it is a sign of vital energy. —For the Celts it was a sacred, magical plant. —In the Middle Ages, clover was a Trinity symbol because of its three leaflets; as a medicinal plant, it sometimes referred to Mary. —The four-leafed clover (see FOUR) is still seen as bringing good luck; however, clover with more than four leaflets is usually considered unfavorable. The FIVE-leafed clover, however, sometimes points to a happy marriage.

Club A weapon for striking or throwing, made of wood or occasionally metal, it is frequently a symbol of brutal force. —In antiquity it was the attribute of Heracles. —In medieval and Renaissance representations of Virtue and Vice, it is an attribute of bravery; when in the hand of a half-clad fool, it represents folly.

Coal A symbol of hidden, occult power or strength, the cold, black coal needs the igniting spark to unleash its dormant energies. Burning coal symbolizes the alchemical transformation of BLACK into RED. —Charcoal, as wood purified by fire, is also a symbol of purity.

Cock It is the herald of the morning SUN. Because of its iridescent plumage and its fire-red comb, it is a sun and fire symbol for many peoples (e.g., Syrians, Egyptians, Greeks). —In Japan it was believed that only the cock's crow summoned the sun goddess each morning from her cave. —Because of its close relationship to dawn, it is a symbol of the victory of LIGHT over darkness as well as an image of vigilance. Folk belief frequently ascribed apotropaic power over night demons to the first cock crow of morning. Moreover, the cock, himself associated with fire but also with vigilance, was supposed to help counter fire, which is represented by the red cock. —His strong procreative drive caused the cock to be seen as a fertility symbol; thus the sacrifice of the cock is sometimes a part of harvest rites. —In the Far East, and also in the art of antiquity, the cock is a symbol of battle, daring, and courage because of its pugnacity. —Among the Germanic tribes and the Greeks, it also played the role of psychopomp (guide of souls). —In Christianity the cock as herald of day is a resurrection symbol and a sign of Christ's return on the Day of Judgment. Because of its elevated position (often situated on church spires), the *weather cock*, as the first to be touched by the sun's rays, symbolizes the victory of the light of Christ over the powers of darkness and is a reminder summoning people to early morning prayer. —In present times, the cock usually symbolizes pride or strutting male behavior.

Coiffure See HAIR.

Colors For ages colors have been carriers of multiple symbolic meanings that are often cast in the basic polarities of warm-cold and bright-dark. See BLACK, BLUE, BROWN, GRAY, GREEN, RED, VIOLET, WHITE, YELLOW.

Colossus It is a colossal statue of gigantic size and proportion. Such statues (particularly of

Colossus: The colossi of Abu Simbel.

Coltsfoot

Coltsfoot

Columbine

Columns: In the Erechtheion, Athens, ca. 420-405 B.C.

gods or rulers) symbolize supernatural powers (e.g., the sitting statues of Abu Simbel; the Colossus of Rhodes, one of the seven wonders of the ancient world).

Coltsfoot It is a composite flower of the aster family found in temperate and northern zones; the shape of the leaves resembles the foot of a colt. Because of its healing powers and the radial arrangement and light yellow color of the blossom, it is associated with Mary.

Columbine A herbaceous plant found in the northern temperate zone, it was originally consecrated to the Germanic mother goddess Freya. In Christian art it is an attribute of Mary.

Column It is a symbol of the link between heaven (see SKY) and EARTH. As a support in a building, it is generally a symbol of stability and support; it can also, *pars pro toto*, be a symbol of the "structure" of a strong community or institution. In its full form, including base and capital, it is symbolically close in meaning to the TREE of life. The base represents the root; the shaft, the trunk; the capital, the foliage (cf. Egyptian, Corinthian, Roman, and Gothic columns). — Sometimes the column is an embodiment of the human form, alluded to by the term *capital* (from Latin *capitellum*, little head) and by the frequent use of caryatids and statues of Atlas in place of columns. —The Bible speaks of the columns upon which the earth rests and which God will topple on Judgment Day. —At the entrance to Solomon's temple, there stood two symbolically important columns, called *Jachin* ("It stands firm") and *Booz* ("In it is strength"); imitations of these columns later played an important role in the temples of the Freemasons. —Independent of architecturally integrated columns, there are single, free-standing columns or pillars in many cultures: for example, the Saxon "Irminsul," probably a symbol of the world pillar supporting the sky (see WORLD AXIS); the numerous triumphal columns of antiquity which symbolized victory (e.g., Trajan's Column in Rome, decorated with scenic bands in relief). —The column also has phallic significance, especially in fertility rituals. —The column of fire and of cloud, by which God led the Israelites through the desert, often occurs as a mystic symbol in religious literature.

Comet It is a celestial body interpreted in many cultures (in antiquity, in the Middle Ages, and also among Indians and in Africa) as an evil omen of famine, war, pestilence, or the end of the world. —In the fine arts, the Star of Bethlehem is often represented as a comet.

Compass As an instrument of the planning, designing intellect, it is a symbol of active creative power and reflective mental activity, as well as of intelligence, justice, moderation, and truth. It is the attribute of various sciences and of their personifications (e.g., geometry, astronomy, architecture, geography). —In ancient China and the occident, the combination of the compass with the T-SQUARE was regarded in esoteric symbolic language as a symbol of the union of the CIRCLE or SKY (symbolized by the compass), and the SQUARE or EARTH (symbolized by the T-square). Such a union represents perfection. —In the symbolic tradition of the Freemasons, various degrees of extension of the compass correspond symbolically to various levels of spiritual development. For example, 90 degrees (corresponding to the T-square) signifies the equilibrium of spiritual and material forces. Various combinations of the T-square and the compass also symbolize the relationship between spirit and matter. A T-square on a compass thus signifies matter ruling spirit; a crossed relationship of the two instruments signifies a balanced relationship between matter and spirit; a compass on a T-square signifies the spirit's mastery over matter.

Compass: The Creator measuring the world with a compass. After a miniature in a French *bible moralisee*, middle of the 13th century.

Condor It is a very large New World vulture, which is an embodiment of solar powers and an image of the SUN in the mythological conceptions of the peoples of the Andes.

Cone Closely associated with the symbolism of the CIRCLE and the TRIANGLE, it is probably related to fertility goddesses (Astarte/Ishtar/Aphrodite). —In other contexts the form of the cone, which strives toward its apex, sometimes appears as the primal image representing spiritual development. It symbolizes the movement away from distracted involvement in the multiplicity of the material world, toward concentration, identity, and self-discovery.

Container: The virgin as container of the divine child. Venetian *Rosario della Gloriosa Vergine Maria*, 1524.

Conifer See TREE.

Container It is a symbol of receiving and holding, and thus frequently a symbol of the womb. Christianity compares Mary, who received the Holy Ghost into herself, with the container. —The container, particularly one made of *clay*, is also a symbol of the body, which is interpreted as the container of the soul. —The New Testament compares the believer to a container of Grace. —Many peoples considered the pouring of a liquid from one container into another as a symbol of the reincarnation of the soul. See CUP, GOBLET.

Contemplation of the Navel See NAVEL.

Copper Among some African peoples it is a comprehensive symbol of light, life, and things efficacious, such as the word or sperm. —In alchemy there is a correspondence between copper and the planet *Venus*, whose nature is described as warm and moist, feminine, and conducive to beauty, leisure, and sensual pleasure. See METALS.

Coral: The coral tree in the ocean. From a picture in Dioscorides's *De Materia Medica*, 5th century.

Coral As an aquatic animal often existing in branched or tree form, it sometimes shares the symbolism of WATER and the TREE. Its symbolic content also embraces the vegetable, mineral, and animal realms, since it looks like a plant and has a hard, calcified skeleton inhabited by living tissue. Because of its red color, it also symbolizes BLOOD.

Cord Like the CHAIN, it is an image of connection or binding, particularly the connection between heaven (see SKY) and EARTH. It is also understood in the sense of heaven's fructification of the earth; hence it is sometimes a symbol of RAIN. —According to Buddhist, Hindu, Neoplatonic, and other world views, the individual spirit is bound to the soul or body by a golden astral cord. —For the Freemasons a cord with knots symbolizes the community of Freemasonry.

Corn A highly valued nutritional plant in some American Indian cultures, it is associated with the cosmos, the SUN, and the origin of humankind. It symbolizes well-being and happiness.

Corn: The Aztec goddess of corn, Chicomecoatl.

Cow As a fertile domestic animal giving MILK, which is vital for life, the cow is generally a symbol of the maternal earth, plenty, and containing protectiveness. —In Egypt it was revered primarily as a representation of the sky goddess Hathor, who was seen as the mother and spouse of the SUN; as the mother of Horus; as the grandmother of the Egyptian king; as the goddess of joy, dance, and music (in the form of a young woman); as the image of hope and the renewal of life; as the living soul of trees; and as the mistress of the mountains and the dead. Among other forms, she could appear as gleaming gold or assume the shape of a lioness (see LION). —In India the cow is revered as the sacred nurturer; the white cow is related to the holy fire. In Buddhism there is a close connection between the cow and the step-by-step progress toward inner illumination; the white cow symbolizes the highest stage of individual existence prior to dissolving in the Absolute. In the Vedic tradition the cow is psychopomp (guide of souls). —For some peoples (e.g., the Sumerians), there was a symbolic relationship between the fertile cow and the MOON and between the cow's milk and moonlight. —In Germanic mythology the cow *Audhumla*, the primal nourisher and protectress, played an important role; she was also closely connected with WATER and RAIN.

Cow: The Egyptian goddess Hathor as cow. Limestone, 18th Dynasty.

Cowl According to monastic tradition, it is usually a symbol of poverty, renunciation of the world, and membership in a religious community. It is associated in Christianity with baptismal garments.

Coyote It is a North American prairie wolf, which in some American Indian cultures is seen as the cause of all evil (specifically of winter and death).

Crab As an aquatic animal, it is often related to the symbolism of WATER or the primal OCEAN. Because of the shell that protects it from the outer world, the crab is related to imagery of the em-

Crab: The astrological sign for Cancer.

bryo and uterus; the references to "mother" and "sea" also connect the crab to the unconscious. Since antiquity, the crab has been seen as a lunar symbol, perhaps because of the crab's form and the influence of the moon on the sea. —In Christianity the crab is a symbol of resurrection because during its development it sheds its shell; hence in the narrower sense it is sometimes also symbolic of Christ. —In Africa it often appears as a symbol of evil. —Cancer, the crab, is the fourth sign of the ZODIAC; its element is WATER.

Cradle It is a symbol of the WOMB and of the safety of early childhood.

Crane In China and Japan it is a symbol of long life and immortality (see STILTS), since it was believed that the crane could live 1,000 years. The white color of its feathers is associated with purity and cleanliness, and the red head-feathers are considered to be signs of vital energy and of the crane's association with fire. —In India the crane is a symbol of malice and betrayal. — Among some African peoples, the crowned crane symbolizes language and thought because of its seemingly comtemplative posture. —Since the crane is a migratory bird, it is also a symbol of spring. Its return in the spring and its striking courting dance made it—particularly for the Greeks and Romans—a symbol of love and zest for life.

Cremation It is a symbol of complete cleansing and of transformation of material substance into spiritual substance (see HEIGHT, SMOKE). Cremation plays a role in funeral ceremonies (the cremation of the body) and in alchemy. See FIRE.

Cremation: The personified spirit departing from the *prima materia* during cremation. Picture from the *Tractatus qui Dicitur Thomae Aquinatis de Alchimia*, 1520.

Crescent Moon It is an attribute of female, especially virgin, goddesses (e.g., Artemis). Possibly with reference to its waxing phase, it is also closely associated in meaning with pregnancy and birth. The relationship that Christian art established between the MOON and the Virgin Mary (often represented as *Immaculata* standing on the moon sickle) probably relates in part to these two complexes of meaning, even if the initial reference is to the apocalyptic woman clothed with the SUN and having the moon at her feet. — In Islam the crescent moon is an image that symbolizes opening and concentration, and it points to victory over death. Since the Crusades, the crescent moon embracing a single star has been an emblem of the Islamic world in general. (In the Near East the Red Crescent organization corresponds to the Red Cross in the West.)

Crescent moon: Mary in the crescent moon. After Dürer.

Crescent moon: The crescent-moon from the flag of Algeria.

Cricket In China it is a symbol of death and resurrection, since it lays its eggs in the earth and, following a larval phase, returns to the surface of the earth as a complete animal. In China and in Mediterranean cultures, the cricket is welcome in the home and at the HEARTH as a bringer of good fortune.

Crocodile Although related to WATER symbolism, the crocodile is a more complex symbol, since it lives both on land and in the water. — It enjoyed special veneration in Egypt, where it was thought to have been born out of the water like

Crocodile: A dead person at the edge of the world river worshipping the Egyptian earth god Geb in the form of a crocodile. Detail from a picture in the *Book of the Dead* of Heri-uben, 21st Dynasty.

the sun; it was revered as a powerful deity (Sebek), simultaneously solar and chthonic. The earth god could also incarnate himself in the form of a crocodile. —Some American Indian cultures saw the crocodile that lives in the primal ocean as the creator of the world; others saw it as the animal that carries the entire world on its back. — In the Bible the name LEVIATHAN is sometimes applied to the crocodile, which in some places refers to Egypt. — In Christian art it approximates the symbolic meaning of the DRAGON.

Crocus It is a genus of flowering plant of the iris family with over sixty varieties. Wreaths of cro-

Crocus

1. Greek
2. Latin
3. Tau (also called the Egyptian cross, or cross of St. Anthony)
4. St. Peter's
5. St. Andrew's
6. Thief's cross ("Y" cross)
7. Moline
8. Double
9. Cross with handle
10. Cardinal's or Patriarch's cross
11. Lorraine
12. Papal
13. Swastika
14. Russian
15. Crosslet
16. Potent (Jerusalem)
17. Jerusalem
18. Botonee
19. Maltese
20. Coptic

cuses are supposed to protect one from drunkenness. The species saffron was especially valued in antiquity; from the stigmas of saffron a yellow dye was prepared, a symbol of light and nobility. The garments of gods and kings were often saffron yellow in color. —Because of its golden pistil, the crocus is a symbol in Christian literature of GOLD and hence of the highest virtue, love.

Cross It is one of the most extensively distributed and oldest symbols. Like the SQUARE, it shares the symbolism of the number FOUR when considered in terms of its outer four points; thus it became an image of the four cardinal directions. In China it was associated with the numbers FIVE and TEN through inclusion of the midpoint. If only the two cross arms are considered, it becomes a symbol of the interpenetration of two opposed realms, primarily of heaven (see SKY) and EARTH, or of time and space. —The cross-shaped arrangement plays a frequent role in the architecture of sacred buildings and of entire cities. The Greek cross, for example, determined the floor plan of many Byzantine and Syrian church structures, and the Latin cross determined that of Romanesque and Gothic churches. —The cross can also be understood as a sign for the CROSSROADS, as the place where the paths of the living and the dead cross. Among some African tribes, it is frequently understood in this sense (as well as in the sense of embracing the entire cosmos, i.e., people and spirits). —In Asia the vertical axis of the cross is a symbol of the active, "heavenly" forces (i.e., the "masculine" principle), whereas the horizontal axis corresponds to the passive forces of water (i.e., the "feminine" principle). Further, the two axes symbolize the equinoxes and the solstices. —The cross inscribed in a CIRCLE mediates between the square and the circle and thus symbolically emphasizes the joining of heaven and earth. It is a symbol of the midpoint, the equilibrium of activity and passivity, and the perfected human being. If the four arms of the cross inscribed in a circle are viewed as spokes, there appears the image of the WHEEL, a sun symbol that occurs not only among Asiatic peoples but also among the ancient German tribes. (The cross without the circle also is sometimes a sun symbol, as, e.g., among the Assyrians.) Another fire and sun symbol occurring initially in Asia and later among the Germanic tribes is the SWASTIKA. —Through Christ's crucifixion, the cross gained a special meaning in Christianity as a symbol of Christ's suffering as well as of his triumph, and hence it is generally a symbol of Christianity itself. (This special meaning of the cross was accepted slowly, since in antiquity death on the cross was considered extremely offensive.) —In Christian art it appears in many forms (most often the Greek or Latin); the ANCHOR is sometimes a disguised cross symbol. The form of the cross also plays a role in the gesture of blessing and in crossing oneself. The very old form of the forked cross points to the symbolism of the TREE of life; in Christian art the blossoming and leafy cross of Christ occurs as symbolic of victory over death (see TREE CROSS). See also ANKH.

Crossroads In most cultures it is a significant place of meeting with transcendent powers (gods, spirits, the dead). It is often close to the symbolic content of the DOOR, since the crossroads can also symbolize the necessary transition to the new (from one phase of life to another; from life to death). To win the favor of the gods or the spirits, obelisks, altars, or stones were erected, or inscriptions were placed at crossroads. Practically everywhere in Europe crossroads were also regarded as the meeting places of witches and evil demons. For this reason, Christians have erected at crossroads crosses, chapels, and statues of the Madonna and the saints. —Among many African tribes the symbolism of the crossroads plays a significant role in ritual acts. —In Greek mythology Oedipus slays his father at a crossroads. The Greeks made sacrifices to a goddess of the (three-way) fork in the road who was often represented in triple form: Hecate, goddess of ghosts and magic, who was also closely associated with the realm of the dead. The statue of Hermes, the psychopomp (spirit guide), stood guard at crossroads and forks in the road. A

Crossroads: The three-headed Hecate, goddess of the crossroads. 4th century.

famous story recounted by Prodikos tells of *Heracles* who, at the crossroads, chose virtue over pleasure. The Romans knew a cult of the Lares of the crossroads, the aim of which was to make fate propitious. —Under late Germanic law, legal proceedings were undertaken at the crossroads.

Crowfoot

Crowfoot It is any of a widely distributed genus (*Ranunculus*) of herbaceous flowering plants of the buttercup family. Used as a medicinal plant in the Middle Ages, it is associated in Christian art with Mary; because it has three leaves, it is also a Trinity symbol.

Crown As a decoration adorning a person's most noble part, it symbolically elevates the wearer. Because of its common raylike spikes, it is related to some of the symbolic aspects of the HORN; because of its circular form, it also shares the symbolism of the CIRCLE. —The crown is always an expression of majesty, power, consecration, or of a solemn, extraordinary status or condition. In most cultures it is worn by the regent. In Judaism the golden diadem is also the sign of the dignity of the high priest. —The crowns of gods and kings were respected by the Egyptians as powerful, magical beings to whom distinct cults and ritual songs were dedicated. —In Buddhism and Hinduism, as in Islam, the crown (sometimes also associated with the LOTUS blossom) signifies the elevation of the spirit above the body. —The Bible speaks variously of the crown (e.g., the crown of life and the crown of immortality, which symbolizes the condition of eternal salvation). —In the Orient as in the Occident, a bride customarily wears a crown, which is considered to be a sign of virginity as well as of her elevation into an esteemed new condition. The deceased, particularly those who never married, sometimes are buried with a crown (see GRAVE) as a symbolic indication of their approaching union with God.

Crown: Mary with crown. From the Mary Column by H. Gerhard, Munich (Marienplatz).

Crown of Thorns See THORN.

Crux Gammata See SWASTIKA.

Crystal A symbol of purity, clarity, and the spirit, it is also related to the symbolic meaning of the

DIAMOND. —As a transparent physical body it symbolizes, in contrast to other material objects, the union of opposites, particularly of spirit and matter. —Because crystal does not burn but can ignite a flame when sunlight passes through it, in Christianity it signifies the Immaculate Conception and thus is also a sign of Mary.

Cube As a body bounded by six squares, it participates in the symbolism of the SQUARE; in addition it is a symbol of things solid, firm, and unchanging, and sometimes of eternity. Among the five Platonic bodies, it represents the earth.

Cuckoo According to Vedic tradition, it is a symbol of the soul before and after incarnation; the body is compared to the foreign nest in which the cuckoo lays her eggs. —In occidental folk belief, the number of the cuckoo's calls is often considered to be an omen of the length of life, marriage, or expected money. —Since the cuckoo was reputed to be lascivious, sluts in the Middle Ages were sometimes called "cuckoos." The Devil was euphemistically called "cuckoo" in German ("The cuckoo fetch you!"). —Cuckoo's eggs are taken (in German figurative usage) as a sign of something of questionable value that has been substituted or insinuated.

Cup (Chalice) It is often a symbol of overflowing abundance. —In the Bible the image of the cup occurs in various contexts: the cup of salvation or fate, which humankind receives from the hand of God; the cup of God's wrath. On the Mount of Olives, Christ speaks of the cup of suffering that awaits him. —As a vessel providing nourishment, the cup sometimes represents the nurturing breast (e.g., in India); as a protective and preserving container, it is also a representation of the WOMB. —Because of its form, it has been associated with the CRESCENT MOON (which also refers to the maternal breast because of the moon's milk-white color). —Cups in ritual use or in religious art often contain the DRAUGHT of immortality. —In paintings, the cup that contains Christ's blood refers, in addition to the celebration of the Eucharist, to Christ as eternal salvation. —Drinking from a common cup or chalice in a community setting

Cup: The cup of the Eucharist. Detail after a painting by J.D. de Heem, ca. 1650.

is a widespread sign in various cultures of participation in and allegiance to a commonly recognized idea, religion, etc. Mutual exchange of drinking bowls symbolizes fidelity (e.g., in Japanese marriage ceremonies). —In Islamic literature the cup occurs as a symbol of the heart; three cups, filled with MILK, WINE, and WATER, symbolize, respectively, Islam (milk as symbolic of the natural and right religion), Christianity (in which wine has a sacred meaning), and Judaism (in which water plays a destructive role in the flood and a beneficial role in the passage through the Red Sea). —The symbolic meaning of the cup is also sometimes close to that of the SKULL. See GOBLET, GRAIL.

Cupola (Dome) In Buddhist, Islamic, Byzantine, and Christian architecture, it is often interpreted as a symbol of the dome of the sky (cupola murals often depict stars, birds, angels, sun chariots, etc.).

Cuttlefish:
Decoration of a porphyry weight. From Knossos, Crete.

Cuttlefish Found in the ornamental art of both the Celts and the Cretans, it is symbolically associated with the SPIDER and the SPIRAL because of its (often curled) tentacles. As an aquatic animal that ejects clouds of a dark liquid in the presence of its enemies, it sometimes represents the powers of the underworld.

Cypress

Cypress Regarded by many peoples as a sacred tree, it is a long-lived evergreen plant symbolizing, like all conifers, long life and immortality. —In antiquity it was regarded as a symbol of death because after being cut down, it does not grow back; hence it was associated with Pluto and the realm of the underworld. —In China the seed of the cypress was associated with the yang principle (see YIN AND YANG); eating the seed was supposed to grant long life.

Daisy A composite flower of the temperate zone, the daisy was sacred to the Germanic mother goddess Freya. —In medieval art it is a common attribute of Mary, signifying eternal life and salvation, but also, like the MARGUERITE, tears and drops of blood.

Daisies

Dance As rhythmically structured and at the same time ecstatic movement, dance has been associated in many cultures with the powers of order and creation. In many myths gods and heroes appear who, through dancing, bring forth the world as well as give it order (often with reference to cyclical changes of the planets, times of day and year, etc.). Ritual dances were regarded in many cultures as the means of establishing a connection between heaven (see SKY) and EARTH and thus were used to call forth rain, fertility, grace, or (especially in the dances of shamans and medicine men) to gain vision into the future. —Symbolic movements are common in dance, particularly HAND movements, which are usually comprehensible only to the initiated. —In China the art of dance as an expression of cosmic harmony is closely associated with the symbolism and rhythm of number. —Among black Africans, dance was originally the transcendental component of practically all rites and actions of daily life. —The Egyptians (among others) had a large number of different ritual dances in which personifications of the gods participated. —The Old Testament mentions dances that express spiritual joy (e.g., the festival dance of the women after David's victory over Goliath, David's dance before the Ark of the Covenant) as well as darker aspects (e.g., Salome's seductive, fatal dance).

Dance: Acrobatic dancer. Sketch on an ostracon from the New Kingdom, Egypt.

Dance of Death See SKELETON.

Dandelion It is a common milky, composite plant. In medieval Christian art, the dandelion is associated with Christ and Mary, probably because of its sunlike, radiant blossom and its medicinal properties. Like many milky plants it is also a symbol of the death of Christ and the martyrs.

Dance: Dancing bayadere. After an Indian Rajput miniature, 18th century.

Darkness See LIGHT.

Dandelion

Dead Nettle

Dawn It is generally a symbol of hope, youth, the abundance of possibilities, and new beginnings. The Greeks personified dawn as the goddess Eos, the sister of Helios (see SUN) and Selene (see MOON); the Romans personified dawn as the goddess Aurora. As the "rose-fingered one" she precedes the chariot of the sun. —In Christian symbolism Mary is sometimes called the moon who brought us Christ the Sun.

Day In contrast to NIGHT, it is a symbol of clarity, reason, and candor (thus the expressions, to see something in the "light of day," to "bring to light"). —The four times of day are often symbolically equated with the four seasons: spring with morning, summer with MIDDAY or sunset, autumn with afternoon, and winter with night. These identifications also play a role in astrology.

Dead Nettle A labiate plant sometimes used in antiquity for medicinal purposes, in medieval Christian art it is an attribute of Mary.

Death's Head See SKULL.

Deciduous Tree See TREE.

Deesis The depiction of Christ enthroned as judge of the world between Mary and John the Baptist, who intercede for the souls. It is often a symbolically abbreviated representation of the Last Judgment.

Deformation Bodily deformity often points to special and secret abilities that may be good or bad. See LAMENESS, ONE-EYED, ONE-LEGGED.

Depth As a symbolic image, it signifies the realm of darkness and of the mysterious (which can arise from the depths), as well as of the essential. In a negative sense it represents evil, drives, and material things.

Desert It is a symbol with negative and positive aspects. —In Islam it occurs usually in the negative sense as the place of error and aberration. —In the Upanishads, the desert is sometimes a symbol of the undifferentiated, primal unity underlying the created world of appearances. —The Bible mentions the desert in connection with abandonment and separation from God and as the place where the demons dwell; however, it is also the place where God can appear with special intensity (e.g., the columns of fire and cloud by which God led the Israelites through the desert; in the desert John the Baptist preached of the coming Messiah). In connection with legends of hermits, the desert is also mentioned in a dual sense: as the place of temptation by demons (e.g., St. Anthony), but also of meditation and closeness to God.

Dew As an expression of the influence of heaven (see SKY) on the EARTH, it is closely associated with the symbolism of RAIN. Because it condenses silently at night, and glistens in the early morning sun (and resembles PEARLS), its symbolic meaning is more mysterious and more strongly accented toward the emotional-spiritual dimension. In the Cabala, for example, it appears (from the TREE of life) as the symbol of redemption and renewal of life. —In China, dew was believed to come from the moon and to impart immortality. —In Buddhism dew represents transitoriness and the nullity of the world. —The Greeks considered dew to be a symbol of fertilization and fertility.

Diamond Symbolically it is usually considered to be the perfection of CRYSTAL and thus represents absolute purity, spirituality, and immutability. —In India it is sometimes a symbol of immortality; Buddha's THRONE is of diamond. —Plato describes the WORLD AXIS as diamond. —European folk belief ascribes various magical properties to diamond. It is supposed to heal illnesses; make poisons harmless; drive away wild animals, witches, and ghosts; make invisible; and make one pleasing to women. —In the Renaissance it was above all a symbol of courage and strength of character.

Dice See CUBE.

Disk Like the CIRCLE, it is often a sun symbol (e.g., in India and Egypt); the image of a winged

Disk: Winged sun disk. After a picture in the grave of the son of the Egyptian king Ramses III.

Dodecahedron

Doe: Artemis with two does.

Dog: A white dog at the feet of Raphael, who appears in human form. Detail from *Tobias and Raphael* by A. Pollaiuolo.

disk represents the course of the sun and, more generally, the flight or ascent to higher spheres. —In China the disk is the symbol of heavenly perfection; a jade disk with a HOLE in the center (the *Pi*) symbolizes the sky or heaven.

Dodecahedron It is a body bounded by 12 flat polygons. Especially significant symbolically is the *pentagonal dodecahedron*, which is formed of 12 equilateral pentagons; it participates in the symbolism of the numbers TWELVE and FIVE. It was thought to be the most perfect of the five uniform, or Platonic, bodies and is consequently a totality symbol. Plato assumed that the cosmos had the form of a dodecahedron.

Doe (Hind) It is a symbol of the animalistic or maternal aspect of femininity. —In fairy tales women or maidens are often transformed into does. —In Greek mythology the doe is sacred to Hera and Artemis, whose chariot is drawn by four does or four STAGS with golden antlers. —In the mythology of the Turks and the Mongols, the doe embodies the female, i.e., the earthy side of the mythological union of heaven (see SKY) and EARTH.

Dog It was probably the first animal to be domesticated by humans. Since ancient times the dog has given rise to complex, often contradictory, symbolic interpretations. In many cultures the dog is associated with death; it guards the realm of the dead and is the psychopomp (spirit guide) or mediator between the worlds of the dead and the living (e.g., Anubis, CERBERUS). The gods of multivocal, nocturnal (or dark) realms sometimes appear in the shape of a dog (e.g., Hecate, the Greek goddess of the CROSS-ROADS). —Because of the dog's acknowledged wisdom, many cultures (e.g., in Africa) regard the dog as the ancestor of civilization and as the one who brought fire to humans. The dog is also associated with the symbolism of the ancestor and progenitor of humankind because of its sexual prowess. —The dog is a nearly universal symbol of fidelity and is (e.g., in Japan) a mythic helper and protector, especially of women and children. —In a negative sense the dog represents impurity, depravity, and baseness (e.g., in the Old Testament and in Islam, which, however, also grants good qualities to the dog). Reviling a person by calling him or her a dog is common practice in most cultures. In the Middle Ages, a degrading punishment was to have to carry a dog; to make hanging on the gallows a worse punishment, dogs were sometimes also hanged with the convicted. —In medieval art the dog is an ambivalent figure; it symbolizes envy, anger, and temptation by evil but also faith and fidelity. Frequently a white dog signifies the quality and piety of the person at whose feet it is pictured; it can also be a symbol of a good marriage. An ugly, usually dark-colored dog, on the contrary, sometimes symbolizes disbelief or heathens. —The dog is the 11th sign of the Chinese ZODIAC and corresponds to AQUARIUS.

Dolphin: Sea journey of Dionysus. From a Greek bowl, ca. 350 B.C.

Dolphin As a strikingly intelligent, friendly, and mobile animal, the dolphin is represented in the myths of many peoples who lived by the SEA. —In the Minoan culture and for the Greeks and the Romans, the dolphin was considered godlike. In Greece it was sacred particularly to the god of light, Apollo, but also to Dionysus (the patron of sea travel), Aphrodite (who was born out of the sea), and Poseidon (the god of the sea). —The dolphin was considered a psychopomp who safely carried the souls of the deceased on its back into the realm of the dead. In this sense it was also associated symbolically in early Christian art with Christ the Redeemer.

Dolphin: Anchor and dolphin. From the Roman catacombs, 2nd century.

Dolphin: Various representations of dolphins on ancient coins.

Dome See CUPOLA.

Door (Gate, Portal) Similar to BRIDGE, it is a symbol of transition from one realm to a new

59

one (e.g., from this world to the next, from the profane to the holy). The idea of a heavenly gate or sun gate that marks the transition into the extraterrestrial, divine realm is widespread. Also the underworld or the realm of the dead often lies, according to the ideas of many peoples, beyond a great gate or door. —The closed door often points to a hidden secret, but also to prohibition and futility; the open door or gate presents a challenge to pass through or signifies an open secret. —The representation of Christ in medieval panels (e.g., in the Tympanon) refers to Christ's saying: "I am the gate." Representa-

Dove: Aphrodite with the dove. Gold foil, Mycenae.

Door: Door of the Tabernacle.

tions of Mary, on the other hand, often make reference to the symbolic interpretation of Mary as the gate of heaven through which the Son of God entered the world. See JANUS.

Dough It is a symbol of unformed material substance or of the union of WATER and EARTH. The working and forming of dough is sometimes also compared with male sexuality and creativity.

Dove In the Near East it is associated with the fertility goddess Ishtar; in Phoenicia, with the Astarte cult. In Greece the dove was sacred to Aphrodite. —In India, and also to some extent among the Germanic tribes, a dark dove was regarded as a bird of death and misfortune. —Islam views the dove as sacred because it was supposed to have protected Mohammed on his escape. —In the Bible, Noah sends out three doves after the flood; one of them returns with

Dove: The dove as the Holy Spirit. After a miniature of the Holy Trinity in the Landgrafen Psalter, ca. 1212.

an olive branch, a sign of reconciliation with God and thus a symbol of peace. The white dove is also a symbol of simplicity, purity, and, especially in Christian art, the Holy Spirit. It sometimes represents the baptized Christian or the martyr (when carrying the LAUREL or the martyr's crown in its beak), or the soul in the condition of heavenly peace (e.g., sitting on the TREE of life or on a vessel containing the water of life). —In connection with the four cardinal virtues, the dove symbolizes moderation. —A pair of white doves is a popular love symbol.

Dragon In the mythical images of many peoples, it is a living hybrid composed of such animals as the SERPENT, lizard, bird, and LION, and it is often depicted with several heads. In many religions it, like the snake, embodies the primal powers that are hostile to god and must be overcome. In this connection a number of dragon-slayer myths have arisen (involving, e.g., Indra, Zeus, Apollo, Siegfried, St. George). —In the Old Testament the dragon (similar to the LEVIATHAN) embodies the continuing effects of the primal chaos, which threatens creation and must be vanquished. In the Apocalypse the dragon, as the satanic principle, follows the woman clothed with the sun who gives birth to the Christ child; the dragon is felled by the archangel Michael. —In sagas and fairy tales, the dragon often appears as the guardian of a TREASURE or of an abducted PRINCESS and thus personifies the difficulties that must be overcome before an important goal can be attained. —Jung sees the myths of battle with the dragon as the expression of battle between the ego and the regressive powers of the unconscious. —In Hinduism and Taoism the dragon is seen as a powerful spiritual being that can produce the DRAUGHT of immortality. —In China and Japan it is revered as bringing good fortune and as frightening away demons. It grants fertility because it is closely associated with the powers of water and hence with the yin principle (see YIN AND YANG); however, above all it represents the masculine, active powers of heaven and thus the yang principle. As demiurge it brings forth from itself the water of the primal origin or the world EGG; its

Dragon: Michael battles the dragon. After an illustration in the *Bamberg Apocalypse*, ca. 1000.

Dragon: From a dragon waistcoat. China, 17th century.

Dragon: The woman of the apocalypse with the seven-headed dragon. After a book illustration of Konrad von Scheyern.

Duck: From a mural in the grave of the Egyptian scribe Harmhab.

opponent is the TIGER. A popular decorative motif is the dragon, or a pair of dragons, playing with the PEARL of desire. As a powerful being mediating the polar principles, the dragon became the imperial symbol. —The dragon is the fifth sign in the Chinese ZODIAC; it corresponds to Leo, the LION.

Draught As the draught or potion of immortality, it is a symbol of heightened consciousness related to the knowledge of eternal duration. The negative complement of this is the draught of forgetfulness.

Drum It is an instrument frequently used in rites and rituals; its rhythmical sound is sometimes (e.g., in Buddhism) equated with the hidden sounds and powers of the cosmos. Often (e.g., among black African peoples) the drum served magically to call down heavenly powers; the war drum in particular was closely associated with the symbolism of LIGHTNING and THUNDER. —In China the sound of the drum was related to the course of the SUN and especially to the winter solstice (i.e., that point when the yin principle exerts its greatest influence but also when the sun, and hence the yang principle, begins to increase its influence again). See YIN AND YANG. —The drum is the symbolic heart of the universe for Native Americans.

Duck In Egypt ducks were favorite sacrificial animals. —In the Far East duck and drake couples, which usually swim together, were considered symbols of conjugal happiness. See KINGFISHER.

Dung Beetle See SCARAB.

Dust It is a symbol in the Bible and in Christian literature of the transitoriness of human life. In Genesis it also represents Adam's countless descendants.

Dwarfs In folk belief they are creatures similar to humans; they are usually small, old men who have the feet of a goose, duck, or bird and who are sometimes alternately visible and invisible, helpful or provocatively malicious. Dwarfs have been interpreted as symbolic embodiments of useful but ultimately uncontrollable natural forces and powers, as well as of experiences and unconscious actions understood only partially or not at all.

Eagle Found extensively as a symbolic animal, usually in connection with the SUN and heaven (see SKY), it is also associated with LIGHTNING and THUNDER. It is the eagle's power, endurance, and heavenward flight that inform the symbol. —In several American Indian cultures the eagle as related to sun and heaven is juxtaposed to the chthonic JAGUAR. Its feathers were used in ritual dress and cult implements as symbols of the sun's rays. —The eagle is seen as the "king" of the birds and since antiquity has been a symbol of kings and gods. In Greek and Roman times it was the companion and symbolic animal of Zeus (Jupiter). In Roman art an ascending eagle bears the ruler's soul, which rises to the gods after cremation of the body. Roman legions carried the eagle on their standards. —In the Bible the eagle is the emblem of God's omnipotence or of the power of faith. —PHYSIOLOGUS ascribes to the eagle the same legendary characteristics as to the PHOENIX; thus in the Middle Ages the eagle was a symbol of rebirth and baptism as well as of Christ and (because of its flight) his ascension. The mystics repeatedly compared the ascending eagle with prayer. Aristotle taught that the eagle looks directly into the sun as it ascends, so it is also symbolic of contemplation and spiritual cognition. As such a symbol (and because of its flight to the heights), the eagle is also the attribute of John the Evangelist (see EVANGELISTS, SYMBOLS OF). —Among the seven mortal sins, the eagle symbolizes pride; among the four cardinal virtues, justice. —Continuing the Roman tradition, the German Empire and later the Federal Republic adopted the eagle. As a sign of sovereignty, it appears in the insignia of many nations. —Jung regards the eagle as a father symbol.

Eagle: *Top*: Single-headed imperial eagle of the Middle Ages. *Bottom*: Double-headed imperial eagle, since 1401.

Eagle: The symbol of the spirit. From *The Hermaphroditic Child of Sun and Moon*, 1752.

Ear It is a symbol of hearing, communication, and of obedience. As the spiritual ear it is, like

Eagle: The symbol of John the Evangelist. Capital in the Cloister of St. Trophime, Arles, 12th century.

Ear: Lo-Han seated. Statue of fired clay, China, T'ang period.

Earth: The earth as *prima materia* suckling the philosopher's son. From Mylius's *Philosophia Reformata*, 1622.

the EYE, symbolic of inspiration (spiritual "hearing" is considered to be older than spiritual "seeing"). —In antiquity the ear was regarded as the seat of memory; pulling on the ear, which was common in judicial proceedings through the Middle Ages, was considered to be an appeal to the witness's memory not to forget specific facts. —A long or broad outer ear was often (e.g., in China) seen as a sign of judgment, wisdom, and immortality. —In Africa the ear often has sexual significance. The outer ear is regarded as phallic while the ear canal, as the receptive organ, is compared with the vagina.

Earth In contrast to heaven (see SKY), it is usually interpreted as feminine, passive, and dark; it often appears in mythology as a female deity. Creation myths sometimes represent the origin of the world as a procreative act in which earth is fertilized by heaven; earth is also compared symbolically to the WOMB. —The earth is not only the womb out of which all life proceeds, but also the grave into which it returns; hence its symbolic meaning corresponds to the ambivalent figure of the "Great Mother," who is both life-giving and life-taking. Ritual burials and subsequent "resurrections" in INITIATION rites sometimes allude to the connection between the death and birth aspects of the earth. —In alchemy the earth is often represented by the inverted triangle cut across with the horizontal bar: ▽. —In astrology it is linked with the signs of CAPRICORN, Taurus (see STEER), and Virgo (see VIRGIN). See ZODIAC.

Easter Egg See EGG.

Easter Bunny See HARE.

Ebony It is a hard, heavy wood that shares the symbolism of BLACK because of its color. According to saga, the throne of the underworld god, Pluto, is made of ebony.

Ecclesia See CHURCH.

Echidna It is a monster of Greek mythology, consisting of a woman's body whose lower trunk is a SERPENT. From her were born various other monsters (e.g., CERBERUS, the CHIMERA, Scylla, and the SPHINX). She is viewed as a symbol of the psycho-physical, spiritual-instinctual dual nature of human beings. —Jung regards her as a symbol of tabooed incest wishes (i.e., the mother as a beautiful young woman whose lower body evokes associations of horror).

Echo According to Indian conceptions, it is an attribute of the JAGUAR (interpreted as a chthonic deity) because of its association with mountains, wild animals, and drumming. —In Greek mythology it is generally a nymph who falls in love with the handsome youth Narcissus. —For many peoples it is a symbol of regression or passivity; it also represents the ambiguous or the shadow and is sometimes associated with the golem.

Eclipse The total solar eclipse is a seldomly occurring event that has long terrified people and has given rise to evil premonitions and prophecies of catastrophe. —In Islam and Buddhism (and in other cultural regions), the eclipse of the sun and of the moon is often associated with the death of the celestial body, which is thought to have been devoured by a monster. —In Chinese the same word is used for the "darkness of a star" and for "eat, devour." The solar or lunar eclipse was interpreted in China as a disturbance of the macrocosm due to a disturbance in the microcosm specifically caused by the emperor or his wives. —The reappearance of the sun or moon after an eclipse is frequently understood to be the beginning of a new cycle or era.

Ecstasy (Intoxication) In many cultures it was closely connected with harvest rites and prayers for fertility. Because it creates the ability to transcend the bounds of everyday consciousness, the ecstasy achieved through dance, music, alcohol, or drugs is commonly considered to be an expression of special connectedness to God.

Egg As the germ of life, it is a widely recognized fertility symbol. —The *world egg* is central to the mythical concepts of many cultures. As the symbol of the totality of all creative forces, it was present at the primal beginning, frequently floated upon the primal ocean, and gave forth from itself the entire world and the elements (or, initially, only heaven [see SKY] and EARTH).

Egg: A serpent, here symbolizing time, spirals about the world egg. From J. Bryant's *Analysis of Ancient Mythology*, 1774.

Egypt

Egg: Mercurius in the philosopher's egg. From *Mutus Liber*, 1702.

—Mythic human figures (e.g., Chinese heroes) were sometimes imagined as breaking forth from eggs. —Because of its simple form, its (often) white color, and the wealth of possibilities resting within it, the egg also is a symbol of perfection. —In alchemy the philosophical egg played an important role as symbol of the *prima materia* from which the philosophical fire hatched the PHILOSOPHERS' STONE. —The yellow yoke often signifies GOLD, and the egg white signifies SILVER. —In Christianity the egg is a resurrection symbol because Christ broke forth from the grave like a mature chick from the egg; the *Easter egg*, which had played a role as a fertility symbol in heathen spring celebrations, thus received a specifically Christian meaning.

Egypt According to the Old Testament, it was the land of slavery for the people of Israel and the land of pagan gods; hence it is symbolically opposite the land of promise.

Eight It is the number of the major directions of the compass card in its simplest form, as well as of cosmic order and equilibrium. —Eight plays an important role in Hinduism and Buddhism. It is usually the number of spokes in the Buddhist WHEEL symbol; the symbolic LOTUS blossom often has eight petals; eight paths lead to spiritual perfection; the Hindu god Vishnu has eight arms, which must be viewed in connection with the eight guardians of the universe. —In Japan, eight stands for a fundamentally immeasurable and uncountable magnitude. —In Christian symbolism eight refers to the "eight days of creation" (i.e., to the regeneration of humanity); it is likewise a symbol of the resurrection of Christ and of the hope for the resurrection of humankind.

Elder

Elder A bush or tree with white, fragrant blossoms and violet-black fruits, it was valued in antiquity as a medicinal plant; touching the elder was considered effective to transfer the disease to the plant. Additionally, the elder was used as a prophylactic against magicians and witches. Cutting down or burning the elder was believed to bring misfortune or death. —Because Judas was supposed to have hanged himself on an elder tree, the elder was associated with the Devil.

Elecampane It is a large, coarse composite herb with yellow ray flowers. Helen is said to have held it in her hands when she was abducted by Paris (hence the Latin name, *Inula helenium*). The herb molly, which Hermes brought to Odysseus so that he could free his comrades from Circe's enchantment, was occasionally thought to be elecampane. (Usually, however, it was considered to be the black hellebore root). —In Christianity, the elecampane seldom occurs as a symbolic plant; it means "redemption."

Elements They are the fundamental principles structuring the world; other basic phenomena from other realms of being are often ascribed to them. —The Chinese doctrine of the elements arose in the second pre-Christian millennium; it embraced water, fire, wood, metal, and earth. Water corresponds to the number one, the depths, winter, and the north; fire to the number two, height, summer, and south; wood, to the

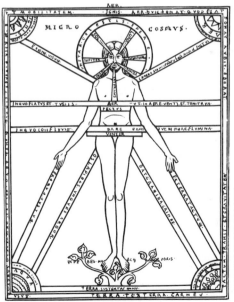

Elements: The human being as microcosm under the influence of the planets and the four elements. After a pen sketch from the *Glossarium Salomonis*, Prufening, ca. 1160.

67

number three, spring, and east; metal to the number four, autumn, and west; the earth, which corresponds to the numeral five, is the mediating element. —Most other cultures, such

Elements: Man at the intersection point of the four elements; after a woodcut by H. Weiditz in *Historia Naturalis*, by C. Plinius Secundus, Frankfurt, 1582.

as the Greek, distinguish four elements (Empedocles was the first to make the distinction): FIRE, WATER, AIR, and EARTH. Since the time of Aristotle, the "fifth element," ether (as the brightly shining high atmosphere lying above the air layer close to earth), was sometimes added; it corresponds to both fire and air. —The doctrine of the temperaments related the four elements to the four temperaments: water to the phlegmatic, earth to the melancholic, fire to the choleric, and air to the sanguine. Likewise the four ages of humanity, bodily fluids and organs, the four times of day, and (as in China) the four seasons were sometimes related to the four elements. —Jung refers to the distinction between masculine, active principles (fire and air) and feminine, passive ones (water and earth). —The Freemasons related the four elements to levels of spiritual development. Human beings are born of earth and are cleansed in a stepwise fashion by passing through air, water, and fire. —The elements were personified during the Renaissance as ancient gods: earth as Cybele, water as Neptune, air as Juno, and fire as Vulcan. —In addition to the four elements of the Greek natural philosophers, the alchemists also conceived of the so-called philosophical elements: SALT, SULFUR, and MERCURIUS (quicksilver).

Elephant: The Indian god Ganesha depicted as an elephant. Sculpture from the 12th century.

Elephant In Asia it is the steed of the ruler and a symbol of power, wisdom, peace, and happiness. It is the steed of the Indian god Indra. Ganesha, the popular son of the god Shiva, the victor over obstacles, is depicted with an elephant's head. In India and Tibet the elephant often appears as the bearer of the entire universe; hence it occurs in architecture as a supporting structure. —In the white elephant are united the symbolic meanings of the elephant and of the color WHITE. According to Buddhist conceptions, before his rebirth as the Buddha the bodhisattva entered the womb of his mother, Princess Maya, as a white elephant; the white elephant thus became a popular symbol of Buddhism. —In Africa the elephant has been revered as a symbol of strength, happiness, and long life. Sometimes one finds an elephant cult that derives from a hunted elephant's forgiving the hunters that have killed it. —According to Aristotle, the male elephant remained chaste during the two-year pregnancy of its mate; hence in the Middle Ages it was associated with the virtues of prudence and moderation (see TEMPERANTIA).

Eleven In Christian symbolism it sometimes represents the number of the sins, since they exceed TEN, the number of the Decalogue.

Elixir See DRAUGHT.

Embryo As it relates to the symbolism of the EGG, it represents still dormant possibilities. —The golden embryo of the Veda symbolizes the principle of life, which is carried by the primal waters (a clear parallel to the then current idea of the *world egg*).

Emerald It is a gemstone that generally shares the symbolism of the color GREEN. —The Indians of Central America associated it with BLOOD (among the Indians, the colors green and RED are expressions of vital energy), the RAIN, and the MOON. —Because of its green color, the emerald is associated in Europe with fertility and thus with moistness, the moon, and spring. —In Rome the emerald was an attribute of Venus. —According to the Book of Revelation, the emerald is among the stones of which the Heavenly Jerusalem is built. —In the Middle Ages the symbolic content of the emerald was manifold. It was regarded as a potently effective talisman because it supposedly originally came from hell; it was especially useful against the infernal powers. It was simultaneously believed that placing an emerald on the tongue enabled one to summon evil spirits and to hold conversations with them. To the consecrated emerald (i.e., one freed of its evil powers) was ascribed the capacity to free those imprisoned. —In Christian symbolism the emerald signifies purity, belief, and immortality.

Enchanter's Nightshade See VALERIAN.

Enlightenment See LIGHT.

Entrails In the folk beliefs of various cultures, entrails possessed meanings related to the future. Particularly widespread was divination using the entrails of sacrificed animals. See LIVER.

Envy See INVIDIA.

Erinyes In Greek and Roman mythology they are the three avenging spirits, especially of crimes against the ties of kinship. (They are also known as the Furies). They are depicted in art as ugly and usually appear with wings, with snakes in their hair and hands, and with torches and whips. —They are often symbolic of a punitive, bad conscience. See EUMENIDES.

Ermine Any of several species of large *weasels* that turn white in winter. Because of its white color it is a symbol of purity, innocence, and incorruptibility; it was often used as fur trim on the robes of rulers to denote nobility. —In Christian art it symbolizes Christ as victor over the Devil, since the ermine hunts and kills SERPENTS.

Etimasie It is a symbolic motif of preparing the throne for Christ's return. Under the cross is the empty throne with the lamb, dove, book of life or scroll, crown, purple cloak, and so on. In the orthodox church it is situated above the ALTAR.

Etimasie: Baptistery of the Orthodox, Ravenna, 5th century.

Eumenides In Greek mythology they are the "forgiving goddesses," often interpreted as symbolic embodiments of divine grace. They are identical to the ERINYES; it is unclear whether the ascription of friendly characteristics to the avenging goddesses is an instance of euphemism or whether the Erinyes, like other chthonic divinities, were both terrifying and beneficent.

Evangelists, Symbols of In Christian art they are the attributes associated with the depictions of the Evangelists; these symbols may also stand for the Evangelists. The angel or HUMAN BEING is associated with Matthew, the LION with Mark, the STEER with Luke, and the EAGLE with John. These associations derive from the vision of the TETRAMORPH described in the Apocalypse of John. The symbols of the Evangelists were originally interpreted in connection with Christ. Through birth, Christ became human; he died like a sacrificial steer; he arose from the grave like a lion; and rose to heaven at the Ascension like an eagle. Later another interpretation became common. The (often winged) human figure for Matthew was related to Christ's lineage and his birth (with the report of which the Gospel According to Matthew begins); the lion of Mark referred to the beginning of the Gospel According to Mark, which reports John's sermon in the wilderness; the steer (as sacrificial animal) of Luke was considered a sign of the beginning of the Gospel According to Luke, which commences with the sacrifice of Zechariah; and the eagle of John symbolized the spiritual heights of the Gospel According to John.

Eve See ADAM AND EVE, SERPENT.

Evening Star Like the MORNING STAR, it is a designation for the bright planet Venus, but in contrast to the morning star, it refers to the evening position of Venus. Because it is considered the herald of approaching night, it is occasionally the Christian symbol of Lucifer.

Excrement Especially among primitive peoples, it was often thought to have valuable powers; sometimes it was symbolically associated with GOLD. —Some African tribes believed that manure piles were inhabited by souls that entered the bodies of women. —The high esteem for excrement led some peoples to practice ritual coprophagy through which they believed they could incorporate the powers of the excreting animal or person into themselves. The early use of excrement in preparation of medicines is also related to these ideas. —From a psychoanalytic perspective, the high value placed on

Matthew

John

Mark

Luke

Evangelists, Symbols of: Detail after a miniature, Pontifical of Chartres, early 13th century.

excrement correlates with the imagery of the early childhood anal phase.

Eye As the primary organ of sense perception, it is closely associated with LIGHT, the SUN, and spirit. It symbolizes spiritual and mental perception, but it is also—as the "mirror" of the soul—the organ of spiritual and mental expression. The right eye is sometimes associated with activity, the future, and the sun; the left with passivity, the past, and the moon. —Buddhism speaks of the third eye as a symbol of inner vision. —In antiquity the eye frequently was a symbol of the sun deity. —In Egypt a common AMULET was the so-called udjat eye, the hawk

Eye: Protection against the evil eye. Mosaic at the doorway of a Roman villa.

Eye: The Egyptian udjat eye. Faience of the late period.

Eye: Head and hand of the Tibetan goddess Tara. Statue in the cloister of Traschilhumpo.

eye of the sky god Horus, resting on a crosier; the eye symbolizes the broad view and omniscience, and the staff the power of the ruler. The amulet was supposed to bestow invulnerability and eternal fertility. —In the Bible the eye is a symbol of the omniscience, vigilance, and the protective omnipresence of God. In Christian art an eye surrounded by sun rays signifies God; an eye in the hand of God signifies God's creative wisdom; an eye in a triangle signifies God the Father in the Trinity. Eyes on the wings of the cherubim (see CHERUB) and seraphim (see SERAPH) refer to their penetrating ability to recognize and know. —Since ancient times apotropaic powers have been attributed to representations of the eye.

Falcon It is generally a solar, masculine sky symbol. In Egypt it was a divine symbolic animal because of its strength, beauty, and high flight; it was sacred to Ra, the sun god. The god Horus usually assumes the form of a falcon or of a human with falcon's head, but other deities also appear in falcon form. —The hooded falcon symbolizes, particularly in the Renaissance, the hope for the light that will illuminate the darkness (as in the motto *post tenebras spero lucem*).

Fan A common device in Babylon, India, China, Persia, Greece, Rome, and in other cultures, it symbolizes sovereign rank, particularly when made of palm fronds or of ostrich or peacock feathers. —In Hinduism the fan represents, among other things, ritual sacrifice, since the sacrificial fires are fanned with it. —Especially in China and Japan, the movement of the fan was associated with defense against evil spirits.

Falcon: Horus in the form of a falcon. Egyptian mural in a grave.

Fat In various cultures it was considered to be a sign of prosperity (and thus was also a valuable sacrifice to the gods), or it was seen to be imbued with the particular powers of the animals from which the fat was rendered. See BUTTER, OIL.

Fates The Greek and Roman goddesses of destiny (also known as *Parcae*) who, through their acts, symbolize the working of fate. According to Hesiod they are the daughters of Night or of Zeus and Themis: Clotho, who spins the THREAD of life; Lachesis, who draws it off the spindle, granting each person his or her own destiny; and Atropos, who cuts the thread of life (see SHEARS).

Feast: Last Supper scene. After a Gospel Book in Corpus Christi College, Cambridge.

Feast As a ritual banquet in many cultures, the feast symbolizes participation in a community and sometimes also in a religiously significant act.

Feathers They are a symbol for many peoples of vegetation, probably because of their leaflike appearance. Because of their raylike form and their intimate relationship to BIRDS, they are also symbolically associated with the sky and the sun. The feather headdress (usually made of the feathers of the prairie eagle) of some North

American Indian tribes is a power symbol closely associated with the sun. —For many peoples feathers served as attributes of social position (e.g., the feather plume on the helmet of the medieval knight).

Fennel Because of its supposed eye-strengthening effect, fennel occasionally signifies spiritual clear-sightedness. Since it also supposedly causes molting in snakes that eat it, it symbolizes periodic renewal or rejuvenation. In the Middle Ages it was considered to be an apotropaic plant. Because of its fragrance and its valuable oil, it is sometimes associated with Mary.

Fermentation For many peoples (e.g., in Africa and India), it is a symbol of matter infused with spirit and of the exuberant power of the imagination. People said of fermented drinks that they had the power to mediate esoteric knowledge; consequently they were often used in ritual acts. —Since the process of fermentation is closely related to that of decay, fermented food stuffs can sometimes also be associated with EXCRE-MENT. —In alchemy, fermentation represents the "ripening" and transformation of organic substance and is also seen in conjunction with the transition from death into life. See LEAVEN.

Fetish Particularly in West Africa, objects such as wood or clay figures, but also parts of animals, etc., that were venerated as magical, beneficial, and protective power sources. Occasionally the object of ritual actions, they were, for example, penetrated with nails, an action that was symbolically supposed to transfer illness to the particular fetish.

Field As a plowed field (see PLOW), it is a symbol of the WOMB. As an unplowed field, it is occasionally a symbol of Mary's virginity.

Fifty In the Bible it is the number for joy and the feast. The 50th day after Easter (originally after the beginning of harvest) was a joyous harvest festival for the Hebrews. Every 50th year the slaves were freed, debts forgiven, and extended rest from work was taken. The first Pentecost, the descent of the Holy Ghost, took place 50 days after Christ's ascension.

Fig Tree Revered as a holy TREE by many peoples, it often symbolizes fertility and abundance (like the OLIVE TREE and the GRAPE VINE). In antiquity it had erotic symbolic significance and was sacred to Dionysus. —In India, a fig tree growing down from heaven symbolizes the world. —The *bodhi tree* is the fig tree under which the Buddha became enlightened (from Sanskrit *bodhi*, enlightenment); in a general sense it is a symbol of knowledge and enlightenment. —Jesus's cursing the unfruitful fig tree in the New Testament is interpreted as a condemnation of the Jewish people; hence in Christian art, a dried fig symbolizes the synagogue.

Fig tree: Symbolic representation of Buddha's enlightenment. Relief from the Stupa of Bharhut (Bhodi Tree Temple).

Finger Among various African peoples, it plays a very complex, symbolic role with manifold references to life and bodily sensations. —In astrological tradition, the THUMB is assigned to Venus, the index finger to Jupiter, the middle finger to Saturn, the ring finger to the Sun, and the little finger to Mercury. —In folk usage, the ring finger is called the heart finger because it was thought to be linked directly to the heart by a special nerve or artery; hence the love and fidelity symbolism of the ring finger, particularly of the left hand (the heart side). —Finger and hand gestures have at all times been aids in emotional and spiritual expression and have been richly developed in Indian art and dance. —In antiquity, sticking out the middle finger was an insult; interlacing the fingers was a defensive gesture. —In Mediterranean lands, "the fig" (i.e., a gesture formed by thrusting the thumb between the index and middle fingers of the closed hand) has for ages been understood as a defensive gesture against the evil eye, as a coarse insult, and as a sexual symbol. —In occidental art a finger laid on the mouth signifies silence. The Christ Child with his finger on his mouth or tongue, however, refers to the Logos as the spoken word. See HAND.

Finger: The "fig" amulet.

Finger Glove See GLOVE.

Fire It is considered by many peoples to be sacred, purifying, and renewing; its power to destroy is often interpreted as the means to rebirth at a higher level (see CREMATION, PHOENIX). Occasionally specific fire gods were honored, such as Agni in India or Hestia in Greece; in China several fire gods were known. —In the Bible, God or the divine is sometimes symbolized by fire. The Apocalypse mentions such images as *fire wheels* (see WHEEL) and animals that spew fire. In the Old Testament God appears as a column of fire (see COLUMN) and in a burning THORNBUSH. —Often fire is associated with the SUN, the LIGHT (or LIGHTNING), the color RED (or BLOOD), and the HEART. In contrast to WATER, which is sometimes said to arise from the earth, fire is often thought to come from heaven (see SKY). —The myths of many peoples speak of a theft of fire, which is interpreted as a crime or sacrilege. —In Greek natural philosophy, fire is either the origin of all being or one of the ELEMENTS. —Simultaneously, however, fire is closely associated with the symbolic nexus of

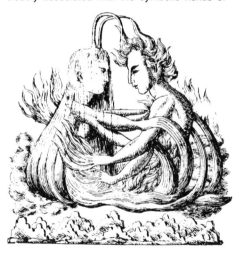

Fire: Indian depiction of the marriage of fire and water, which each have four hands, symbolizing their efficacy.

destruction, war, evil, the demonic, hell, or divine wrath. The burning of Sodom and Gomorrah was often understood in the Middle Ages to be a preview of *hellfire*. —Production of fire through friction was associated in many cultures with sexuality; the origin of fire is frequently ascribed to a sexual act of mythic beings or animals. —The apotropaic effect of fire plays a role among numerous peoples; for example, among the Germanic tribes the HEARTH fire, which drove away evil spirits, must never be extinguished. —In alchemy, fire is often symbolized by the upward-pointing equilateral triangle. —In the ZODIAC, fire is linked with the signs of ARIES, Leo (see LION), and SAGITTARIUS. See FLAME.

Firefly Because of its ability to glow in the dark, it is sometimes a symbol of the soul's ongoing life after death. —In China it is traditionally associated with students, since the firefly's light was supposedly the only source illuminating their books at night.

Firewater See ALCOHOL.

Fire Wheel See FIRE, WHEEL.

Fish Closely related symbolically to WATER, its vital element, it is also a symbol of fertility and death. As a symbol of life and fertility, it is a TALISMAN found in many places. —In Egypt, most varieties of fish were thought to be holy, but they were often simultaneously viewed as threatening and uncanny. —The fish is one of the oldest secret symbols of Christ, probably because of the baptism in water; later the Greek designation for fish (*ichthius*) was interpreted as an acrostic for the words *Iesous Christos Theou Huios Soter* (Jesus Christ, Son of God, Savior). Baptized Christians saw themselves as fish who had been reborn in the baptismal waters. As an embodiment of Christ, the fish also symbolizes spiritual nourishment and, especially when pictured along with BREAD, the eucharist. —The fishes (Pisces) are the 12th and last sign of the ZODIAC; their element is WATER.

Fish: Two fishes with an anchor. Licinia's gravestone.

Fishes: The astrological sign for Pisces.

Fishermen See NET.

Five A particularly significant numeral because it is (a) the sum of the first even and the first uneven numbers (i.e., TWO and THREE, insofar as ONE is not taken to be an actual number), and (b) the midpoint of the SQUARE, conceived as a quaternity (see FOUR). For the Pythagoreans it symbolized marriage and synthesis as the union of two and three. Five is the number of the fingers on one hand (and can signify this), the senses, the wounds of Christ, the pillars of piety in Islam. —Five played a special role in China as symbol of the midpoint (see CENTER); moreover, the Chinese knew five colors, five fragrances, five tones, five planets, five metals. In addition, five is the number of the harmonious union of YIN AND YANG. —In Hinduism five signifies, among other things, the number of the life principle. The god Shiva was sometimes imagined with five faces (the fifth, looking upward, was identified with the WORLD AXIS and was usually not depicted); he was sometimes worshiped in the form of the five LINGA-representations. —The alchemists sought in the *quintessence* (the fifth essence, i.e., the fifth element in addition to the other four) the spirit that generates and preserves life; the fivefold ornamentation found occasionally in Christian churches of the Middle Ages is possibly related to these ideas. See PENTAGRAM.

Flag It is a symbol of sovereignty as well as of national or group allegiance. In war it signifies military honor and fidelity, which are to be defended with the sacrifice of one's own life if necessary. The fluttering flag often represents starting out or the power to create future change. —In the symbolism of Christian art, Christ or the Lamb carries the flag as a sign of resurrection and of the victory over the powers of darkness.

Flame To a large extent it is symbolically identical with FIRE and often appears *pars pro toto* for fire (e.g., as the fire of the Holy Ghost in representations of the miracle at Pentecost or of Christ's baptism). The extraordinary power and the destructive force associated with the "fieriness" of speech are sometimes graphically depicted by fire that appears in place of the tongue or comes from the mouth. Vices such as greed, envy, and lust are also symbolized as fire.

Flaming Sword See SWORD.

Flamingo It is associated in the Upanishads with the symbolism of LIGHT.

Flammeum See RED.

Flint It is a symbol of LIGHTNING for many primitive peoples.

Floods Representing the violent aspect of WATER, which often devours or indiscriminately buries everything in its path, floods also symbolize dangerous passions. —Throwing oneself into the flood signifies the courageous step into the unknown. —In the Bible floods are signs of decline and death. See WAVES.

Flute It is an instrument often associated with shepherds. —The sound of the flute is sometimes interpreted as the voice of angels or of mythic or enchanted beings. —In Islamic cultures, the sound of reed pipes, which are played for the dervishes' dances, symbolizes the call of the soul that is separated from God and that wants to return to the heavenly realms.

Fly In the Far East the fly symbolizes the immaterial or the restlessly wandering soul. —The fly is primarily associated with illness, death, and the Devil. There was a widespread belief that demons of illness threatened people in the form of flies. The principal Devil mentioned in the Bible is *Beelzebub* (from Hebrew *Ba'al zebhubh*, lord of the flies, a perversion of the original Canaanite deity Baalzebul), often represented as a fly. He plays a role in folk belief, especially in magic spells. —In Persian mythology the principal of opposition, Ahriman, slips into the world as a fly.

Fly: Beelzebub. From Collin de Plancy's *Dictionnaire Infernal*, 1845.

Fog It is a symbol of the indefinite, of the transition from one condition to another, or of the fantastic. According to the mythological ideas of many peoples, it was the primal substance of the world. —Depictions of fog often occur in Japanese painting. See CLOUDS.

Foot It is that part of the human and animal body most closely associated with the EARTH. As the organ of locomotion, of "stepping out," it is related to the will; for instance, in folk customs and in law, "placing one's foot on something" was understood to be a sign of taking possession. Particularly in antiquity it was customary to place one's foot on the vanquished enemy as a sign of total dominance. —Arising on, or stepping off with, the right foot was considered as early as the time of the Romans to bring good fortune, but with the left foot such action augured bad luck. —Bare feet are often a sign of humility (e.g., when entering a mosque or a sanctuary); in monastic orders bare feet are an expression of poverty. —Demonic beings are often represented with animal feet (e.g., depictions of the Devil with feet of rams or horses; or DWARFS or female demons with feet of geese or ducks). —Kissing the foot (of those of higher rank) was—considering the "lowliness" of the foot—symbolic of profound submission. —Washing of feet (see HAND AND FOOT WASHING), which in the Orient is an act of hospitality, is a symbol of humility and love when performed by someone of higher rank. On Maundy Thursday, foot washing is customary in the Catholic church as a symbolic repetition of Jesus's washing the feet of his disciples. —In the psychoanalytic view, the foot is often given a phallic meaning.

Foot Washing See HAND AND FOOT WASHING.

Foreigner In all religions that see the next world as the legitimate home of humanity, the foreigner is a symbol of the original, homeless condition of people on earth. See PILGRIM.

Forest In the religious ideas and folk beliefs of many peoples, the forest plays a significant role as a sacred and mysterious realm where good and evil gods, spirits and demons, wild men, fairies, and female wood, moss, and forest spirits dwell. Sacred groves, which offer protective asylum, have symbolic meaning in many cultures. Consequently, pictures of the forest, or of the forest as the scene of dramatic events, point symbolically to irrational but also to hidden things. —As a place of seclusion from the affairs of the world, the forest, like the DESERT, is a favorite dwelling place of ascetics and hermits and is thus a symbol of spiritual concentration and introversion. —The dark forest, which conceals its secrets, often occurs in German fairy tales, sagas, poetry, literature, and song. —Psychoanalysis regards the forest as a symbol of the unconscious; as a symbolic reference it can manifest in dream images as well as in actual anxiety when an individual confronts a dark forest. Sometimes it is also interpreted as a symbol of woman (especially the forested hill).

Fortitudo The personification of *bravery*, one of the four cardinal virtues, it is frequently depicted with the CLUB, SWORD, shield, LION, and banner of victory.

Fortress. As a fortified place of dwelling, often situated on a pinnacle or surrounded by a FOREST, it is a symbol of protection and safety. In the Bible and in Christian symbolism, it signifies refuge in God or faith, which protects against the demons. Occasionally hell is depicted as a dark, sometimes subterranean, fortress with numerous dungeons and chambers.

Fortuna The Roman goddess of fate, but later the goddess only of good fortune, she is identified with the Greek goddess TYCHE and often appears in the art of the Renaissance. As the personification of chance or changing luck, she is usually depicted as standing on a WHEEL or sphere. A frequent attribute of Fortuna is the HORN of plenty. See BLINDFOLD.

Fortuna: The *Fortuna* of V. Solis the Elder.

Forty In the Bible it is the number for expectation, preparation, penitence, fasting, and punishment. The waters of the flood flowed for 40 days and 40 nights; Moses waited 40 days and 40 nights on Mt. Sinai before he received the tablets of the law; the city of Nineveh did penance 40 days to escape God's punishment; the Israelites were 40 years in the wilderness; Jesus fasted 40 days in the wilderness; after the resurrection, Jesus appeared to his disciples during a period of 40 days. —With reference to Christ's fast, the Christian church practices a 40-day fast (Lent) before Easter.

Fountain It is symbolically associated with WATER, but also with deep secrets and access to hidden springs and sources. Descent into the well (e.g., in fairy tales) often symbolizes the path to esoteric knowledge or to the realm of the unconscious. Plunging into the water of the well corresponds symbolically to drinking a particular elixir (see DRAUGHT) that grants immortality, youth, and health (e.g., the *Fountain of Youth*). —In the Bible the well is symbolically connected to cleansing and purification, blessing, and the water of life.—In Arab lands, wells with square stone enclosures often represent paradise.

Fountain: The fountain of life as *fons mercurialis*. From the *Rosarium Philosophorum*, 1550.

Fountain of Youth

Fountain of Youth See FOUNTAIN.

Four As a symbolic number it is closely associated with the SQUARE and the CROSS. It is the number of the cardinal directions and hence of the primary winds, the seasons, the elements (AIR, EARTH, FIRE, WATER), the temperaments, the rivers in paradise, the Evangelists, the stages of life (childhood, youth, maturity, old age). As a principle that divides and orders space, it is primarily a symbol of the earth and thus often of wholeness. See TETRAMORPH.

Four: The four winds. Old woodcut.

Fourteen A number significant in Christian symbolism as the double of the sacred number SEVEN, it is also the number of goodness and mercy (e.g., Catholic saints number 14).

Fox In Japanese and Chinese myths, it plays a significant role as a wise, demonic, partly good, partly evil animal with knowledge of magic and the ability to metamorphose into many other shapes, especially human ones. —In some Indian cultures the fox is a symbol of sexual lust. —In Europe it often symbolizes cunning and slyness. In medieval art it appears as a symbol of the Devil, lies, injustice, intemperance, greed, and lust.

Fox: Aesop listens to the words of the fox. From a bowl in the Vatican, ca. 450 B.C.

Freemasonry A secret fraternity that was founded during the Enlightenment, it adheres to no particular religion, but its symbolism, which involves building, construction, and light, has been incorporated into cultlike rites. It strove for the "world brotherhood of light" and the exercise of the "royal art" (i.e., skilled "stone mason work" on one's own ego and on building up the "temple of humanity"). The rich and manifold symbolism of Freemasonry drew extensively on the craft customs of the medieval guild of stone masons.

Freemasonry: The sign for steadfastness. From the Lodge of Johannis.

Frog Closely associated with WATER and particularly with RAIN, it is often considered to be a lunar animal and in China is bound to the yin principle (see YIN AND YANG). In China there was a belief in a seasonally changing rulership of frog and QUAIL analogous to the polar pair PHEASANT and SERPENT. —In Japan the frog presages good fortune. —In India there is the idea of the great frog that overthrows the world; the frog is also seen as a symbol of dark life trapped in matter or, in a positive sense, as mother earth. —In the Bible the frog is considered to be an unclean animal. —In Egypt there was a frog-headed goddess who assisted at birth and imparted long life and immortality; the frog was above all a resurrection symbol, probably because of its change of form during development and the assumption that it arose annually in the spring from the slime in the Nile. —For the church fathers the frog was a symbol of the Devil or (because of its perpetual noise) the heretic. —In medieval folk belief, the frog was a witch's animal, and frogs' bones were used as a love spell.

Frond See FAN.

Fruit It is a symbol of ripeness and completed development. Several fruits of different varieties often symbolize abundance, fertility, and well-being. —The forbidden fruit of paradise, not precisely described in the Bible, varies depending on the country in which it is artistically depicted; forbidden fruits include the APPLE, grapes, and cherries. They symbolize the temptation to sin.

Furies See ERINYES.

Game It is often a symbol of battle fought according to rules and waged against other persons or against obstacles to be overcome. —Games were originally associated with sacred actions; sometimes magical or prophetic significance was ascribed to their outcome. —In connection with vitally important events (e.g., the harvest), games were also an expression of thanks to the gods (for example, as symbolic representation of the battle of the elements, or of victory of vegetation over the elements). See CHESS.

Garden It is a symbol of earthly and heavenly paradise and of the cosmic order. —In the Bible, in contrast to the holy city (see JERUSALEM, HEAVENLY), which symbolizes the end of time, the garden is an image of the primal, sin-free condition of humanity. The Song of Songs compares the garden with the beloved. — In the garden of the Hesperides of Greek mythology, there grew the TREE with golden apples, which is usually interpreted as the tree of life. — As a refuge from the world, the garden is closely associated symbolically with the oasis and the IS-LAND. — The walled garden, which can be entered only through a small portal, symbolizes the difficulties and obstacles that must be overcome prior to attaining a higher level of spiritual development. The enclosed garden also symbolizes the intimate areas of the female body.

Garden: Fountain in a walled garden, symbolizing constancy and truth under difficult circumstances. From Boschius's *Symbolographia*, 1702.

Garlic Perhaps because of its strong odor, which was thought to produce the power to banish, many peoples believed that garlic was a medicament against the evil eye, evil spirits, and (especially in Central Europe) vampires. In Greece merely saying the word garlic was supposed to grant protective power.

Garment See CLOTHING.

Gate See DOOR.

Gauntlet See GLOVE.

Garlic

Gazelle A symbol of speed, it is associated (e.g., in India) with air and wind. — In the Semitic world, the gazelle is the essence of beauty, specifically because of its eyes. — Since it was said to have particularly acute vision, it is sometimes a Christian symbol of penetrating spiritual knowledge or insight. — In the fine arts the gazelle is frequently depicted as a sacrifice or a victim that is pursued or slain by wild, predatory animals; it is a symbol of something noble and defenseless destroyed through brutality. — In psychoanalytic interpretation these images represent self-destructive tendencies arising from the unconscious.

Gemini See TWINS.

Gems As hard, durable, sparkling rare minerals that can be polished or ground to shape, they represent "terrestrial stars," which are images of the heavenly light of truth on earth. For gem-specific meanings, see AMETHYST, CRYSTAL, DIAMOND, EMERALD, JADE, JASPER, SAPPHIRE, TURQUOISE). Gems were used to decorate such objects as the crowns of royalty and the breastplate of the high priest of the Old Testament; utopian buildings and cities such as the Heavenly Jerusalem (see JERUSALEM, HEAVENLY); and fairy-tale and heavenly castles.

Genuflection A ritual symbolic action that was often legally binding, it is a sign of reverence, humility, and submission.

Giants They are huge, humanlike creatures (e.g., Titans, Cyclopes) that appear in the myths and fairy tales of most peoples. Probably originally viewed as embodiments of overpowering natural forces, they are the enemies of the gods in most mythologies; in fairy tales they usually eat humans, and in folk tales they are often clumsy louts. —Sometimes there are positive images of primal giants who were involved in the creation of the world or who support it. —The battle against the giants probably symbolizes the assertion of humans over nature.

Giant: Detail from the Gundestrupp bowl depicting a giant. Relief in silver, Celtic, 1st century B.C.

Ginseng Because of the humanoid shape of its root, it is considered in China to be endowed, like the MANDRAKE, with life-prolonging powers. Since people ascribed to it the power to strengthen virility, it was associated with the yang principle (see YIN AND YANG).

Girdle Because of its circular form and its function of holding something in place, it is a symbol of strength, consecration, fidelity (i.e., a bond to a person, group, or task), protection, and chastity. Taking a person's girdle or belt signifies robbing that person of connections, strength, and sometimes also of dignity. —In India the guru's putting a girdle on one is an essential part of spiritual consecration. —In the Bible the girdle is mentioned as a symbol of readiness ("girded loins and shod feet"). —Among the Indians, Greeks, and Romans there was the custom of the bridegroom's loosing the girdle. —The girdle of Venus was prized as irresistibly and magically efficacious. —In the erotic realm, the girdle also has a separative and concealing function. The first girdle of which the Bible speaks is the girdle of fig leaves with which ADAM AND EVE hid their genitals. The angels were thought to be girded as a sign of their strength and their control over their sexual energy; the girdles of monks, hermits, and priests (serving the Mass) have the same meaning. Prostitutes during the Middle Ages were forbidden to wear either VEIL or girdle. —The virtue of easing birth was ascribed to the girdles of various saints.

Glass Like CRYSTAL, it is a symbol of LIGHT because of its transparency. In medieval pictures, glass that lets all things shine through without being affected itself is a symbol of the Immaculate Conception.

Glove Especially in medieval knighthood, it was an important symbol in law and sovereignty. A glove thrown at another was understood to be a sign of challenge ("throwing down the gauntlet"); however, a blow struck with the hand was forbidden as unchivalrous. Knights and later cavaliers carried the glove of a revered woman on their helmets or in their hats. —The wearing of *finger gloves* was for a long time a prerogative of the nobility and hence a symbol of their station in life. —In Freemasonry gloves are a part of the ritual garb; they are usually WHITE and signify purity as well as the work to be done. —In the Catholic church the use of gloves symbolizes purity and dignity.

Gluttony See GULA.

Goat As a useful domestic animal since ancient times, the female goat is associated with fertility cults and demonic powers. In Greek mythology, Zeus as a child is suckled by the she-goat Amalthea (see also AEGIS, HORN). —In India, among other places, the female goat represents the *prima materia*, an embodiment of the primal mother (probably because the word for *she-goat* and the word for *unborn* are homonyms). —The male goat is considered to be the positive or negative embodiment of male sexual powers. In Greek mythology it is a sacrificial animal (sacred to Dionysus) and also the steed of Aphrodite, Dionysus, and Pan. —In the Bible the male goat is a sacrificial animal that takes the sins of the people upon itself; in this context the scapegoat, as proxy, is banished into the wilderness. It is also seen as a stinking, unclean, demonic animal, symbolic of the damned at the Last Judgment. —In the Middle Ages the Devil was pictured with the horns and feet of a ram or a goat. The he-goat was also considered to be the obscene steed of witches and of lust personified. See CAPRICORN.

Goat: The billy goat as witch's steed. Detail from a woodcut in Praetorius's *Blockes-Berges Verrnichtung*, Leipzig, 1669.

Goblet As a vessel for drink passed from person to person, it is a symbol of friendship and association. —In the Bible it is an ambivalent symbol: as the cup of wrath, it is a sign of God's judgment; as the cup of blessing and joy, it is a symbol of God's presence. See CUP.

Gold It has always been considered the most noble metal. It is ductile, shining, capable of being polished, and within wide limits proof against heat and acids; hence it is a symbol of immutability, eternity, and perfection. Primarily because of its color, it has been universally identified with the SUN or with FIRE; consequently it is also a symbol of (especially esoteric) insight and knowledge. —In Christian symbolism, gold represents love, the highest of the virtues. —The golden ground on medieval murals is always a symbol of heavenly light. —The idea of gold as the most intimate and most sacred secret of the earth is widespread. —The alchemists' attempts to make gold from base metals, which related to the PHILOSOPHERS' STONE, were originally associated with the quest for purification of the soul (which is symbolized by gold). —Gold is sometimes given negative symbolic meaning as the essence of all earthly goods; hence it is synonymous with MONEY and a symbol of greed or attachment to the world. See EXCREMENT.

Golden Age See AGE.

Golden calf: The dance around the golden calf. Relief in the Regensburg Cathedral, 14th century.

Golden Calf According to the Old Testament, it is a calf (or STEER) idol made by Aaron on Sinai, which the Israelites worshiped while Moses received the tablets of the Law. It symbolizes the perpetual temptation of the Israelites to succumb to the Baal cults. —The dance around the golden calf is today a symbol of exaggerated striving for material goods.

Golden Fleece In Greek mythology it is the fleece of the golden ram, which was guarded by a DRAGON and which Jason and the Argonauts stole after overcoming numerous difficulties. —According to Jung, the golden fleece represents goals that, contrary to the judgment of mere thought, are nevertheless attained in the development of the individual.

Golden Pheasant See PHEASANT.

Goldfinch It is a bird that reputedly lives on THISTLES, but because it sings so beautifully, it was a symbol in the Middle Ages of Christ (especially of the Christ Child) and an image of the faithful soul purified through suffering.

Good Shepherd See SHEPHERD.

Goose: The Egyptian primal goose. Drawing from a papyrus.

Goose In Egyptian mythology it plays an important role as the primal goose that either lays the world EGG or, in other versions, hatches from it. Wild geese were considered in Egypt and China to be mediators between heaven (see SKY) and EARTH. —In Greece the goose was sacred to Aphrodite; in Rome it was dedicated to Juno. It was considered to be a symbol of love, fertility, marital fidelity, and vigilance; thus the geese at the Capitol were said to have saved it during the destruction of Rome in 387 B.C. —In Russia, central Asia, and Siberia, the word *goose* is a customary name for a beloved woman. —For the Celts the goose was symbolically close to the SWAN, and like the swan was considered a messenger from the spirit world.

Goose grass A common plant related to wild tansy and wild agrimony, it was supposed to grant likableness, eloquence, cleverness, and wit to people who carried the root. It was considered to be a symbol of maternal love, and thereby of Mary's love, because the leaves fold over the bud when it rains and form a protective roof.

Gordian Knot See KNOT.

Gorgoneion The head of a Gorgon (see GORGONS), which had a grotesque, horrific appearance with open maw, bared teeth, protruding tongue, and often a beard. It is a symbol of the terrifying aspect of divine powers and an apotropaic sign affixed to temples; a Gorgoneion is also affixed to the center of the AEGIS.

Gorgons In Greek mythology they are three sisters, Euryale, Stheno, and Medusa, who are ugly monsters, the sight of whom turns the viewer to stone. They are represented with SERPENTS in their hair or on their GIRDLES and are often winged. They are frequently interpreted as symbolic embodiments of the horrific aspect of the numinous. When spoken of in the singular, the Gorgon usually refers to Medusa, the mortal among the three sisters, whom Perseus decapitated. In later times she was often depicted as young and beautiful. See GORGONEION.

Gorgon: The Gorgon from the west gable of the Artemis Temple in Corfu.

Gourd Because of the great number of its seeds, the gourd, like such fruits as the POMEGRANATE and LEMON (see also ZEDRAT LEMON), symbolizes fertility. —Among black African peoples and others it is also a symbol of the WORLD EGG and the WOMB. —In Taoism it is revered as the nourishment that grants long life and bodily immortality. —In China two dried gourd halves from which one drinks symbolically represent the two halves of a unity that has been broken apart. —In Christian art the rapidly growing and rapidly decaying gourd often signifies the brevity and frailty of life.

Grafting The fruits of grafted trees were regarded by the Jews as the product of an unnatural act that interfered with the divine order, thus the fruit of such trees was forbidden. —In Christian art of the Middle Ages, a grafted scion signified conversion, ennoblement, and a new beginning brought about by grace.

Grail In medieval literature it is a holy object. —In France it was usually a container that held the host, the communion bowl, or the bowl in

Grapevine:
Heinrich Seuse
contemplates
Christ in the
grapevine.
Woodcut by
A. Sorg,
Augsburg, 1482.

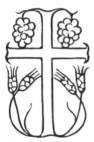

Grapevine: The
cross with grapes
and ears of grain,
a symbol of the
Eucharist.

Grapevine: The
return of the
scouts sent to the
Promised Land.
From a children's
Bible, ca. 19th
century.

which Joseph of Arimathea caught the blood of Christ. —In the German version of *Parzival* by Wolfram von Eschenbach, the grail is a STONE with wonderous powers that dispenses food and grants eternal youth. It is a symbol of the highest heavenly and earthly happiness and also of the Heavenly Jerusalem (see JERUSALEM, HEAVENLY). It was attainable only by the pure because it symbolized the highest level of spiritual development, which could be achieved only after having endured spiritual adventures.

Grape See GRAPEVINE.

Grapevine It is a symbol of abundance and life. —In Greece it was sacred to Dionysus; with reference to the Dionysian mysteries, which celebrated the god of ecstasy as lord of death and of the renewal of life, wine was also a symbol of rebirth. —In Jewish and Christian symbolism, the grapevine is a sacred plant with manifold meanings. It is regarded as a symbol of the people of Israel (God's concern for the Israelites is compared to people's concern for their grapevines), and as the tree of the Messiah; the Messiah is compared in the Old Testament to a grapevine. Christ equated himself with the true grapevine that, as a living root, bears the faithful as its branches (i.e., only those who draw their strength from him can truly bear fruit). —The enclosed and protected *vineyard* is a symbol of the chosen people; later it also referred to the holy church. —The *grape*, brought back from the Promised Land, is a symbol of promise; on early Christian sarcophagi it represents the

promised afterlife into which the deceased have entered. See WINE.

Grass See HAY.

Grasshopper See CRICKET, LOCUST.

Grave As a barrow or tumulus, it may be an allusion to holy MOUNTAINS. The form of numerous tombs or monuments (and also urns, such as the so-called *house urns*) refers symbolically to the idea of a dwelling (i.e., house, temple, etc.) for the deceased. —As the place of death but also of rest, of being cared for, and of the hope of rebirth, the grave is sometimes associated psychoanalytically with both the loving and horrific aspects of the Great Mother.

Grave Stone See STONE.

Gray Consisting equally of BLACK and WHITE, it is the color of mediation and compensating justice, as well as of intermediate realms (e.g., in folk belief it is the color of the dead and of spirits that walk abroad). In Christianity it is the color of the resurrection of the dead and of the cloak that Christ wears as judge at the Last Judgment.

Green The color of the plant kingdom, particularly of awakening springtime, it is also the color of water, life, and freshness. It mediates between the RED of hellfire and the BLUE of heaven. Often green is the opponent of red, but sometimes (as the color of life) it also represents red. As the color of the annual renewal of nature, moreover, green is the color of hope, long life, and immortality. —In China the color green is symbolically associated with lightning and thunder, WOOD, and the yin principle (see YIN AND YANG). —In Islam, green is the color of material and spiritual salvation, wisdom, and the prophets. —The mythological ideas of many peoples reveal close connections and transformations between red and green. In Africa, for example, green, which represents the feminine, is sometimes seen as proceeding from the masculine red. —The alchemists often saw the transformation processes as the interactions among realms that were symbolized by the masculine red and the feminine green. The "green light" plays a role for alchemists and occultists. It oc-

Grasshopper: The vision of the apocalyptic grasshopper or locust. After a picture in the *Apocalypse of Saint-Sever, Satan et les Sauterelles,* 11th century.

Grave: Various types of "house-urn" graves.

curs in nature and during the burning of various chemical substances, as well as in the form of the extremely infrequently observed "green ray" of the rising or setting sun. It is a symbol of illumination, and is associated with life and death. The alchemists also saw the so-called secret fire, which was "the living spirit," in the image of a green, translucent, and fusible CRYSTAL. In alchemy, green in compound forms such as "green lion" and "green dragon" usually designates solvents that are capable of dissolving even GOLD. —The Christian artists of the Middle Ages sometimes painted Christ's cross green as a sign of the renewal brought about by Christ and as an expression of humanity's hope of return to paradise. In medieval art green also has a negative meaning as the color of poison and of a threatening glance (e.g., green-eyed demonic creatures).

Green Woodpecker See WOODPECKER.

Griffin A fabulous animal of antiquity that had the head of the EAGLE, body of the LION, and wings, it was considered to be a solar symbolic animal. —For the Greeks it was sacred to Apollo and Artemis; it symbolizes strength and vigilance because of its penetrating glance. —Since as eagle it belongs to the sky and as lion to the earth, it was symbolic in the Middle Ages of the twofold divine-human nature of Christ; as a solar animal it was also symbolic of resurrection.

Griffin: Copper engraving by M. Schongauer.

Grimace See APOTROPAIC FIGURES, BES, GORGONEION.

Ground Ivy It is a creeping labiate flower with mostly blue-violet blossoms. In the Middle Ages it was used frequently for medicinal purposes; in this connection it was often a symbol of Mary. A wreath made of ground ivy plucked on Walpurgis Night was supposed to impart the ability to recognize witches on the following day.

Grove See FOREST.

Ground ivy

Gula The female personification of *gluttony*, one of the seven mortal sins, she rides on a SWINE or a FOX with a GOOSE in its maw. Gluttony is also symbolized by such animals as the BEAR, RAVEN, and WOLF.

Hair It was viewed in many cultures as the real bearer or symbol of strength (e.g., the hair of Samson in the Old Testament). The significance of hair sacrifices (e.g., among the Greeks when one was admitted to citizenship and at wedding and burial ceremonies; in Christianity since the Middle Ages vis-a-vis certain saints) as a sign of devotion and allegiance or as penance becomes clear in light of the high esteem placed on hair. The tonsure of monks and clerics is probably significant in this context. —Among the ancient Germanic tribes and in the Middle Ages, cutting off a person's hair had symbolic value judicially and was understood to be a way of dishonoring a culprit. —In various cultures, especially those that were magically oriented, a person's shorn hair could signify the actual person and was used accordingly in certain practices. —The *coiffure* also has symbolic significance. Wild, tangled hair, sometimes interlaced with snakes, alludes to horrific deities, the Furies, etc. (e.g., in Hinduism and in Greek mythology). Various hair styles also signified occupations, castes, classes, ages, and gender. In ancient Egypt, for example, children wore a long strand of hair on the right side. —Long, loose hair, especially on men, was a sign of freedom or noble lineage; for women in the Middle Ages it was the sign of virgins (but also of whores). Long, uncut hair (such as that worn by yogis, hermits, or members of modern subcultures) can be a sign of conscious hostility to civilization. At different times people went without cutting their hair during wars, a trip, or as an expression of mourning (the Greeks of the Archaic Epoch, however, cut off their hair as a sign of mourning). —Sometimes the color of the hair carried a symbolic significance: blond hair was associated with light; RED hair in the high Middle Ages was considered a sign of evil.

Hair: The child Horus with side lock of hair.

Halo (Glory Gloriole) It is a symbol in Christian painting (and sometimes in sculpture) of divinity, high rank, or sovereignty. Modeled on the NIM-BUS of antiquity, the halo is a round, usually golden, area or spray of rays about the head of persons (in contrast to the AUREOLE and the MAN-DORLA). Originally associated with Christ, the

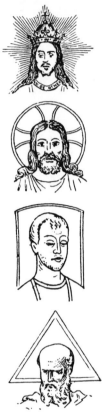

Lamb, God the Father (often a triangle), and the dove as the Holy Ghost, it is often depicted with the Christ monogram or the CROSS as a "cross nimbus." It was later used with Mary, angels, apostles, prophets, and saints. When used for living persons, it was usually SQUARE in shape.

Hammer Originally a weapon, it is a tool that symbolizes power and strength. Because the hammer was often associated with thunder, it was associated in Germanic mythology with the thunder god, Thor. —In antiquity it was the tool of Hephaestus, the god of fire and of the smithy. —In some cultures magical protective powers against evil are ascribed to ritually forged hammers. —In northern Europe numerous representations of hammers are found (e.g., on gravestones); these may have to do with signs that are supposed to protect the peace of the deceased against evil influences. Sometimes hammers also appear as disguised cross symbols. —In Freemasonry the hammer symbolizes will power guided by reason. —In jurisprudence the hammer possesses symbolically binding significance in auctions and other business dealings. —After the death of the Pope, a golden hammer is struck three times on the walls of the death chamber in order to force death to express itself.

Halo: Variations on the halo (from top to bottom): halo or rays; disk with cross for Christ; rectangular halo for living persons; triangle halo for God the Father.

Hand It is a symbol of activity and power. Finding oneself in the hands of a ruler or of a god means being in that person's power, but also standing under that person's protection. —Shaking or offering the hand or hands is a sign of friendly openness, devotion, or forgiveness; consequently for ages it has also been an essential symbol of the marital bond and has extensive symbolic significance judicially. —In Buddhism a closed hand signifies keeping silent about esoteric secrets; hence the open hand of the Buddha implies that he has no secret to keep. In addition, both Buddhism and Hinduism know a multitude of hand gestures, the symbolic meaning of which is fixed and which play a significant role in art and ritual dance; they can, for example, express threats, devotion, meditation, admiration, prayer, argumentation, and fearlessness. —In most cultures hand and FIN-

GER languages are a means of communication and expression. In Africa, laying the left hand with closed fingers in the right hand is generally understood to be a sign of submission and respect; in ancient Rome a similar meaning was conveyed by concealing one's hands in one's sleeves. In antiquity, covered or veiled hands were generally customary when one approached high dignitaries or received presents from them. Sometimes this gesture occurs later in Christian art as an expression of religious reverence; it is customary in Christian liturgical acts when holy objects are carried by the laity. —The difference in symbolic significance of RIGHT AND LEFT hands is widely attested. For example, it plays a role in the blessing by laying on of hands, which as a rule is done with the right hand and is often understood as a real transfer of powers. — In Christian art, God's intervention is often symbolized by a hand reaching down out of the clouds; generally the hand of God has been interpreted as the incarnated Logos. Since the Middle Ages, folding the hands has been the gesture of prayer. —To this day raising one's right hand when taking an oath is legally binding. See GLOVE.

Hammer: Thor's hammer Mjollnir as an amulet. Silver, 10th century.

Hand and Foot Washing In almost all religions people wash (especially their hands) before holy actions as a sign of ritual purification. —Pilate washed his hands, symbolically expressing his denial of responsibility. —In the Orient, washing the feet of strangers and guests was understood to be an act of kindness. Christ's washing the feet of his disciples was both a demonstration and a symbol of his serving love; his action has been reenacted since the seventh century in the Catholic liturgy of Holy Thursday. See BAPTISM, BATH.

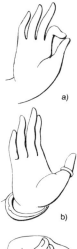

Hare Often equated with the *rabbit*, it is a lunar symbolic animal because it sleeps during the day and awakens at night, and because it is prolific. In the fairy tales and sagas of many peoples, the MOON is consequently depicted as a hare (or the bright and dark spots on the moon are said to be hares). Because of its fertility (also possibly because it habitually descends into furrows in the earth), the hare is closely as-

Hand: Examples of hand gestures in India: **a.** Cinmudra or wakhy-anamudra, signifying meditation or teaching. **b.** Abhaya, signifying granting of protection. **c.** Suci or tarjani, signifying threat.

Hand and Foot Washing: Jesus washing the feet. After a picture in the Gospel Book in the Cathedral of Speyer.

Hare: Hare or rabbit sitting in the crescent moon, depicted as a bowl filled with the water of life. Mexican, Codex Borgia 55.

sociated with the earth, which is understood as Mother, and hence it is also a symbol of the perpetual renewal of life. —The facetious idea of the *Easter bunny* reinforces the fertility symbolism because the EGG is an additional fertility symbol. Since the hare's numerous progeny are attributed to its great sensuality, the hare is also associated with sex. —It is sometimes a symbol of anxiety and cowardice because of its timidity, and of vigilance because of its supposed ability to sleep with its eyes open; it also symbolizes the rapid passing of life because of its speed. —In the Bible the hare is mentioned as an unclean animal.

Harp See LYRE.

Harvest It is a symbol of fulfillment. In Christian art it often represents the Last Judgment.

Hat It sometimes symbolizes the head or the thoughts; changing hats may also signify changing one's views or opinions, or one's occupation or role.

Hawk It is a predatory bird widely recognized as a death symbol in Christian art of the Middle Ages.

Hawthorn Christ's crown of thorns was supposed to have been made of hawthorn. In the Middle Ages, it was a symbol of caution (which one needs in order to pick it unharmed) and of hope.

Hay As dried (i.e., "dead") grass it is a symbol in the Bible of the transitoriness of the world and of human life.

Hazel It plays a role in folk belief and magic, probably because it is flexible, it is not struck by lightning, and it blossoms early. It was valued as protection against evil spirits and snakes. The hazel switch was a favorite instrument of gold and water diviners, since it supposedly moved when held over veins of gold or water. It was also used to cast magic spells.

Heart As a vital, central organ in humans, it is associated with the symbolic meaning of the CENTER. —In India the heart is thought to be the place of contact with Brahman, the personification of the absolute. —In ancient Greece it originally represented thought, feeling, and will; it later acquired a more spiritual meaning. —In Judaism and Christianity the heart is seen above all as the locus of emotional forces, particularly of love but also of intuition and wisdom. —Islam sees the heart as the seat of contemplation and spirituality; it is thought to have various colored layers cloaking it and is made visible through excitement. —In the Egyptian religion, the heart played an essential role as the center of the will and of vital and spiritual energy. In the embalmed mummy it was left along with a SCARAB, since weighing the heart at the judgment of the dead determined the fate of the person after life. —Christian art, especially since the mysticism of the high Middle Ages, developed an extensive heart symbolism (e.g., the flaming, pierced heart of Christ, Mary, the saints). —Today the heart generally symbolizes love and friendship.

Heart: The heart of Jesus. Master E.S., copper engraving, 1467.

Heart: The heart as popular symbol of love.

Hearth A symbol of the house, the human community, warmth, safety, care, and shelter, the family, wife, and woman. In the religious ideas of many peoples it has played an important role. In prehistoric times the deceased were buried next to the hearth; it frequently served as a site for cult and ritual practices.

Heaven See SKY.

Heavenly Ladder See LADDER.

Heavenly Portal See DOOR.

Heavenly Jerusalem See JERUSALEM, HEAVENLY.

Hedgehog It is an animal revered in China and Japan as a symbol of wealth. —In Mesopotamia, central Asia, and sometimes South America (possibly because of its quills), it was regarded as a solar animal that was associated with fire and thus with civilization. —According to PHYSIOLOGUS, in the Middle ages it symbolized the Devil; it also appears as a symbol of greed, voracity, and—because of its quickly erected quills—anger. In a positive sense it was seen as a hunter of SERPENTS and thus as an opponent of evil.

Height: The union of height and depth. Detail from a picture by Maria Prophetissa in Maier's *Symbolia Aureae Mensae*, 1617.

Helmet: Greek helmet.

Hermaphrodite: Hermaphrodite on the crescent moon. From Mylius's *Philosophia Reformata*, 1622.

Height It is the symbolic visualization of the realm of the spirit and the divine. To attempt to ascend a height symbolizes moral and spiritual development.

Hellfire See FIRE.

Helmet It is a symbol of strength, invulnerability, and invisibility.

Hem As a border, it is symbolically significant particularly in the Near East. Kissing or touching the hem was considered a gesture of reverence or submission. —Cutting off the hem, however, was for some peoples a humiliating punishment or at least the symbolic expression of one's power over another person; it was sometimes done in conjunction with the symbolically related act of cutting off the HAIR.

Hen It is a symbol of caring, protective motherliness, sometimes in the exaggerated, caricatured sense. See COCK.

Herbs They are symbols of the hidden power and modesty of inconspicuous plants, which often have healing properties.

Hercules at the Crossroads See CROSSROADS.

Herdsman See SHEPHERD.

Hermaphrodite It is a symbol of the coexistence or mediation of the opposites, as well as of the perfect or complete human being. In many religions the deity was thought to be of both sexes. In the Symposium, Plato reports the myth of the primordial hermaphrodite. —In alchemy the PHILOSOPHERS' STONE, which is supposed to be created through the reunion of the male and female principles, is often represented as a hermaphrodite. See MERCURIUS, REBIS.

Hero According to psychoanalytic dream and fairy tale interpretation, the hero is often the embodiment of victorious ego powers.

Heroic Age See AGE.

Heron In Egypt it was considered to be a sacred bird; the bird Benu (see PHOENIX) sometimes appears in heron form. —Because of its long beak it symbolizes the fathoming of hidden wisdom as well as curiosity (that sticks its beak or nose in everywhere). —Like other animals that destroy SERPENTS, it was a Christ symbol in the Middle Ages. —Due to its ash-colored plumage, the gray heron was regarded as a symbol of penance. —Since, according to Pliny, the heron can shed tears of pain, it is also symbolically associated with Christ on the Mount of Olives.

Hexagram (Seal of Solomon, Star of David) A six-pointed star formed from two superimposed or intertwined triangles, it occurs primarily in Judaism, Christianity, and Islam; in principle it also underlies the Indian YANTRA. In the widest sense, the hexagram is a symbol of the interpenetration of the visible and the invisible worlds. —In Hinduism it symbolizes the union of the YONI and the LINGA. —In alchemy it represents the union of all opposites, since it comprises the basic forms of the signs for the elements: FIRE △ or AIR △, and WATER ▽ or EARTH ▽. There are numerous speculations in alchemy that proceed from a correspondence of the individual lines or points of the hexagram and the planets, metals, qualities, etc. —The Star of David is a symbol of the faith of Judaism and the national emblem of Israel. —Jung sees the hexagram as representing the union of the personal and nonpersonal realms or of the masculine and the feminine.

Hexagram: Symbol of the union of fire and water. From Eleazar's *Uraltes Chymisches Werk*, 1760.

Hind See DOE.

Hippopotamus Feared in Egypt because of its voracious appetite, it was seen as an embodiment of evil powers and as a symbol of brutality and injustice. The female hippo, however, was revered as a symbol of fertility in the form of a hippopotamus goddess who was frequently depicted pregnant and standing upright; she was known as the protectress of women. —In the Old Testament the hippopotamus symbolizes brutal power, which God alone can subdue.

Hole It is a symbol of opening and of departure into the unknown, but also of nothingness and lack. It may also represent female genitals. —The Chinese jade disk with a hole, called *Pi*,

Hippopotamus: The Egyptian hippopotamus goddess Thoeris, supported by the hieroglyph meaning "protection." Statuette of green slate, 26th Dynasty.

Hole: A jade Chinese heaven symbol, Pi. Late Chou period.

is a symbol of heaven; the hole represents the spiritual matter shining into the world.

Honey Often associated with MILK, it represents sweetness, gentleness, or the highest earthly or heavenly good, and hence the condition of perfect bliss (e.g., of Nirvana). As a substantial, nutritious food, it also symbolizes vital energy and immortality. —In China, honey was closely associated symbolically with the earth and the midpoint or CENTER; hence there always had to be some honey among the dishes served to the emperor. —In antiquity, honey was considered to be a mystical food because, among other reasons, it was extracted by an innocent insect (see BEE) from innocent blossoms, which were touched but not destroyed. Honey symbolized spiritual insight, knowledge, and dedication, as well as calmness and peace. —There are isolated instances of initiation rites in which it was customary to wash the hands not only with WATER but first with honey, since honey was valued for its medicinal properties and was thought to provide internal cleansing. —Because of its golden yellow color, honey was sometimes associated with the SUN. —According to Jung, honey represents the self (the maturational goal of the individuation process). See MEAD.

Hood: Hermit. Detail from a drawing by Urs Graf, 1512.

Hood It is a garment of various gods, demons, magicians, and monks. In addition to its practical use, it signifies concentration of spiritual power or self-concealment. Covering the head with a VEIL or a hood during initiation rites sometimes symbolizes death.

Hoopoe It is any of a family of Old World nonpasserine birds having a slender curved bill. In Arabic poetry and literature it is a messenger of love. —Its crest of feathers, reminiscent of horns, and the smelly liquid that it sprays at enemies make the hoopoe a symbol of the Devil; hence it is also associated with witches and sorcerers.

Horn Because of its important function in the animal kingdom, it is a symbol of strength and power in the physical and spiritual senses. Consequently Dionysus, Alexander the Great, and Moses are often depicted with horns (although such depictions probably stem from an error in translation, namely, the confusion of *facies coronata* [haloed] and *cornuta* [horned]). —Horns were used by many peoples as AMULETS. —The sacrificial altar of the Israelites bore horns pointing in the four cardinal directions as a sign of the omnipotence of God. —The horn having a shape similar to the moon sickle is associated with lunar symbolism. —Horned animals are often considered fertility symbols; the horn itself is a phallic symbol. —In a negative sense, the symbolic significance of the horn appears in the many depictions of the horned Devil. —Jung referred to the ambivalent symbolic significance of horns. Because of their form and power, they embody the masculine, active principle; because of their lyrelike, open form, however, they also represent the feminine, receptive principle. Horns therefore may symbolize spiritual balance and maturity. —The *horn of plenty*, which is the attribute of Fortuna or of the personification of autumn, is a symbol of the superabundance of good fortune and of rich harvest; originally it was thought to be the horn of the GOAT Amalthea or of the river god Achelous, whose horn Heracles had broken off in battle.

Horn: The horned Moses. From the *Moses Well* of C. Sluter, Carthusian Monastery of Champmol, Dijon.

Horn of Plenty See HORN.

Horse Early representations of horses appear in Paleolithic caves (see ROCK PAINTINGS). They continued to play a great role in most cultures through the Industrial Age, hence the rich symbolism associated with this animal. —Originally the horse was considered to be a chthonic creature that was associated with FIRE and WATER, forces of life and of danger. Thus in many parts of Europe and the Far East it was said that its hooves could strike springs of water from the ground. The horse also appears in relation to the lunar realm. It was closely associated with the realm of death (e.g., in central Asia and among many Indo-European peoples) and consequently appears as psychopomp (spirit guide); for this reason it was also sometimes buried with the dead or sacrificed when a person died. —The dark side of horse symbolism appears in Zoroastrianism, where Ahriman, the spirit of opposition, is often embodied in the

Horn: Horned devil; detail from a representation in *Le grant kalenderier et compost des Bergiers*, Troyes, 1496.

Horse: Sassanid winged horse. 10th century.

form of a horse. Also associated with the negative aspect of horse symbolism are the part-human, part-horse creatures of Greek mythology (CENTAURS, satyrs, sileni), the horse component of which usually represents uncontrolled drives. —The winged horse of Greek mythology, PEGASUS, is related to the light symbolism of the horse that developed later (e.g., in China, India, and in antiquity) and is complementary to the chthonic. The white horse in particular was regarded as a solar and heavenly animal; it became the steed of the gods and a symbol of force subdued by reason (see, e.g., the well-known simile of the two horses in Plato's *Phaedrus*, or the representations of joy and victory on the graves of martyrs). —As a symbol of youth, strength, sexuality, and masculinity, the horse is part of the dark and light sides of the above-mentioned symbolism. —The horse is the seventh sign in the Chinese ZODIAC and corresponds to Libra (see SCALES). See also RIDER.

Horseshoe Considered by many peoples to be capable of warding off misfortune and bringing good luck, it is possibly connected to the positive aspect of the symbolism of the HORSE.

MYN GLAS LOOPT RAS

Hourglass:
From a picture in
a work by Joost
Hartgers,
Amsterdam,
1651.

Hourglass It is a symbol of passing time and death. Because it must be inverted each time the sand has run through, it also sometimes represents the end and the new beginning of cycles or epochs, or the alternating influences of heaven (see SKY) on the EARTH and vice versa. —Among the four cardinal virtues, the hourglass symbolizes moderation.

House As an ordered, enclosed area like the CITY or the *temple*, it symbolizes the cosmos or cosmic order. —Graves were sometimes shaped like houses to signify the last dwelling place of humans. —Like the temple, the house is sometimes a symbol of the human body and is often thought (e.g., in Buddhism) to offer the soul a habitation for only a short time. Occasionally (e.g.,in psychoanalytic dream interpretation) the symbolic body-house relationship is developed in greater detail. The facade of the house corresponds to the external appearance; the roof to the head, spirit, or consciousness; the cellar to the instincts, drives, or the unconscious; the kitchen to psychological transformations.

House Urns See GRAVE.

Human Being The human being, as well as parts and processes of the human body, appear in many cultures as representing relationships outside of the individual. The interpretation of the human as the *microcosm* in reference to the universe is widespread. —Often human body parts, organs, or fundamental substances are associated with other realms: the bones (as the supporting framework) with the EARTH, the head (as the seat of intellect or spirit) with FIRE, the lungs (as the organ of respiration) with AIR, and blood (as the fluid substance uniting all the others) with WATER. The healing arts of earlier times were based to a great extent on the assumption of correspondences among phenomena of the human body and phenomena in the rest of the universe (see ZODIAC). —The (often winged) human form is the attribute of St. Matthew (see EVANGELISTS, SYMBOLS OF).

Human Being: The human being as the microcosm, showing light and shadow areas. After a picture in Robert Fludd's *Utriusque Cosmi Historia*, Oppenheim, 1619.

Hundred For intellectual systems using the decimal system, it is the essence of a multiplicity completed in a greater totality. In Christian literature, 100 occurs as a symbol of heavenly bliss; the number 1,000 has a similar significance.

Hunt As a goal-oriented pursuit of prey, it is a symbol of the passionate striving for spiritual goals (e.g., in Christian mysticism, the hunt signifies the soul's quest for Christ). —As the victory over or the destruction of wild animals, it also represents the victory over coarseness, disorder, and ignorance (e.g., in the Near East and Egypt).

Hydra It is a serpent monster of Greek mythology that has numerous (usually nine) heads and lives in the swamps of Lerna (hence it is also called the Lernaean Hydra); for each head cut off, two new ones grow back again. Heracles conquered it by burning away each neck. It is a symbol of difficulties and obstacles that multiply in the course of accomplishing a task.

Hyena In Africa it is a symbolic animal of ambivalent meaning. As a voracious, shy scavenger, the hyena symbolizes coarseness and cowardice; as an animal having a powerful bite and a keen sense of smell, it symbolizes power, knowledge, and cleverness. — In medieval art it represents greed; the hyena-headed, apocalyptic DRAGON symbolizes the cardinal vices.

Hyperboreans They are a fabled people said in antiquity to live in the farthest northern reaches (beyond the north wind, personified as Boreas). It is unknown to what extent an historical people gave rise to this idea. In myth the land of the Hyperboreans came increasingly to symbolize a place of light and bliss where Apollo sometimes retreated; later, political utopias were situated there.

Hyssop It is a small, white- or blue-blossomed labiate herb with white, spicy leaves. In Judaism and in Christian ritual it served as a fan or brush for sprinkling the blood of sacrificial animals or holy water (which sometimes also contained hyssop). Since the inconspicuous plant grows on stony ground, it was also regarded as a symbol of humility. — In medieval art, it was associated with Mary because of its frequent use as a medication.

Ibis A sacred bird of the Egyptians, it is the symbol and incarnation of the moon god, Toth, who invented writing and was also the god of wisdom. The curved shape of the bird's beak refers to the CRESCENT MOON; the pointedness and length of the beak are associated (as is the HERON) with plumbing the depths of wisdom.

Icarus In Greek mythology, he is the son of Daedalus, who made him wings held together with wax. In spite of his father's warning, Icarus flew too close to the SUN; the wax on his wings melted and he plunged into the sea. He symbolizes limitless demands or unreasonable adventuresomeness, which leads to downfall.

Imperial Orb See APPLE.

Incense It is a material used in rituals by numerous peoples because of the symbolic ideas connected with the scent, the SMOKE, and the compounding from various resins. The ascending smoke symbolizes the prayers rising to heaven; the scent is supposed to drive away evil spirits and influences; the RESIN symbolizes permanence. — In Christianity, incense was initially used in burials and has since been used for liturgical purposes.

Initiation To many primitive peoples it represents the entry—accompanied by ritual practices—into a new phase of life, especially into the role of the sexually mature adult; it is linked to tests and symbolic actions (see CIRCUMCISION). A process of transformation usually also takes place, which is understood to be both symbolic and actual and which generally embraces the phases of shedding the old role, of solitude, and finally of return and becoming part of the community again. — In the narrower sense, initiation is frequently a prerequisite of acceptance into secret societies or mystery religions. Living through a symbolic death (sometimes even in actual graves and coffins set aside for that purpose) and a spiritual resurrection at a higher level often play a significant role in initiation rites. Some rites involve practices that suggest a symbolic return to the WOMB and rebirth from it. In addition there are usually other tests to be passed that relate symbolically to the development of particular moral and spiritual abilities. See LABYRINTH.

Intoxication See ECSTASY.

Invidia The female personification of *envy*, one of the seven mortal sins, she rides on a DOG with a bone in its mouth or on a DRAGON. Envy is also symbolized by the SCORPION, DOG, and BAT.

Ira The female personification of anger, one of the seven mortal sins, she rides on a BEAR or a wild boar and is also symbolized by the DOG, HEDGEHOG, and TORCH.

Iris It is a plant of the northern temperate zone having swordlike leaves. — In Greek mythology the goddess Iris is the embodiment of the rain-

Ibis: The ibis-headed Egyptian god Toth at the judgment of the dead. Detail from a funereal papyrus, Ptolemaic period.

Incense: Sacrifice offering of incense. Relief on the Osiris temple of Abydos, Egypt.

Iris

105

bow. The name *iris*, which in Greek means RAIN-BOW, is also associated symbolically with the reconciliation between God and humanity. —Valued in antiquity for its medicinal properties, it was a symbol in the Middle Ages of Mary.

Iron A widely distributed symbol of power, durability, and inflexibility, it was sometimes contrasted in China to COPPER or bronze as the less noble metal. Iron and copper participate in the opposition of the symbols WATER-FIRE, north-south, BLACK-RED, YIN-YANG. Iron has not, however, been viewed as less valuable in all respects and in all cultures; in particular, meteoric iron fallen from the sky has often been thought to be divine. —Iron and iron implements have been seen as protection against evil spirits, but also as the instruments of such spirits. In the Old Testament iron tools were forbidden in the building of Solomon's temple and of altars because people feared that iron could drive out the numinous powers present in the altar stone. For similar reasons the use of iron instruments for the slaughter of sacrificial animals was avoided in various cultures. —In alchemy, iron corresponds to *Mars*, which was described as masculine, as the planet of battle and strife, as hot and dry, and as causing lightning, storms, wildness, and mercilessness. See METALS.

Iron Age See AGE.

Island As a separate, self-contained realm to which access is difficult, it frequently symbolizes something special, complete, or perfect. It occurs sometimes (e.g., in dreams) as a place to be reached only in the future, when utopian wishes will be realized. —It is also imagined to be a carefree place in the world beyond (e.g., the *Isle of the Blessed* in Greek myth where the beloved of the gods dwell after physical death). —In a negative sense it represents the renunciation of the world through the avoidance of coming to terms with life.

Ivory Because of its white color and unchanging smoothness, it is a symbol of purity and constancy. See IVORY TOWER.

Ivory tower It is a symbol of arrogance, unworldliness, or aesthetic distance from the world. —In Christianity, Mary is sometimes compared to an ivory tower, which represents the tower of David (i.e., Mary is the pure CONTAINER that bore the offspring of David's lineage). See IVORY, TOWER.

Ivy Like most evergreen plants, it is a symbol of immortality. Because of its unchanging green color and its climbing habit, but also its "nestling, snuggling" character, it became a symbol of friendship and fidelity (e.g., in ancient Greece it was given to brides and grooms at weddings). —Because of its need to lean and cling, ivy is sometimes also a feminine symbol. —The vigorous, green plant was a symbol in antiquity of vegetative powers and of sensuality, and it played a significant role in the cult of Dionysus; thus, for example, the maenads (bacchantes), satyrs, and sileni were crowned with ivy and the THYRSUS was decorated with it.

Ivy

Jackal Often regarded as an animal that slinks about graveyards and feeds on corpses, it was believed to be an evil omen when it appeared. Sometimes it is a symbol of greed and anger. —The animal head of the Egyptian god Anubis is often considered to be the head of a jackal, but it is more likely the head of the jackal-like greyhound.

Jade In China jade, like GOLD, is closely associated with the yang principle (see YIN AND YANG) and thus symbolizes vital energy and cosmic forces. It is an image of perfection and a symbol of the union of the five heavenly virtues (i.e., purity, immutability, clarity, euphony, and kindness) as well as the union of moral qualities and beauty. Jade was used as a universal medicament, was valued as nutrition for immaterial beings, and was the medicine that granted immortality or long life and protected the bodies of the deceased from decay. —In Central America jade symbolized the soul, the spirit, the heart; because of its green, transparent color, it was also related to vegetation, water, rain, and blood (because of the occasional interchangeability of the symbolic meanings of RED and GREEN).

Jackal: The Egyptian god Anubis. Detail from a mural in the tomb of Ramses I, Valley of the Kings, 19th Dynasty.

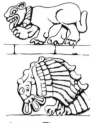

Jaguar: The jaguar and the eagle. Representation on the pyramid of Quetzalcoatl, Tula, Mexico.

Jaguar Among American Indians, particularly those of Central America, it is a chthonic being related to the powers of the MOON and to the hidden secrets of the EARTH; for this reason it is sometimes also a psychopomp (spirit guide). The twilight of evening is pictorially represented as the sun being swallowed by a giant jaguar. The jaguar, however, is also associated with the sun during the nocturnal movement of the stars (see *black* SUN). The jaguar is said to be the lord of the mountain ranges, the wild animals, the echo, and the drum call; it is called "heart of the mountain." Often it is symbolically contrasted to the EAGLE (which is associated with the sky and the sun). —Among the Indians of South America is found the legend of a four-eyed jaguar, perhaps a symbol of the profound wisdom of chthonic powers.

Janus: Depiction on a Roman copper coin.

Janus One of the oldest Roman deities, Janus is the god of the DOOR. He is depicted as having two faces, one looking outward and one inward (i.e., watching over the coming and the going). In this sense he is generally the protector of all beginnings and transitions (such as the beginning of the year, the first month of which is named after him). —Later the Janus-head also became a symbol of ambiguity or of the good and the evil side of the same thing.

Jasper It is a variety of chalcedony (a type of translucent quartz) having impurities. When it is broken or fractured, new stones appear to arise in it; therefore it symbolizes pregnancy and birth (a traditional idea that came from the Babylonians via the Greeks and Romans and was common in medieval times). —In the Middle Ages jasper was particularly prized because it was designated in the Apocalypse as the first cornerstone of the Heavenly Jerusalem (see JERUSALEM, HEAVENLY). (Usually, however, the jaspoid opal was meant, which was called "the orphan" in the crown of the Holy Roman Emperor). —The term *jasper* has undergone such frequent mutations in meaning that what is ascribed to it cannot always be deciphered unambiguously.

Jaws See MOUTH.

Jerusalem, Heavenly The city described in Revelation as having TWELVE gates on a square ground plan, it is a symbol of the anticipated end of the world when God will dwell among his chosen people. The city rests on twelve cornerstones (of JASPER, SAPPHIRE, agate, EMERALD, onyx, carnelian, chrysolite, beryl, topaz, chrysoprase, jacinth, and AMETHYST) on which stand the names of the twelve apostles; the twelve gates are twelve PEARLS.

Jerusalem, Heavenly: After a book illustration in the *Bamberg Apocalypse*, ca. 1020.

Jet Also known as black amber, it is a very dense carbon that takes a high polish. As an AMULET it was a widely known preventative against harmful influences (e.g., against the evil eye, poisons, illnesses, bad weather). —In the Middle Ages and in later times it was a symbol of mourning because of its deep BLACK color and was thus frequently worn during mourning.

Jewelry Precious ornaments, often set with gems, symbolize special status, power, and esoteric knowledge, but also material riches. In a negative sense jewelry represents vanity and the mere external appearance of all earthly things. —Among many peoples the wearing of AMULETS as jewelry was regarded as having an apotropaic effect.

Journey As a goal-directed movement along a path or road on which obstacles must often be overcome, it symbolizes the course of life. In a more specialized sense, it represents the quest for spiritual goals that are embodied as the Promised Land, the Isle of the Blessed (see IS- LAND), castles, or sacred places (often on MOUN- TAINS). —Rites of initiation sometimes took the form of a series of tests that, like a journey, the initiate had to undergo (e.g., in Chinese secret societies, the Greek mysteries, among the Freemasons). —Common to many cultures is the idea of a journey that the deceased must undertake after death (see the Egyptian and Tibetan *Book of the Dead* for extensive accounts). Such a journey after death signifies the purification and further development of the soul. —Buddhism compares the cycle of births (i.e., the sequence of incarnations of the spiritual individuality until its final redemption in Nirvana) to a journey.

Justice: Detail of Justicia seated on the terrestrial sphere. Woodcut by a German master of the 16th century.

Jupiter See TIN.

Justice See JUSTICIA.

Justicia The female personification of *justice*, one of the four cardinal virtues, she is often represented with the attributes of the SCALES, SWORD, BLINDFOLD, and lawbook. As an enforcer of the law, Justicia also appears with a severed head in her lap.

Key: Peter with the key to heaven. From a wing of the altar of the former baptismal church of St. John the Baptist, Worms, ca. 1250.

Key The symbolic meaning of the key has to do with its power to open and to lock. Janus, the Roman god of DOORS (later usually known as the god of beginnings), is generally represented with the doorkeeper's staff and key. —In Japan the key is regarded as a symbol of good luck because it opens the door to the storeroom (and, in an extended, spiritual sense, to hidden treasures). —In Christian art it symbolizes the two-fold authority given to St. Peter to loose and to bind (cf. also the two keys in the Pope's coat of arms). —In the Middle Ages the gift of the key was regarded as a symbolic legal act that granted full power of authority (e.g., giving the key to the city). —In esoteric symbolic language, the possession of the key often signifies the condition of being initiated. —In fairy tales and folk legends, the key appears as a symbol of impeded access to secrets or (as in folklore and folk song) as an esoteric symbol.

Kidney It is an organ regarded by primitive peoples as well as by Jews as the seat of feelings, special power, and passion. The expression "heart and reins" (reins means kidneys), as a designation of a person's inner powers, is found in the Old Testament. —In the Middle Ages the kidneys were thought to be the seat of the emotions and especially of the sexual drive.

King The king is often understood to be the embodiment of God, the sun, the sky, the center of the cosmos, or the mediator between heaven (see SKY), human beings, and EARTH. —Jung regarded the dream image of the old king as an archetype representing the wisdom of the collective conscious. The king in fairy tales (and especially the process of "becoming king") often symbolizes the hoped-for goal of ego development. — In alchemy the king sometimes corresponds to the PRIMA MATERIA.

Kingfisher Any of numerous nonpasserine birds that frequently fly in pairs, the kingfisher is a symbol of marital happiness, especially in China. — In Christian symbolism it signifies resurrection, since according to the medieval view, the kingfisher annually renews its entire coat of feathers.

King: The king as *prima materia* devouring the son. After a picture in Lambsprinck's *Figurae et Emblemata*, 1678.

King's Way In contrast to crooked, indirect paths, the King's way is the correct, straight way; it symbolizes the continued development of the imperturbable soul toward its inner goal. In the Middle Ages, for example, it was the usual designation for the monastic and meditative path to God.

Kiss Probably originally perceived as the breath (see WIND) of the soul, it was also thought of as transferring power and as life-giving. — The kiss is usually an expression of spiritual devotion and a sign of reverence. In addition to its actual erotic significance (which in the marriage ceremony can assume symbolic character), the kiss also has sacred meaning. In Egypt, for example, the feet of the god-king were kissed, a form of deference to rulers, priests, and judges common in many cultures. — In antiquity one kissed the threshold of the temple, the altar, and the divine image. In current Islamic practices, kissing the black rock of the Kaaba is the goal and high point of the pilgrimage. — In the early Christian church, the kiss of peace or brotherhood symbolized solidarity (cf. the Easter kiss of the Eastern Orthodox church). In profane contexts, the kiss of brotherhood also symbolizes solidarity in a community (e.g., among communist comrades) and, with reduced symbolic significance, is the kiss of greeting among relatives and friends. — In Christianity, kissing such objects as the altar, the cross, the Bible, and the relics of saints is also understood as spiritual union. — In the Middle Ages the kiss symbolized reconciliation. — Kissing the hand (like "throwing a kiss") is perhaps related to magical ideas and

Kiss: The kiss of Judas. After a miniature from the psalter of Heinrich von Blois.

may represent the kiss in general. —The *Judas kiss* signifies a kiss bestowed as an act of betrayal.

Kite A kind of hawk, it was considered by the Greeks to be sacred to Apollo; because of its high flight and sharp sight, it symbolized prophecy. —In Japan the kite (especially the golden kite) was believed to be a divine bird.

Knife As a sharp cutting tool (like the SHEARS), it is a symbol of the masculine, active principle that works on the feminine, passive material. —In Hinduism the knife is an attribute of horrific deities. —In many cultures it is also seen as warding off evil, a belief that possibly derives from the symbolic meaning of IRON. —A knife in the hand of Old Testament figures is a circumcision knife, which alludes to membership in the covenant.

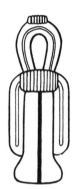

Knot: Knot of Isis.

Knot It is a symbol of linking, bonding, or the connection to protective powers, but also of complications and obstacles. —Among the Egyptians the knot symbolized life and immortality; the Isis knot, a sort of ANKH, with arms at its sides, was a widely used AMULET. —As a symbol of love and marriage, the knot occurs sometimes in wedding rituals. —In the Islamic world the knot is a protection-giving symbol; Arab men, for example, sometimes tie knots in their beards as protection against the evil eye. —The symbolic significance of untying the knot is widespread and various. Buddhism compares the sage's releasing himself from the world of mere appearance to untying a knot. Death is also sometimes compared to untying a knot. Untying knots is a symbol of opening oneself; in Morocco, for example, a husband could sleep with his wife only after he had untied seven knots on his clothing. —Alexander the Great's cutting of the *Gordion knot* is proverbial as a symbol of resolute action; in a negative sense, it is a symbol of raw impatience.

Kola Nut

Kola Nut Because of its bitter taste, it symbolizes among black African peoples the difficulties of life and victory over them; it is thus a symbol of the virtues of friendship and fidelity that contribute to this victory.

Labyrinth Originally it was the designation for the palace built by Daedalus on Crete for King Minos's confinement of the MINOTAUR. It had numerous passages and intricate mazes. Ultimately it came to refer to all mazes in architecture and art. —Passage through a maze or labyrinth was sometimes a part of INITIATION rites, symbolizing both the discovery of the hidden, spiritual center and the ascent from darkness to light. —In many old churches, labyrinths represented on the floor symbolize human life with all its tests, difficulties, and detours; the center symbolizes the expectation of salvation in the shape of the Heavenly Jerusalem (see JERUSALEM, HEAVENLY).

Labyrinth: Floor pattern in the Church of St. Vitale, Ravenna, 6th century.

Ladder In varying forms it is a symbol of the uniting of heaven (see SKY) and EARTH; in this connection it is associated symbolically with the RAINBOW. It represents ascent, stepwise increase, or development. The number of rungs may correspond to a sacred number (often SEVEN), and the individual rungs sometimes are of different colors (e.g., in Buddhism) or are made of various metals (e.g., in the Mithras mysteries); often they correspond to various steps in a spiritual initiation. —The Bible mentions Jacob's dream of the *heavenly ladder* on which angels ascend and descend; the ladder is a symbol of the living relationship between God and humanity. —In Christian art the ladder of virtue is depicted on which virtuous persons, threatened on all sides by demons, climb step by step to the top. —As a place of spiritual development, the cloister was sometimes compared with the ladder (Cistercian and Carthusian cloisters are often called "Scala Dei"). See STAIRS.

Ladder: The ladder of virtues. After a miniature from Zwettl.

Lady's Mantle The herb *Alchemilla vulgaris*, which is associated with Mary, was sometimes colloquially called "Our blessed Lady's night mantle" because of the form of its leaves.

Lady's Slipper A variety of orchid so called because the form of its blossom suggests a slipper, it was also sometimes called "Kriemhilda's helmet" and is associated in many legends with the Virgin Mary.

113

Lady's Slipper

Lamb: The Easter lamb. Terra-cotta, from the studio of A. della Robbia.

Lake (Pond) The lake is interpreted graphically as the earth's open EYE. —It is sometimes considered to be the dwelling place of subterranean beings, fairies, nymphs, and water spirits, who entice humans in order to draw them into the subterranean realms. —In dream imagery the lake is symbolic of the feminine or of the unconscious.

Lamb (Sheep) Because of its simplicity, tolerance, and white color, it symbolizes gentleness, innocence, and purity. In antiquity the lamb and the RAM were the most common sacrificial animals; thus they became symbols of Christ and his sacrificial death. In Christian art a lamb in the midst of other sheep, or standing to the side, refers to the Lamb of God, who bears the sins of the world. Groups of lambs or sheep also represent the faithful or the church of the martyrs (here Christ appears in the role of the good SHEPHERD). The Last Judgment is sometimes represented by Christ separating the sheep from the goats. —The sheep is the eighth sign of the Chinese ZODIAC and corresponds to Scorpio (see SCORPION).

Lameness It is an expression of weakness or woundedness. Like BLINDNESS, lameness or limping can be symbolic of spiritual inadequacy. However, like blindness, being ONE-EYED, or having a humpback, lameness also can allude to unusual abilities in specific realms (as in the case of witches, magicians, and fire gods, e.g., Hephaestus). In Greek mythology lameness is a punishment of the gods for disobedience (Hephaestus limps because he sided with his mother, Hera, against his father, Zeus). —According to folk belief, the Devil is lame on one foot because his fall from heaven was his own fault.

Lamp A graphic representation of the irrepresentable LIGHT, which is often interpreted as the personal spiritual light of spiritual beings. Striking or extinguishing a light may thus signify the birth or death of a person. In antiquity particularly, the light was simply a symbol of life and death. —The pottery *oil lamp* is a symbol of humanity. It is made of clay; the oil (see OILS) contains a sort of "vital energy"; when it is lighted, it appears as the bearer of spirit, symbolized by the FLAME. — In the biblical simile of the sensible and the foolish virgins, the lamp carefully filled with oil is a symbol of spiritual vigilance and readiness. — Setting lighted lamps on graves is a common practice in Christianity and other religions; it refers to the idea of a divine light beyond death. See LANTERN.

Lamp: The sensible (*left*) and foolish (*right*) virgins with a lighted or an empty oil lamp. Two woodcuts from a series by N. M. Deutsch, 1518.

Lance (Spear) Like all weapons it is a symbol of war and power. It commonly represents the sun ray, which is a phallic symbol, and is also associated with the WORLD AXIS. — In Christian art animals that have been impaled on lances often allude to vices that must be overcome. For this reason, the personifications of virtues are frequently depicted with lances as attributes. In the narrower sense, the lance is an attribute of the cardinal virtue of valor. — The Eucharistic use of a small lance in the Orthodox church refers symbolically to the lance of Longinus, who confirmed that Christ was dead by thrusting his lance into Christ's breast. (The lance of Longinus played a great role in the Middle Ages, e.g., in the GRAIL legend.)

Lantern To a great extent it corresponds symbolically to the LAMP. Lanterns are often placed

Lantern: From the temple in Nikko, Japan.

in Japanese temple and garden settings as symbols of the light of spiritual clarity.

Lapis Lazuli Because of its blue color and the numerous golden flecks embedded in it, lapis lazuli is a symbol of the firmament. —In the Orient it is prized as protection against the evil eye.

Lapis Philosophorum See PHILOSOPHERS' STONE.

Larch It is a conifer of the northern temperate zone. In Siberia, the world TREE was imagined to be a larch on which the sun and the moon ascended and descended in the forms of a golden and a silver bird.

Lark As a bird that flies straight up into the sky and builds its nest in the earth, it is a symbol of the union of SKY and EARTH.

Larkspur Any of a genus of the crowfoot family, in the Middle Ages it was associated with the knightly nobility because of its spurlike blossoms, and thus it symbolized knightly virtues. In paintings of Mary it also symbolizes her honor as Mother of God.

Larkspur

Laurel Like all evergreen plants, it is an immortality symbol. —In antiquity it was believed to be physically and morally cleansing. The power of granting poetic inspiration and prophecy was also ascribed to it; in addition, it was thought to protect one from lightning. It was sacred principally to Apollo. —It first appeared in the context of triumphal processions because of the cleansing powers ascribed to it; people wanted to cleanse themselves of the blood spilled in war. Later it became a symbol of victory, triumph, and the immortality granted by victory. In this sense it was also used as a decoration, usually in a wreath, for outstanding accomplishments in the sciences and the arts, especially the literary arts.

Laurel: Wreaths of laurel on ancient coins.

Lavender A very spicy, fragrant, inconspicuous blossoming labiate flower of the Mediterranean regions, it has been used since antiquity for bathing, washing, and medicinal purposes. In the Middle Ages it sometimes referred symbolically to the virtues of Mary.

Lead Because of its high specific gravity, it is a symbol of heaviness or of oppressive burden. In alchemy lead is identified with *Saturn*, who is often represented as a stooped old man with a SCYTHE, or as a grey dwarf; he was said to cause one to feel cold, damp, ill, and melancholy. In a positive sense, Saturn is associated with philosophy and generally with systematic thought and asceticism. —In Christian symbolism lead occasionally refers to humankind burdened with sins. See METALS.

Leaf Generally a symbol of the plant kingdom, it has widespread ornamental use in agrarian cultures. —In the Far East the leaf is a symbol of happiness and well-being; a branch with leaves symbolizes the cooperative work of individuals on a common effort. —In Christianity a three-petaled leaf (see CLOVER) signifies the Trinity, and a four-petaled leaf signifies the CROSS, the four Evangelists, or the cardinal virtues. —As Adam and Eve's first clothing after the Fall, the fig leaf (see FIG TREE) symbolizes modesty and chastity.

Leaven In early Judaism it was sometimes a symbol of decomposition, spiritual corruption, and impurity. Consequently, sacrificial breads offered to the gods almost always had to be unleavened. During the Exodus of the Israelites from Egypt, which took place at night, unleavened bread was taken along to eat, since there was no time to let fermentation take effect; the annual Jewish Feast of Passover, also called the Feast of Unleavened Bread, is the symbolic reenactment of the Exodus from Egypt; the unleavened bread is thus a symbol of promise.

Left See RIGHT AND LEFT.

Legume It is a symbol of embodiment, the husk of the soul and the spirit.

Lemon It is a symbol in Judaism of the human heart. —In the Middle Ages it was regarded as a symbol of life and as protection against forces hostile to life (i.e., against magic spells, poison, pestilence). It was placed in graves and was also used in such rites as baptism, marriage, confirmation, and communion. In the late Middle

Ages, it was a symbol of purity and an attribute of Mary.

Leo See LION.

Leopard It is a symbol of wildness, aggression, battle, and pride. —In China the leopard was considered a lunar animal, in contrast to the solar LION. —In African myths, it is associated with the light of the morning sun. —In antiquity the leopard was an attribute of Artemis and Dionysus; it symbolized strength and fertility, and in this sense it also played a role in the Dionysus (or Bacchus) cult. Because of its wild leaping it was compared with the maenads. See PANTHER.

Leopard:
Maenad with leopard. From a bowl of the Brygos painter, ca. 450 B.C.

Lernaean Serpent See HYDRA.

Letters In most cultures letters of the alphabet carry specific symbolic meanings. For example, Islam distinguishes between airy, fiery, earthy, and watery letters that, as materializations of the Divine Word, are all bearers of specific meanings (e.g., with reference to past, present, and future). —In the Cabala an entire system of mystical speculations is presented, which has to do with the form of the individual letters as well as with definite numerical values. —In antiquity the seven Greek vowels (for e and o there are two letters each) symbolized the spirit, or the seven heavenly spheres and the seven heavenly bodies moving in them; the consonants, on the other hand, symbolized matter. The ALPHABET, as a union of vowels and consonants, and thus of "spirit" and "matter," and as the totality of all linguistic signs, symbolized the totality and perfection of the entire cosmos; consequently it was also used apotropaically. Its occasional use from early Christian times into the Middle Ages on gravestones, for example, probably reflects this meaning. See ALPHA, ALPHA AND OMEGA, OMEGA, TAW.

Leviathan:
Catching the leviathan with the sevenfold rod of the tribe of Jesse, Christ crucified as bait. From Herrad von Landsberg's *Hortus Deliciarum*, 1180.

Leviathan Originally a monster of Phoenician mythology, symbolizing chaos, it usually lived in the sea; there was the constant threat that it would arise again and endanger the existing order. —In the Bible and in Christian art (where it is similar to the CROCODILE, DRAGON, SERPENT, or WHALE) the Leviathan appears as chaos, the Devil, or the Antichrist vanquished by God.

Liber Mundi See BOOK.

Libra See SCALES.

Light An omnipresent phenomenon that is known in its effects but is to a great extent incomprehensible in its essence, it is a common symbol of immateriality, spirit, and God, but also of life and happiness. A yet finer distinction exists between the light of the SUN, symbolizing inspiration and spiritual vision, and the light of the MOON, which, as reflected light, symbolizes indirect knowing via rational, discursive thought. —Light often occurs in contrast to *darkness*, which in such cases usually represents the failure to recognize, spiritual dullness, morally underdeveloped or inferior realms and conditions, death, misfortune, or mystery. —The spatial concepts "above" and "below" (see HEIGHT and DEPTH) correspond symbolically to the relationship of light and darkness. —Practically all fundamental principles based on a twofold division of the world make reference to the differentiation of light and darkness (e.g., Ormazd and Ahriman, YIN AND YANG, angels and demons, spirit and matter, male and female). For many peoples the idea of an ascent from darkness to the light plays an important role in the development of both the individual and humanity; numerous initiation rites are also based on this duality. —The separation of light and darkness as the positing of the primal order at the creation of the world occurs in the cosmogonic concepts of many peoples. —Mystics speak sometimes of a darkness that lies "beyond" (in contrast to "below") the light of knowledge and that symbolizes the fundamental inscrutability of God. —In art an AUREOLE, NIMBUS, or HALO visually expresses the spiritual illumination of a person. See ECLIPSE, FIRE.

Lighthouse See TOWER.

Lightning A symbol or expression in many cultures of divine power, which appears as terrifying or creative. In many cultures lightning and THUNDER were thought to be caused by the highest god (e.g., Jupiter/Zeus, Indra). —In the Bible lightning is associated with God's wrathful judgment; a punitive God of fire, lightning, and

Light: Personification of light. Detail after an Alsatian miniature, 12th century.

Lightning: Zeus hurling a thunderbolt. Greek bronze miniature, first quarter of the 5th century.

Lightning: Detail from a depiction of the *Apocalypse of John*. Woodcut by M. Greyff, 1492.

Lilies of the Valley

thunder is depicted. —Zeus, the hurler of lightning bolts, can be seen as a fructifying, illuminating deity as well as a punishing one. —Particularly in the Orient, a relationship exists between lightning and storms or rain; hence the symbolic connection of lightning and fertility, and the phallic significance of lightning. —Until recently, people in some areas of Asia and Europe have made milk offerings to pacify lightning.

Lilies of the Valley As a medicinal plant used against numerous ailments, it was a frequent attribute of Christ and Mary. It sometimes appears in depictions of the Annunciation in place of the LILY. It symbolizes the salvation of the world.

Lily: Kaiser Frederick I (Barbarossa) with a lily scepter. After a miniature from the Weltchronik, Altdorf (now called Weingarten), last quarter of the 12th century.

Lily The white lily is an old, widely found symbol of light; it also represents purity, innocence, and virginity, especially in Christian art (particularly in depictions of Mary, e.g., in connection with the Annunciation by the archangel Gabriel). Its connection to purity, innocence, and virginity may have to do with the sublimation of an originally phallic meaning ascribed to the lily because of the striking form of its pistil. A lily, shown extending from the mouth of Christ as judge of the world, is a symbol of grace. —In the Bible, "lilies of the field" are mentioned as a symbol of trusting devotion to God. —The lily is also an ancient regal symbol and plays an important and varied role in heraldry. It can, for example, refer to the patronage of the Mother of God or, when represented with three distinct leaves, to the Trinity.

Lime tree (Linden) A tree revered by Germanic and Slavic peoples as being sacred, it was thought to divert lightning and, when touched, to draw diseases to itself. Often it grew in the center of communities or groups of buildings (hence the lime tree in the court, cemetery, at the well, in the village center). —In contrast to the OAK, the lime tree is often considered to be female or feminine.

Linga (*pl.* **Lingam**) A phallic image common in India; it is also a symbol of the Hindu god Shiva. It occurs both as a naturalistic copy and as a truncated column, often with a square base, an

Lime Tree (Linden)

eight-sided central shaft, and a cylindrical upper part (frequently having one or more heads). It symbolizes the divine, the masculine creative power, and probably also the WORLD AXIS. The female counterpart is the YONI. A linga entwined by the kundalini SERPENT symbolizes the power of knowledge or cognition; in conjunction with the yoni, it is a symbol of awakening cognition and the union of form and matter.

Linga: Phallic symbol of the Indian god, Shiva.

Lion The "king" of terrestrial animals (the EAGLE is the "king" of birds), the lion is a common symbolic animal that usually has solar significance or some connection to light, probably because of its strength, golden color, and shaggy mane radiating around its head. The lion's relationship to light is also expressed in the characteristic attributed to it of never shutting its eyes. Further characteristics that give rise to the lion's symbolic meanings are its courage, wildness, and supposed wisdom. —Representations of lions on royal thrones and in palaces are images of power and justice. —In China and Japan the lion, like the DRAGON, was believed to frighten away demons and often was depicted as the guardian of the temple. —Egyptian, Assyrian, and Babylonian temples were often guarded by lion statues. —In Egypt representations of two lions with their backs to each other symbolize the rising and the setting sun, East and West, yesterday and tomorrow. —In the cult of Mithras the lion symbolizes the sun. —The Indian god Krishna, as well as the Buddha, are compared to lions. —Because of the lion's intractable power, it was also closely associated in antiquity with fertility and love gods (e.g., Cybele, Dionysus/Bacchus, and Aphrodite/Venus).— The Bible frequently mentions the lion in both a positive and negative sense: God resembles the lion in his power and justice; the tribe of Judah is compared with a lion; Christ himself is called "the Lion of Judah"; the Devil is associated with the ravening lion. —In the Middle Ages the lion symbolized the resurrection, in part because of the idea, attested by many authors, that lions are born dead and after three days are awakened to life by their father's breath. Representations of roaring lions sometimes symbolize the

Lion: Youthful deity in the rising sun, supported by two lions symbolizing the eastern and western horizons. After a picture in the funereal papyrus of Heri-uben, 21st Dynasty.

Lion: Bronze statue of a lion in Braunschweig.

Lion: The astrological sign for Leo.

resurrection of the dead on the Day of Judgment. —In reference to the negative, threatening aspect of the lion, some medieval depictions show lions devouring people or other animals, symbolizing malevolent, threatening, or punitive powers. —The lion's strength has similar negative meaning in representations or mythic stories of heroes (e.g., Heracles, Samson) hunting or fighting lions, which represent untamed wildness. —The winged lion is an attribute and symbol of St. Mark (see EVANGELISTS, SYMBOLS OF). —In heraldry the lion usually occurs with reference to its strength and often appears on coats of arms and as bearing coats of arms. —The lion (*Leo*) is the fifth sign of the ZODIAC; its element is FIRE.

Live-Forever A yellow-blossoming perennial with fleshy leaves (*Sedum triphyllum*), it was supposed to protect against lightning and storms, according to folk belief. As a long-lived plant it was also a symbol of eternal life (its Latin name is *sempervivum*).

Liver: An eagle eats Prometheus's liver, representing his vital energy. From a Cretan bowl.

Liver It was believed among various peoples to be the seat of vital force, desires, anger, and love. Predictions of the future were made from the livers of animals; the Babylonians and the Etruscans had highly developed systems of interpretation. —Eating liver was supposed to give one the power to dissolve magic spells.

Lizard Because of its liking for the SUN, it is closely associated with LIGHT and sun symbolism. The lizard often appears as a symbol of the soul, which seeks the LIGHT (of knowledge, God, the life beyond). It is depicted in this context on ancient burial monuments and funeral urns, as well as in Christian art. The representation of Apollo as the lizard slayer (*sauroktonos*) derives from this meaning. It symbolizes the yearning of the soul to die at the hand of the god of light, and through death in the light to attain the life beyond. —In the Middle Ages a link was established between the lizard and the yearning for Christ (reported, for example, in *Physiologus*). Having become blind in old age, the lizard regains its sight if it creeps through an eastward-pointing cleft in a stone wall and gazes uninterruptedly into the rising sun; likewise an individual, whose inner eye has begun to darken, should gaze at Christ as the sun of justice. —The annual molting of the lizard made it a symbol of renewal and resurrection. —Sometimes the lizard has a negative symbolism in hot climates, where its frequent appearance corresponds to periods of heat and drought.

Locust The migratory locust represents voracity and destruction, because it devastates entire districts in great hordes. —In the Old Testament the plague of locusts that descends on Egypt is an affliction sent by God. —The locust vision in the Apocalypse is interpreted as either a symbol of heretics or of demonic powers. —In China the occasional rapid increase in the numbers of locusts was seen as an expression of a disturbance in the cosmic order, and as a symbol of numerous progeny and hence of happiness and well-being.

Lodestone Magnetic oxide of iron, or lodestone, was called *lapis amoris* in antiquity because, like love, it exerted a power of attraction. —In the Middle Ages it was a symbol of God's power to attract his creatures and was thus also called *lapis gratiae* (stone of grace). —In a widely told fable of the Middle Ages, a magnetic mountain in the sea drew all passing ships to it, causing them to go aground; the mountain was a symbol of the sins on which the SHIP of life must necessarily be destroyed because it was not oriented to Mary, the sea star.

Lorelei See SIRENS.

Lotus Any of various water lilies, as a symbol it plays a significant role in Egypt, India, and the Far East. Since at sunset it closes its blossom and retires into the water, and only at sunrise reappears and opens its flower, it is an ancient light symbol. The white, blue, or red blossoms that rise out of murky water symbolize purity overcoming impurity. —In Egypt the lotus, which bears the sun in itself, was believed to have arisen out of the primal waters and hence represented the watery origin of the world; thus it was closely linked to the sacred, life-giving Nile. It was an attribute of various deities, was

Das.lₓₓuij.Capitel.

Lodestone: The lodestone pulling the nails out of a ship. Woodcut, 1509.

Lotus: Smelling the life-giving fragrance of the lotus blossom. Detail after a mural in the Grave of the Night near Thebes, 18th Dynasty, ca. 1400 B.C.

used in connection with funereal and sacrificial rites, and played an important role in temple architecture and ornamentation. The scent of the fragrant blue lotus was believed to renew life. —The lotus is richly symbolic in Buddhism and Hinduism. The bud of the lotus flower floating on the primal waters, like the *world egg*, symbolizes the totality of all unmanifested possibilities before the creation of the world. (It is also a symbol of the human heart.) The opened blossom represents creation. The eight-petaled lotus flower symbolizes all the directions of the compass and thereby cosmic harmony; in this connection it often occurs as a yantra. Brahma is usually depicted sitting on a lotus leaf; Buddha is shown either on or emerging from a lotus blossom. The "jewel in the lotus" (*mani padme*) is Nirvana, which is already latent in the world. The thousand-petaled lotus blossom symbolizes the totality of all revelations. In India there is also a distinction made between the red lotus blossom as solar and the blue as lunar. —The association of the lotus or the water lily with ideas of purity continued into the European Middle Ages in superficial form. Since its seed and root were believed to calm sensual drives, they were recommended to monks and nuns as a medicament.

Lychnis

Lust See LUXURIA.

Luxuria The female personification of *lust*, one of the seven mortal sins, she rides on a SWINE or a RAM. Its symbols include the SIRENS and the MIRROR.

Lychnis A common meadow flower in Europe and northern Asia that has showy, rose-red flowers, it is an attribute of Mary in medieval Christian art.

Lynx It is an animal that usually refers to the Devil in medieval symbolism. Since people ascribed to it the ability to look through walls, the lynx appears in representations of the five senses as the personification of the sense of sight.

Lyre (Harp) It is a symbol of divine harmony and of the harmonious union of SKY and EARTH.

Lyre: Orpheus with the lyre. From a krater from Gela, ca. 450 B.C.

—The lyre is an attribute of the Greek god Apollo and a common symbol of music and poetry. —The sound of the lyre was sometimes believed (e.g., in the myth of Orpheus) to have magical powers, especially of taming wild beasts. —In the Bible, playing the harp is an expression of thanks to and praise of God.

Magical Squares Having a flat surface divided into square fields similar to the chessboard, the magical squares usually have *numbers* inscribed in them in such an order that the sum of each horizontal, each vertical, and each diagonal row yields the same value. At one time they had magical significance symbolizing harmony. There are also magical squares based on letters (e.g., the Sator Arepo formula).

Magpie It is a bird that signifies evil, persecution, or early death in Medieval Art.

Maiestas Domini A symbolic representation in Christian art of the eternal majesty of Christ exalted, it consists of a frontal view of the enthroned Christ, often with raised right hand and the book of life in his left hand. Christ is frequently surrounded by the symbols of the Evangelists (see EVANGELISTS, SYMBOLS OF) or the 24 elders of the Apocalypse, and is often enclosed in a MANDORLA.

Mallow Any of a variety of herbs of the family Malvaceae (including cotton, okra, hollyhock, hibiscus) of the northern temperate zone, they were used as medicaments. Since antiquity, the leaves of the mallow were seen as signifying a plea for forgiveness; in Christian art the mallow sometimes appears in this sense.

Mallow

Mandala It is the Hindu term for CIRCLE. In Indian religion the word came to designate circular or rectangular meditation images that were abstract or that contained representational elements. The mandala symbolically represents religious experiences, and as a meditation aid it is intended to assist the meditator's union with the divine. —Jung considered mandalas to be individuation symbols. See YANTRA.

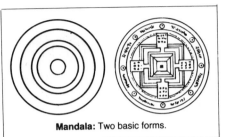

Mandala: Two basic forms.

Mandorla: Christ in the mandorla. After a miniature, Pontifical of Chartres, early 13th century.

Mandorla An almond-shaped AUREOLE that shares the symbolic meaning of the MANDALA, since early Christian times it has been used primarily for representations of the glorified Christ.

Mandragora See MANDRAKE.

Mandrake It is a Mediterranean herb (*Mandragora officinarum*) of the nightshade family, which, according to German folk belief, grew from the semen of the hanged. (Hence the root was also called *Galgenmaenlein*, gallows manikin.) The long, tapering rootstock frequently has a forked shape reminiscent of the human form. Mandrake has been used extensively since antiquity as a healing and magical substance and as an aphrodisiac. Various peoples (e.g., the Egyptians and the Hebrews) consequently saw the mandrake as a magically effective love and fertility symbol. —In medieval folk belief the mandrake was reputed to have the power to bring good fortune, fertility, and riches; since then there have been many references to this (e.g., in colloquialisms and proverbs). See GINSENG.

Mandrake: From *Hortus sanitatis* (German edition), 1485.

Manna According to the Old Testament, it was a miraculous food that fell from heaven for the children of Israel during their wanderings in the

Manna: Rain of quail and manna. Byzantine octateuch in Smyrna, first half of the 13th century.

126

wilderness as they fled Egypt. According to Talmudic tradition, it was created on the evening of the sixth day of creation. It was also interpreted by Jewish and Christian authors to be a symbol of the Logos. In addition, it is a symbolic designation for every sort of supernatural nourishment.

Marabou See STORK.

Marguerite A flower of the family Compositae, with white, radiating petals, it was compared with the PEARL (the Latin *margarita* means *pearl*), but also with shed drops of blood. In Christian paintings of the Middle Ages it alludes to the sufferings and death of Christ and the martyrs.

Marguerite

Marigold An ancient medicinal plant of the aster family having golden yellow to orange blossoms, it appears in medieval Christian paintings as an attribute of Mary and as a symbol of salvation.

Marionette A jointed puppet that is suspended from and manipulated from above by strings, wires, or sticks, it is a symbol of a person's dependency on superior powers; in a narrower sense it is symbolic of a personality without will, directed from without.

Marigold

Marriage In many religions it is the symbol of the union of (usually personified) divine forces, of humans with God or gods, of the soul with the body, or—especially in alchemy—of the opposites. For example, in antiquity there was the union of the divine pair Zeus (Jupiter) and Hera (Juno) as well as numerous unions of Zeus (Ju-

Marriage: Marriage symbolizing the union of the opposites in alchemy. From *Rosarium Philosophorum*, 1550.

Mask: Two
Greek theater
masks.

piter) with mortal women. —In the Old Testament the marriage of Yahweh with the Israelites is mentioned; in the New Testament there are various references to the Christian church as the bride of Christ. As a symbolic expression of their marriage with Christ, nuns in the Catholic church receive VEIL, WREATH, and RING when they are accepted into the convent. See SACRED PROSTITUTION.

Mars See IRON.

Masculine-Feminine See LIGHT, YIN AND YANG.

Mask An ancient form of an expressive facial disguise, it served to frighten enemies, was used in magical rites, and depicted spirits and the personified powers of people and animals, usually with noticeable emphasis on certain stereotyped character traits. —On the sarcophagi from late antiquity, the theater masks allude to life as a play. —Today the mask is generally understood to be a symbol of the concealment of the ego behind an artificial appearance.

Maya See VEIL.

Mead A fermented (see FERMENTATION) drink of HONEY and WATER, in Germanic mythology it is the drink of the gods and heroes. The intoxicating effect was variously interpreted as a sign of the transmittal of divine powers to humans.

Melon Like most fruits with many seeds, it is a fertility symbol.

Menhir An upright stone having ritual or cult significance, in the broadest sense it is a phallic symbol and thus also a symbol of power and protection. It may be associated with the symbolism of the WORLD AXIS.

Menhir:
Gollenstein
menhir near
Blieskastel,
Neolithic,
ca. 2000 B.C.

Mercurius (Mercury) It is the ancient Roman god of commerce (later equated with Hermes). It is also the name of the planet closest to the sun. —In alchemy it is the designation for *quicksilver* (the terrestrial counterpart to the planet), the *prima materia* (the basic, original stuff or substance), or the PHILOSOPHERS' STONE. Along with SALT and SULFUR, quicksilver was considered to be one of the "philosophical" elements and world principles; it represented the volatile (i.e., the spirit). Mercury was interpreted as HERMAPHRODITE in contrast to the "masculine" planets (Sun, Mars, Jupiter, and Uranus) and the "feminine" planets (Venus, Saturn, and Neptune); consequently it played an important role as symbol of all the practices of alchemy that mediate the opposites.

Mercury See MERCURIUS.

Metals In terms of their symbolic meanings, metals are ambivalent. The working of metals (see SMITH) was often seen in connection with the fires of hell. On the other hand, the extraction of metals from their ores and their chemical analyses were symbolic of purification and spiritualization. —Jung saw in the "subterranean"

Mercurius: Mercurius as the solar-lunar hermaphrodite, standing on the sphere of chaos. From Mylius's *Philosophia Reformata*, 1622.

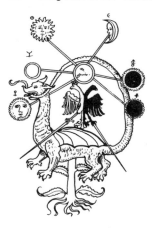

Metals: The seven planets of antiquity (Mercury as the seventh in the center) to which the alchemists assigned certain metals.

character of metals a symbol of sexuality, which needs refining or purification. —In initiation rites (and also in Freemasonry) the initiate sometimes removes all metal objects worn on the body as a sign of purification or of renouncing all earthly goods. —In specific metals the alchemists saw correspondences to the seven planets known to antiquity:

Sun = gold
Moon = silver
Mercury = quicksilver (in antiquity, steel and tin)
Venus = copper
Mars = iron
Jupiter = tin (in antiquity, brass or electrum)
Saturn = lead

Meteorite See STONE.

Microcosm See HUMAN BEING.

Midday (Midnight) Like the summer and winter solstices, midday and midnight are temporal turning points that for ages have had special significance. In China they are considered to be the high points, respectively, of yang and yin influences (see YIN AND YANG). —According to the esoteric view, midnight is the time when the spiritual (in contrast to the physical) SUN stands at the zenith; consequently, midnight is associated with contemplation, initiation, and spiritual knowledge and insight. —In folk belief midnight is the witching hour when contact with spirits, poor souls, etc., can most easily be established. —In fairy tales the midnight hour, and the bright hours of day when no shadows fall, are the times of mysterious happenings. —The midday heat of summer was believed in antiquity to be the hour of Pan.

Midgard Serpent See SERPENT.

Midnight See MIDDAY.

Milk As the first and most nutritious food, it symbolizes in many cultures fertility, spiritual and intellectual nourishment, and immortality. Because of its color and mild taste, it is often associated with the MOON, which, in contrast to the sun, radiates a mild, white light. —In some parts of Asia and Europe it was thought that LIGHTNING or the fires it set could be extinguished with milk. —According to Indian cosmogonic ideas, the universe was originally a sea of milk that was transformed into BUTTER, the first food for living creatures, by a huge paddle or by whiplashes (see WHIP). —Christian art, which often depicts the Mother of God nursing (*Maria lactans*), distinguishes between the good mother, who bestows truth, and the evil mother, who suckles SERPENTS at her breast. —Milk in connection with HONEY occurs in antiquity and in the Old Testament as the essence of the highest divine goodness and of the blessed life (e.g., milk and honey flow in the promised land). Consequently milk and honey play an important role in various ancient mystery cults. In the practices of the early Christian church, milk and honey appeared as a liturgical symbol; they

Milk: The Egyptian king nursed by Isis, appearing in the form of a sacred tree that gives milk. From the grave of Thutmose III.

were offered to the candidate for baptism as a sign of the promise of salvation the first time he or she received communion.

Milky Way In the religious ideas of many peoples, probably because the moon seemingly scendent one. The Milky Way was compared with such things as a white snake (e.g., in some Indian cultures), a river, footsteps, spilled milk, a tree, and an embroidered garment. Sometimes (e.g., in the Far East and among Germanic tribes) it was believed to be the path that the souls of the deceased had to follow; many primitive peoples also understood it as the abode of the dead. In Japan, India, and Egypt, the Milky Way was seen as the river of a fertile land on whose banks the gods dwelt. —For some peoples it was close in symbolic meaning to the RAINBOW. —Occasionally it was understood to be a tear in the dome of the sky through which the heavenly fire shone into this world.

Millet A foodstuff eaten in many areas by the common people, it was considered in China to be a symbol of the fertile earth and the natural order.

Mill, Mystic In a medieval allegory illustrating the relationship between the New Testament and the Old Testament, the wheat of the Old Testament is ground in the mystic mill into flour, from which the believers' bread of life is made.

Mill, Mystic: Capital on a column in Vezelay, France, middle of the 12th century.

Mimosa It is any of a large genus of herbs, shrubs, or trees with bipinnate leaves. The leaves of the *touch-me-not* (*Impatiens Noli Tangere*) variety collapse at the slightest touch; it is consequently a symbol of sensitivity and bashfulness. —The yellow-blossomed mimosa (often equated with the true ACACIA) symbolizes light and the certainty of salvation.

Minotaur A fabulous creature of Greek mythology with a human body and a STEER'S head, the Minotaur was held captive by King Minos in the LABYRINTH. Yearly or every seven years Athenian youths and maidens were offered to it as food; with the help of Ariadne's THREAD, Theseus vanquished it. It symbolizes dark, destructive forces that work invisibly; it sometimes also has the same symbolic meaning as the CENTAUR.

Minotaur: Theseus slays the Minotaur. After a picture on a Greek plate.

Mirror: Mirror representing vanity. From S. Brant's *The Ship of Fools*, Basel, 1494.

Mistletoe

Moloch: After a picture in Athanasius Kircher's *Oedipus Aegyptiacus*, Rome, 1652.

Mint See PEPPERMINT.

Mirror With reference to the imaging and reflective function of thought, it symbolizes knowledge, self-knowledge, and consciousness, as well as truth and clarity. —It is also a symbol of the creation, which "reflects" the divine intelligence, as well as the pure human heart, which, for example, God (in Christian mysticism) or the Buddha merges into himself. The mirror is associated metaphorically with the eye or face (as the mirror of the soul). —Because of its clarity, the mirror is a sun symbol and also a moon symbol (as an indirect source of light); because of its passivity it symbolizes the feminine. —In China it represents the contemplative, wise person who does not act. —In Japan, where the mirror symbolizes the perfect purity of the soul as well as the sun goddess, sacred mirrors are found in numerous Shinto temples. —Due to its likeness to the reflective surface of water, it is used by some black African peoples as a symbol of water in magical rain rites. —In the art of the Middle Ages and the Renaissance, the mirror is a symbol of vanity and lust, as well as of intelligence and truth. In medieval art it also symbolizes the virginity of Mary, in whom God "mirrored" his own image in the form of his son. —Folk belief of various peoples ascribes apotropaic powers to the mirror.

Mistletoe A parasitic shrub, it was widely regarded as a preventative against illness, lightning, and magic spells, and as bringing good fortune. Since it is evergreen, it is an immortality symbol; it plays a significant role, especially in Celtic customs, at the new year.

Moloch Originally a Canaanite god to whom human sacrifices were made, later it became a general symbol of forces that harm or destroy human beings (specifically, inhuman political systems).

Money In the broadest sense, it is a symbol of economic goods. —As the abstract form of all earthly goods, money, like GOLD, has been interpreted from the moral viewpoint as a symbol of attachment to the world and also as greed. —As minted coin (like the SEAL), it is sometimes a Christian symbol of the faithful soul that carries the image of God in it (as the coin carries the image of the king, for example). —From the psychoanalytic perspective, money is closely associated with EXCREMENT.

Monster Probably a personification of anxieties (see CERBERUS) that relate to the external world and to threatening aspects of one's own psyche. —In the Bible the monster LEVIATHAN embodies the order opposed to God. —The monster, which must be fought and overcome, occurs in sagas and fairy tales as the guardian of treasures or as the abductor and guard of a virgin; from a psychoanalytic viewpoint this can be interpreted as symbolizing difficulties and tests in the course of personal development.

Money: The money shitter of Goslar.

Moon It plays a significant role in the magical and graphic religious symbolism of most peoples, probably because the moon seemingly "lives" (due to its perpetually changing shape), it is related to various vital rhythms on earth, and it is an important referent in measuring time. In this regard it used to play a more important role than the SUN in the ancient Orient. Among many peoples it was worshiped as a god or (usually) goddess (e.g., among the Greeks as Selene; among the Romans as Luna). —Because of its waxing and waning and its general influence on the earth, especially on the female, it is closely associated with female fertility, rain and the moistness, as well as with every sort of becoming and passing away. —Among many peoples there were special rites that were supposed to strengthen or save the moon at the time of the new moon or the dark of the moon, which were understood to be times of weakness or threat to the nocturnal heavenly body. —In contrast to the sun—which generates its own light, is usually interpreted as masculine, and is related to the yang principle (see YIN AND YANG)—the moon usually appears as a symbol of the mild, dependent feminine and is linked to the yin principle. Less often there occurs (e.g., among Germanic-speaking peoples) the idea of the moon as an (old) man. In many myths the moon appears as sister, wife, or beloved of the sun. In astrology and in depth psychology the moon is

Moon: The moon represented as Luna holding branches(?) and a horn, walking on the clouds with two wheels and the astrological sign for Cancer. Woodcut, 15th century.

Moon: As female principle, Luna. Vatican, 15th century.

sometimes symbolic of the unconscious, fertile passivity, and receptivity. See CRESCENT MOON, HARE, MILK.

Moor See SWAMP.

Morning Star Like the EVENING STAR, it is a designation for the bright planet Venus, but here it refers to the morning position of Venus. Heralding each new day, it signifies perpetual renewal or eternal return; it is a symbol of light victorious over darkness and is also a Christian symbol of Christ or Mary.

Mortal Sins These are sloth (personified by ACEDIA), avarice (AVARITIA), gluttony (GULA), envy (INVIDIA), anger (IRA), lust (LUXURIA), and spiritual pride (SUPERBIA).

Mortar A vessel in which substances are crushed or ground with a club-shaped pestle, often symbolizing the feminine principle worked on by the masculine principle. Like the pestle, it is a popular sexual symbol.

Moth Irresistibly drawn to the light and consumed by it, the moth is a symbol of the soul's mystic, selfless, self-sacrificial love of the divine light.

Mountain Because it often reaches into the clouds, it is a symbol of the joining of heaven (see SKY) and EARTH, as well as of spiritual ascent (see LADDER) and higher development achieved with great labor. —Holy mountains commonly signify the dwelling places of the gods. Spiritually significant events take place on mountains (e.g., the Chinese emperor made offerings on the peaks of mountains; Moses received the Ten Commandments on Mount Sinai). —Because of its great, immobile mass, the mountain is also a symbol of imperturbability. —For the Sumerians it represented undifferentiated primal matter. —The concept of the mountain as the midpoint or WORLD AXIS is widespread. —For some peoples, the realm of the dead or the dwelling place of certain deceased persons is in the depths of a mountain.

Mourning Veil See VEIL.

Mouse The Romans believed white mice to be good omens. —In medieval folk belief mice

Mouth: The Egyptian king Ay performing the ceremony of opening the mouth of his deceased predecessor, Tutankhamen (depicted as Osiris). Detail from a mural in the grave of Tutankhamen.

were embodiments of witches or the souls of the deceased; white mice, on the other hand, were sometimes seen as the embodiments of unborn children. The mouse plague was thought to be a punishment from God. —In contrast to true mice, the shrew, a mouselike creature, was revered by the Egyptians as a sacred animal.

Mouth As the organ of speech and the breath, it symbolically embodies the power of the spirit and of creativity, especially by "inspiring" the soul and life. As the organ of eating and devouring, it also symbolizes destruction, particularly the mouths of monsters (the "jaws of hell"). —The ceremony of opening the mouth that was performed on Egyptian mummies was supposed to enable the deceased to speak the truth before the gods, and to eat and drink again. —In the paintings of the Middle Ages, little black demons that come out of the mouth signify evil words and lies. Christ as judge of the world often appears with a SWORD or with a sword and a LILY which come out of the mouth.

Mouth: The mouth represented as the jaws of hell. Detail from an English miniature, second half of the 13th century.

Mugwort The plant *Artemisia vulgaris*, several varieties of which were considered to be brides' plants and consequently were associated with Mary, the heavenly bride. See WORMWOOD.

Mulberry Tree It is a tree associated in China with the rising SUN. Arrows shot in four directions from a bow made of mulberry wood (or from the wood of the PEACH tree) were supposed to drive away evil influences.

Mulberry Tree

Mullein A plant common in Europe, Africa, and Asia, it was used in antiquity as a medicament to protect one from anxiety and against misfortune. In the Middle Ages it was associated with Mary.

Mushroom An edible fungus that is a symbol, especially in China, of long life, possibly because when dried it can be stored for long periods of time. Supposedly it thrives only in peaceful and ordered times and thus is also a symbol of wise government. —In some parts of Africa and Siberia the mushroom symbolized the (newborn) human soul.

Mussel As a form of aquatic life, it is often an attribute of sea gods. The white mussel is closely

Mullein

Myrrh

Mussel: The birth of Venus from the mussel. After Botticelli.

associated (e.g., in China) with the MOON (and hence with the yin principle; see YIN AND YANG). —As "the foam born" (*anadyomene*), Aphrodite is sometimes represented standing on a mussel shell. The mussel's association with Aphrodite (and in India with Lakshmi, the goddess of happiness and beauty) may have to do with several factors: its resemblance to the female genital, its symbolic relation to the fertile WATER of the SEA, and its harboring of the beautiful PEARL, which grows inside it. —As an object sometimes included in Christian burial, the mussel symbolizes the grave from which humanity will arise on the Day of Judgment. The mussel became a symbol of Mary because she carried Jesus, the "precious pearl," in her womb and because of the medieval belief that the mussel remained virginal and was fertilized by dew drops.

Myrrh It is the resin produced by several species of *Commiphora (Balsamodendron)*, especially *C. Myhrra*. Because of its fragrance and its healing effects, myrrh played an important role in Indian, oriental, Jewish, and Christian rituals and was an ingredient of the holy anointing oil of the Israelites; in the Bible it is mentioned as one of the gifts of the three kings to the infant Jesus. Due to its bitterness, medicinal properties, and use in mummifying corpses, it symbolically referred to the sufferings and death of Christ as well as to the penance and asceticism of faithful Christians.

Myrtle It is an evergreen, white-blossomed tree or shrub of the temperate zones. The Jews saw in it a symbol of divine favor as well as of peace and joy. —In antiquity the myrtle was sacred to Aphrodite and was consequently a love symbol; as an evergreen plant, it was also a symbol of immortality. In contrast to the LAUREL, which adorned victors after bloody battles, the myrtle WREATH symbolized the victory won without bloodshed. —The myrtle wreath for brides was customary as a sign of joy among the Jews; in antiquity brides adorned themselves with wreaths of roses and myrtle, alluding to the goddess of love and marriage, Aphrodite. Today the bride's wreath of myrtle often symbolizes virginity.

Nakedness Since ancient times, nakedness has been a polyvalent symbol. —In reference to the clearly apparent sexual appeal of the body, nakedness (which is viewed negatively in the Biblical tradition in contrast to the Greek) symbolizes seduction and lust; it was often an element in magical love practices. —When nakedness represents openness and candor, it symbolizes purity and truth (hence the phrase "the naked truth"). —Adam and Eve's nakedness in paradise is a symbol of their innocence before the Fall. —As renunciation of CLOTHING (which can represent attachment to the world), nakedness also symbolizes asceticism; as a reminder that human beings are all born naked, it symbolizes unconditional subjugation to the will of God. —The condemned criminal was sometimes stripped of clothing as a sign of loss of membership in the community. See also VEIL.

Narcissus A bulbous plant, a common member of the amaryllis family, it withers after flowering and appears again in the spring as one of the most striking blossoming plants. In Greece it is associated symbolically with sleep. It was planted on graves as a sign of the relatedness between sleep and death. It is also a symbol of spring and fertility. —In Asia it represents good fortune. —Because of its straight stem, among the Arabs it symbolizes the upright person acting according to God's commandments. —In medieval art it is sometimes a symbol of Mary (probably because of its lilylike appearance).

Narcissus

Nard Oil See VALERIAN.

Navel In the myths of various peoples, it is a symbol of the center of the world, from which all creation is supposed to have originated. The *omphalos* at Delphi, a cylindrical stone rounded on the top, was famous as a symbol of the union of the realms of the gods, humans, and the dead. —The POLESTAR was considered to be the navel of the sky, around which the vault of the heavens appeared to rotate. —*Contemplation of the navel*, a meditation on the basic principles of humanity and the cosmos, is practiced in Indian yoga and sometimes in the Orthodox church.

Navel: The omphalos of Delphi as world navel.

Nest It is a symbol of safety, protectedness, and rest. In medieval art birds in nests often symbolize the peace of paradise.

Net: The apostles as fishermen with a net. Panel from the ceiling of a church, Zillis.

Net It is a symbol of extensive interconnectedness, but especially of catching and gathering. —Oriental deities are sometimes represented with nets by which they subjugate or draw humans to them. —In Iran, humans, especially mystics, are depicted with nets by which they seek God. —In the New Testament the net appears as a symbol of God's effects; it is also alluded to when the apostles are called "fishers of men." In this sense a net with FISH may represent the church. —From the perspective of depth psychology, catching fish is an expression of an active coming to terms with the unconscious.

Night: Winged genius representing night and day. Detail from the Genesis mosaic, San Marco, Venice, early 13th century.

Night In contrast to DAY, it is a symbol of the mysterious dark, the irrational, the unconscious, and death, but also of the protective and fertile WOMB. See MIDDAY.

Nightingale Because of its sweet and simultaneously plaintive song, it is a symbol of love (especially in Persia) but also of yearning and pain. —In antiquity its song was regarded as a good omen. —In folk belief the nightingale is a damned soul, but also a harbinger of a gentle death. —In Christian symbolism it is an image of the longing for heaven.

Nimbus In ancient and oriental art (especially painting), it is a circular area or corona of rays about the head of a god, hero, saint, etc., possibly representing the SUN or a CROWN. It is a symbol of divinity, majesty, illumination, or sovereign authority. See HALO.

Nine As the treble of the sacred number THREE, it signifies completeness or wholeness. —In China the nine-story pagoda is a symbol of heaven. —In antiquity the sum of human arts and sciences was personified as the nine muses. —Nine is the number in Christian symbolism of (among other things) the choir of angels. See NINETY-NINE.

Ninety-Nine In Christianity, probably with reference to the "perfect" symbolic number NINE, it is the number of the word *Amen*, calculated according to the numerical value assigned to the Greek letters: alpha (1) + mu (40) + eta (8) + nu (50). — The significance of the 99 PRAYER BEADS in the Islamic rosary probably also has to do with the symbolism of the perfect nine.

Noli Tangere See MIMOSA.

Nose It occurs sometimes in literature as a disguised symbol of the penis.

Null It is a symbol of nothingness and worthlessness. With reference to the numbers following null (zero), it also symbolizes the beginning.

Numbers In most cultures and religions, numbers are carriers of symbolic meaning with often complicated significance. Numbers were frequently regarded as expressions of the cosmic and human order or (for the Pythagoreans) of the harmony of the spheres. The even numbers were generally understood as masculine, bright, or good, and the uneven numbers as feminine, dark, or evil. Sometimes the interchangeability of numbers and LETTERS played a role (e.g., in the Cabala). Attention was repeatedly paid to the relationships among numbers in architecture, sculpture, painting, music, literature, and in sacred and profane customs and usages (e.g., the medial section). — The assignment of symbolic significance to specific numbers was based on theoretical considerations related to a particular counting system.

Nut The symbolism of the *walnut* corresponds closely to that of the ALMOND. — In Christian literature the nut is mentioned as a symbol of humanity. The green husk stands for the flesh, the hard shell for the bones, and the sweet kernel for the soul. As a Christ symbol, the bitter-tasting hull embodies the flesh of Christ that suffered the bitter passion; the shell represents the wood of the cross; and the kernel, which nourishes and whose oil gives light, represents Christ's divine nature.

Oak For many Indo-Germanic peoples it is a sacred tree. The Greeks (particularly in Dodona) dedicated it to Zeus, the Romans to Jupiter, and the Germanic tribes to Donar (probably because of its majestic form and because it draws lightning to itself). Since antiquity it has been a symbol of strength, masculinity, and steadfastness because of its hard, durable wood; in antiquity and the Middle Ages it was also a symbol of immortality because its wood was thought to be imperishable. —In eighteenth-century Germany the oak became a symbol of heroism; since the early nineteenth century, oak foliage has been used in the victor's WREATH.

Obelisk It is a tall stone pillar with a square cross-section that tapers as it rises and terminates in a pyramid. In Egypt it was a symbol of the sun god; its apex was struck in the morning by the first rays of the SUN. Its directionally accented form symbolized the connection between the EARTH and the heavens (see SKY) or the sun.

Oak

Oil Lamp See LAMP.

Oils Oils are regarded in many cultures as the bearers of special powers. Olive oil in particular—as the product of the OLIVE TREE, which bears fruit on poor soil—symbolizes spiritual power, but since it burns in the oil lamp, it is also a light symbol. —In the mythological conceptions of Shintoism, wherein the primal waters consisted of oil, it symbolizes the undifferentiated original condition. —In the Eleusinian mysteries oil was used as a symbol of purity. In Mediterranean countries oil sacrifices (i.e., oil poured on stone altars) was a sign of prayer for fertility. —Anointing with oil plays an important ritual role in various religions. In Judaism, for example, things (e.g., the Stone of Bethel) and people (priests, prophets, and kings) were anointed with oil as a sign of divine blessing and of God-given authority. The Latin word *Christus* (as well as the Hebrew, *mashiah* and the English *messiah*) means "anointed"; hence it designates the royal, prophetic, and priestly power of Jesus. —Oil (also mixed with balsam and spices; see CHRISM) is sometimes used in Chris-

Oak: Oak wreath decorating a military order.

tian ritual for consecration (e.g., in BAPTISM, consecration of priests, extreme unction).

Olive Tree It has been cultivated since ancient times, and is rich with symbolic meaning. In Greece it was sacred to Athena and was regarded as a symbol of mental strength and knowledge (since it also provided oil for lamps, it was associated with LIGHT), purification (because of the cleansing power of the oil), fertility and vital energy (since it is very hardy and can live several hundred years), and victory, as well as peace and reconciliation (due to the soothing effect of its oil). —With reference to the olive branch brought back by the dove Noah sent from the ark, the olive tree and its branches are regarded in Christianity as a sign of reconciliation with God and of peace. See also OILS.

Obelisk: Obelisk with hieroglyphs, in front of the pylon of the temple in Luxor, 19th Dynasty.

Om (Aum) It is a holy meditation symbol of Hinduism, Buddhism, and Jainism with a profusion of esoteric meanings. It is believed to be immortal and inexhaustible and is interpreted as the symbolic expression of the creative spirit, the word, or (with reference to the three component sounds) the three human conditions (waking, dreaming, and deep sleep), the three times of day (morning, midday, evening), and the three faculties (action, cognition, volition).

Omega The last letter of the Greek alphabet, in Christianity especially it is a symbol of the end and of the perfection of the world. —Teilhard de Chardin called the goal toward which humankind strives the "point omega." See ALPHA, ALPHA AND OMEGA, TAW.

Olive Tree: Noah's dove with the branch from the olive tree. Woodcut by G. Marcks.

Omphalos See NAVEL.

Onager It is a wild ass of Asia that is difficult to domesticate. In the Bible it is a symbol of the person who will not listen to reason and, more broadly, of obstinate Israel that will not bend to God's commandments. —It is also a symbol of the hermits living in the desert. —Since the onager is often represented with a horn on its forehead, it serves as a phallic variant of the UNICORN.

One It is a symbol of the yet undifferentiated primal origin, as well as of the totality into which all

Om: The sacred syllable as script.

Onager: After an etching by M. Merian.

One-Eyed: Blinding of the one-eyed Polyphemus. From an ancient Greek vase, 6th century B.C.

Orchid

things and beings strive to return. As a unity it is thus a symbol of God but also of individuality. As a graphic symbol the number one sometimes referred symbolically to humans (because of the erect form of the numeral). In earlier speculations, the number one was often not considered a numeral in the narrower sense (see TWO).

One-Eyed Like BLINDNESS, LAMENESS, or having a humpback, having one eye usually signifies a limitation, but it also expresses capacities of a particular sort, such as unusually primitive powers (e.g., Cyclops, Polyphemus) or divine knowledge (e.g., Odin).

One-legged It is an attribute of beings (e.g., gods, witches, magicians, animals) that in the mythological conceptions of many peoples is responsible for RAIN and THUNDER. In China, for example, the appearance of a one-legged bird was an omen predicting rain; dances done on one leg were supposed to bring rain.

Orange Like most fruits with many seeds, it is a fertility symbol.

Orchid It is a plant found usually in warm, moist regions. Many terrestrial orchids (e.g., the varieties native to Europe and adjoining areas) have testicle-shaped tubers (the Greek *orchis* means testicle). —In antiquity they were regarded as an aphrodisiac and a fertility symbol. They were seen as a favorite food of satyrs, were used for love magic, supposedly protected against illness and the evil eye, and granted good luck in gaming and in making one rich. —The Chinese used orchids in spring festivals to drive out evil spirits. —The spotted orchid was originally sacred to the Germanic mother goddess Freya and later to Mary.

Oriole In China it is a bird symbolic of spring, marriage, and joy.

Ostrich The Egyptians regarded the feathers of the ostrich as symbolic of truth and justice (the bird was the embodiment of Maat, goddess of the world order). —According to medieval natural philosophy (see PHYSIOLOGUS), the ostrich does not brood its eggs itself but only watches them incessantly until the young hatch. Hence the ostrich egg was regarded as a symbol of meditation. According to other conceptions, the ostrich lets the SUN hatch its eggs; hence it represents Christ, who was resurrected by God. The ostrich egg is also regarded as a symbol of the virgin motherhood of Mary. —In the negative sense the ostrich, which deserts its eggs, is a symbol of ungodly humanity. The ostrich with its head in the sand is also symbolic of the mortal sin of sloth. Presently the ostrich refers to people who close their eyes to unpleasant facts.

Ostrich: The sun hatching the egg of the ostrich. Detail after a painting depicting Mary, Ottobeuren, ca. 1450-60.

Otter It is a lunar symbolic animal. In some American Indian cultures and in Africa, its pelt plays a role in initiation rites. In Europe it sometimes occurs as psychopomp ("spirit guide").

Ouroboros See UROBOROS.

Oven It is symbolically related to FIRE. In AL-CHEMY it is especially important in the transformation processes of metals, AIR, EARTH, and WATER, and hence in the associated mystical and moral processes. —The oven, particularly for baking bread, symbolizes the womb; consequently "being in the oven" can be interpreted as a return to the embryonic condition, and being cremated in the oven as a symbol of death and rebirth.

Ostrich. From an Egyptian picture, 20th Dynasty.

Owl As a night bird that cannot tolerate the light of the sun, it is often contrasted to the EAGLE. —In Egypt and India the owl was the bird of the dead; from antiquity to the present, the owl and its call are considered uncanny and are taken as omens portending misfortune or heralding death. —In China it played an important role as a fear-inspiring animal associated with LIGHTNING (which lights up the night), the drum (which penetrates the stillness of night), and the yang (see YIN AND YANG) principle (intensified to the point of destruction). —Since it sees in the dark and is thought to be serious and pensive, it also symbolizes wisdom, which penetrates the darkness of ignorance; in this context it became an attribute of the Greek goddess of learning, Athena. —The Bible counts it among the unclean animals. —In Christian symbolism it appears negatively as the image of spiritual darkness, but

Owl: Owl on an ancient Athenian coin.

positively as a symbol of religious knowledge or Christ, as the light that illuminates the darkness.

Ox In contrast to the STEER, the ox is a symbol of peaceableness and good-natured strength. —Ox and water buffalo are sacred and beloved sacrificial animals in the Far East and in Greece. In the Far East the water buffalo is the steed of sages (e.g., of Lao-tse during his journey to the West). The bison or buffalo, the great grass-eating animal of the North American plains, was called *wakan* by the Sioux (denoting sacred power, mystery, and energy). For Native Ameri-

Ox: *Left*: Soap-stone seal with a representation of a humpback ox. From Mohenjo-Daro. *Right*: Ox and ass at the manger of

Jesus. Relief on the baptismal font of the Stiftskirche in Freckenhorst, first half of the 12th century.

cans, its meat offered wholeness, its bones were used for tools, its skin provided clothing and shelter. The White Buffalo Maiden (Sioux) was the bearer of the Sacred Pipe to the people; as a vessel with a stem (symbolizing the feminine and masculine parts), it was smoked to become a bridge between heaven (see SKY) and EARTH. —Like the ass, the ox almost always appears in depictions of the nativity of Christ. —The ox is the second sign of the Chinese ZODIAC and corresponds to *Taurus* (the STEER or bull).

Ox-Eye Daisy See DAISY.

Packing See WRAPPING.

Palm The date palm in particular is a tree of over 65 feet in height, with a supple trunk not broken by the wind; it can reach an age of 300 years. For the Babylonians it was a holy tree. —In Egypt it was probably associated with the symbolic meaning of the TREE of life and was often the model for shaping COLUMNS. —In antiquity the branches of the palm were used as victory symbols in public games. For the Greeks it was the tree of light and was sacred to Helios and Apollo. Its Greek name, PHOENIX, suggests a close symbolic relationship to the fabled bird of the same name. —Palm branches are a widespread symbol of victory, joy, and peace; the evergreen fronds of the palm are a symbol of eternal life and resurrection. In Christian art the palm branch frequently occurs as an attribute of martyrs. —According to Jung the vertically growing form of the palm is a symbol of the soul.

Palm: Palm as the tree of life. From a sarcophagus in the mausoleum of Galla Placidia, Ravenna, 5th century.

Pansy It is a variety of violet. The botanical name *Viola tricolor hortensis* points to the frequent presence of three colors in the pansy blossom, for which reason it often occurs as a symbol of the Trinity. —Greatly divergent symbolic meanings are ascribed to the pansy. It is regarded as a symbol of the shyness of young maidens, the fidelity of lovers, and envy.

Pansy

Panther The black LEOPARD is commonly called a panther. In contrast to the spotted leopard, it is a less wild symbolic animal. In *Physiologus* it is reported that following every feeding, the panther sleeps three days and then gives off a marvelous fragrance that irresistibly attracts people. The panther was therefore regarded as a symbol of lust and sensuality, but also (because of awaking after three days) as a symbol of Christ's death and resurrection.

Parasol It is a symbol of the canopy or vault of heaven. —In antiquity the parasol was carried by servants and held over the king or emperor as a symbol of power and dignity. —In China and India it often had several levels and symbolized the heavenly hierarchies.

Parasol: The king with a parasol. Sassanid relief, 5th century.

Parcae See FATES.

Peace Pipe Also called a calumet, the ceremonial tobacco pipe of the North American Indians is smoked with all those involved on occasions of making peace and treaties, and as a sign of friendship. It is usually considered a primordial image of a human creature whose power and immortality it symbolizes. Particularly with reference to its SMOKE, it sometimes represents the connectedness of humans with nature as well as with heaven.

Peach Tree Primarily because of its early flowering, it is a Chinese symbol of spring and fertility. The wood of the peach tree, like that of the MULBERRY TREE, was regarded in China as having effective powers against evil influences; similar effects were ascribed to its fruit. The tree, blossom, and fruit were also regarded as symbols of immortality. —In Japan the peach blossom symbolizes virginity.

Peacock It is regarded as a solar bird in India and other places, probably because of its FAN- or WHEEL-shaped tail. It is the steed of various deities (e.g., of Buddha). —With a SERPENT in its beak, it symbolizes light vanquishing darkness. The beauty of its plumage was considered to have resulted from the transformation of the poison it had absorbed in its battle with the serpent. —Probably because of its beauty, the peacock was assigned in antiquity to Hera (Juno). —In Islam the peacock's outspread tail represents the universe and the full moon or the midday sun. —In early Christianity, representations of the peacock likewise occur as sun symbols and as symbols of immortality and the joy in the afterlife. —The peacock's tail, or "wheel," which contains all colors, was regarded in esoteric tradition as a totality symbol. —In the symbolism of the Middle Ages the peacock embodies the vice of *pride* (SUPERBIA). —Because of its pompous courting behavior, the peacock has been regarded in modern times as a symbol of self-satisfied conceit and vanity.

Peacock: The peacock wheel as a symbol of wholeness. From Boschius's *Symbolographia*, 1702.

Pearl It is a common lunar and feminine symbol (e.g., in China it is closely associated with the MOON, WATER, and woman, and hence the yin principle; see YIN AND YANG). Because of its spherical form and its inimitable luster, the pearl is recognized as a symbol of perfection. —Its hardness and durability make it a symbol of immortality in such places as China and India. The "flaming pearl" was regarded in China as a sun symbol and as an image of the highest value. —Among the Greeks the pearl was a symbol of love, probably because of its beauty. —The intact pearl was regarded in Persia as a representation of the virgin. Moreover, in Persian myth pearls were associated with the primal shaping of matter. —The most profound and widespread significance of the pearl is that, hidden in the oyster or MUSSEL (i.e., in the darkness), it grows at the bottom of the sea, thus symbolizing the child growing in the mother's womb as well as the light shining in the darkness. Many peoples share the idea that the pearl arises from "light seeds" or dew drops that fall from the sky or the moon. In particular, Gnosticism and Christianity emphasize this complex of meanings and often relate it to Christ as the Logos born of the flesh (Mary). —The gates of the Heavenly Jerusalem (see JERUSLAEM, HEAVENLY) are twelve pearls. —In folk belief pearls are identified with tears. —The pearl necklace is a symbol of the unity formed from multiplicity.

Pear Tree Combining fruit wood with a white blossom, because of its delicacy and transience it is a symbol of mourning. —In the Middle Ages the pear tree (probably because of its pure white blossoms) was a symbol of Mary. —Because of its shape, which suggests the female form, the pear has been construed sexually in psychoanalytic dream interpretation. —In folk belief many pears indicate the blessing of many children.

Pegasus In Greek mythology it is the winged horse that sprang from the severed head of the Medusa (see GORGONS). Hippocrene, the sacred spring of the Muses, is supposed to have arisen where the hooves of Pegasus struck the ground; thus Pegasus later became a symbol of intellectual, and especially poetic, creativity.

Pelican According to *Physiologus*, it is a bird that kills its unruly young (in other accounts the

Pelican: The pelican rending its own breast. Relief in the cathedral paradise, Muenster, Westphalia, 1235.

young are killed by a SERPENT), but after three days it reawakens them to life with blood drawn from self-inflicted wounds. It is a symbol of sacrificial maternal and paternal love. In medieval art and literature, the killing of the young was overshadowed by the legend that the pelican feeds its progeny on its own blood until it dies; hence it became a widespread symbol of Christ's sacrificial death. — In the imagistic language of the alchemists, the pelican symbolizes the PHILOSOPHERS' STONE, which dissolves itself (i.e., "dies") to let the LEAD and the GOLD arise from it.

Pentagonal Dodecahedron See DODECAHEDRON.

Pentagram It is an ancient magical sign consisting of a five-pointed star drawn with one continuous line. —For the Pythagoreans it was a symbol of health and knowledge. —The Gnostics depicted it on ABRAXAS cameos. —In the Middle Ages it was a common sign used to ward off demonic powers and female night spirits, among others. —As a self-contained form, it represents Christ as the ALPHA AND OMEGA; as a five-pointed form, it signifies the five sacred wounds of Christ. —In witchcraft, the inverted pentagram depicts the Devil's goat, the WITCH'S FOOT, and the reversal of man's true nature.

Pentagram

Peony In China it is a symbol of wealth and honor. —It was regarded in antiquity as protection against the wiles of satyrs and fauns. —In the Middle Ages it was often used as a medicinal and magical plant; the seed of the peony served as an AMULET. As the "rose without thorns," it is a common symbol of Mary in medieval paintings.

Peppermint It is a labiate flower having a strongly aromatic oil. Valued in antiquity as a medicinal plant, it is a symbol in Christian art of Mary because of its healing properties.

Periwinkle

Periwinkle A creeping perennial indigenous to southern and central Europe, it has leathery, evergreen leaves and blue blossoms. Like all evergreen plants, it represents eternal life and fidelity; it was also valued as a protection against witches and magicians.

Phallus A universal sign of fertility, of special as well as cosmic forces, and of the source of life, it is consequently used as an AMULET and worshiped as a ritual image (e.g., as an essential part of the ancient herm). See also LINGA.

Pheasant In mythological conceptions, especially those of China, it is a symbol of cosmic harmony because of its song and dance; its call and the sound of its beating wings are associated with THUNDER and thus with storms, RAIN, and spring. The pheasant was related to the yang principle (see YIN AND YANG). In the course of the seasons it was thought to transform itself into the SERPENT (related to the yin principle) and back again into the pheasant. —The *golden pheasant* was closely associated in antiquity and in the Middle Ages with the PHOENIX.

Phallus:
Herm of Siphos.

Philosophers' Stone In alchemy, the *lapis philosophorum* is a substance that on the basis of laborious processes could supposedly be made from the *prima materia*. The philosophers' stone was supposed to transform base metals into precious metals and to have a rejuvenating and healing effect. In these processes an important role was played by the separation and reuniting of opposites, particularly of the feminine and the masculine, for which reason the philosophers' stone is often represented as hermaphroditic (see HERMAPHRODITE). Attempts to find the philosophers' stone probably represented symbolic actions that accompany psychologically and religiously motivated strivings: through a sort of death, the initially formless *prima materia* decomposes into its basic constituents and experiences a resurrection on a higher level in the form of the philosophers' stone. —Jung interpreted these procedures as the individuation process.

Phoenix For the Egyptians it was a sacred bird (Bennu or Boine), which was originally seen as a wagtail and later as a HERON or a heron-headed golden FALCON. It was regarded as the embodiment of the sun god (who was supposed to have alighted on the primal mound of earth at the creation of the world), of the daily course of the sun, and of the yearly flooding of the Nile.

Phoenix:
Phoenix arising from the ashes. Romanesque carving on a choir chair, Abbey of Champeaux.

149

—This reference to ever-recurring renewal was reinterpreted by the Greeks, Romans, and the Christian church patriarchs (especially with reference to Physiologus), resulting in the widespread symbol of the bird that is consumed in fire and then renewed from the ashes at specific intervals (every 500, 1,000, or 1,461 years). In this form the phoenix is a symbol of Christ, as well as a general symbol of immortality and of resurrection victorious over death.

Physiologus The designation for a group of natural history books that probably derive from an Alexandrian source. In *Physiologus* are found, for example, fabulous animals and fabulous characteristics of known animals, which are often interpreted in biblical and Christian terms. In the Middle Ages there were various Latin versions ("bestiaries") from which numerous ideas in Christian animal symbolism derive.

Pi See DISK, HOLE.

Pisces See FISH.

Pilgrim In the imagery of many religions, the pilgrim signifies earthly human life, which is not final but merely a transition to another life.

Pine

Pine In antiquity *Pinus* was the designation for all cone-bearing trees. In a narrower sense the pine is a fertility symbol (probably because of its constant production of new cones). —The Scotch pine is a conifer of the northern temperate zone. As an evergreen tree and because of its incorruptible resin, it is a symbol in China and Japan of immortality; in Japan, moreover, as a tree that endures wind and weather, it symbolizes vital energy and the personality that masters the difficulties of life unharmed. Two pines are a symbol of love and marital fidelity. —The *pine cone* (and sometimes the cone of the Aleppo pine, the resin of which preserves wine) crowned the THYRSUS staff of Dionysus and his retinue. —In Christian symbolism it is closely associated with the TREE of life, whose crown it forms in many representations.

Pine: Ancient bronze pine cone from a fountain in the Vatican.

Pine Cone See PINE.

Pitcher In Indian art it is sometimes a symbol of overabundant fertility and plenty; it also symbolizes the DRAUGHT of immortality. —In China it is a symbol of heaven and especially of thunder (because of the sound one can produce by striking an empty pitcher). —In early Christian art the branches and leaves growing out of a pitcher or the birds drinking from it refer to the water of life contained in it.

Plantain It is a symbol in China of fertility because of its many blossoms and seeds.

Plants As the lowest and also most fundamental level of the organic world, plants represent the unity of all living things. In mythological tales there are many examples of the complete or partial transformation of plants into humans and animals and vice versa. —The plant's perpetual change, which involves growth, flowering, maturation, and death, from sowing to harvest, makes the plant kingdom as a whole a symbol of cyclical renewal. —Plants in fertile abundance are the essence of Mother Earth.

Plant: Leaf mask.

Plow In many cultures the plow working the earth is equated with man fertilizing woman; the plow is consequently a phallic and a fertility symbol. Plowing, according to widespread folk belief, was regarded as the fertilization of the earth or as the connection between heaven (see SKY) and EARTH brought about by humans.

Plumb line It is a symbol of the perpendicular and sometimes of the WORLD AXIS. Especially in Freemasonry, it symbolizes spiritual balance and the upright spirit. In art it is a symbol of architecture, geometry, moderation, and justice.

Plum Tree Because its early flowers appear on a leafless tree, it is a symbol in the Far East of spring, youth, and purity. —The plum is sometimes understood in psychoanalytic dream interpretation as a female sexual symbol.

Point It is a symbol, particularly in meditation, of the CENTER or of the coincidence of all realities, all potentialities, or both. It is usually represented as a midpoint of a CIRCLE.

Polestar The star about which the vault of the heavens appears to rotate; hence it was regarded as the center of the cosmos, NAVEL of the world, gate of heaven, hub of the cosmos, or the highest peak of the world MOUNTAIN.

Pomegranate:
Woodcut of a pomegranate. From the Ten Bamboo Hall.

Pomegranate Like other seedy fruits (see GOURD, LEMON, ORANGE, TOMATO), it is a fertility symbol, for which reason it was sacred in Greece to Demeter, Aphrodite, and Hera. With reference to this symbolic meaning, newly wedded women in ancient Rome wore wreaths of pomegranate branches. In India the juice of the pomegranate was considered to be a remedy for infertility. Opening the pomegranate is sometimes also seen symbolically as deflowering. —Because of the bright red color of its flesh, the pomegranate is a symbol of love and blood, and thus life and death. —For the Phoenicians the pomegranate was closely associated with the SUN and signified life, power, and renewal. —The pomegranate is a Judaic symbol of faithfulness to the law of the Torah. —In the Middle Ages the fragrance and the many seeds of the pomegranate were interpreted as symbols of the beauty and the many virtues of Mary. The spherical form, the multitude of seeds, and the fragrance also signified perfection and the endless number of characteristics of God's goodness. The multitude of seeds, contained in one husk, could also be understood as a symbol of the church; the red juice was associated with the blood of martyrs. The pomegranate, which has a hard and inedible husk but which contains sweet juice, is also a symbol of the perfect Christian, particularly of the priest.

Poplar

Pond See LAKE.

Poplar Because its foliage trembles at the least breath of air, it is a symbol of pain and lamentation. The Greeks regarded it as a tree growing in the underworld, and in that connection it symbolizes the laments of the dead.

Poppy A flower sacrificed to Demeter in the Eleusinian mysteries, it is a symbol of the earth but also of sleep and forgetfulness.

Portal See DOOR.

Pot It is a common symbol of the WOMB, and thus of woman. See CONTAINER.

Poppy

152

Prayer Beads Rosaries, common to many religions, consist of a cord or chain with knots or beads, the individual elements of which symbolize various spiritual facts, attributes, prayer forms, or names of saints, of the illuminati of gods, etc. —The customary Buddhist rosary has 108 beads and corresponds to the various developmental levels of the world. —The Islamic rosary has 99 beads, which symbolize the 99 names of Allah. —The rosary of the Catholic church is the physical representation of a series of prayers. Beginning with an "Our Father," one says ten "Hail Marys" followed by a "Glory Be to the Father" as one contemplates certain events from the life of Jesus; the sequence is repeated four more times (for a total of five decades of prayers).

Pride See SUPERBIA.

Prima Materia See MERCURIUS, PHILOSOPHERS' STONE, WATER.

Primrose It is a perennial herb of the genus *Primula* (from Latin *primus*; originally in the name *primula veris*, firstling of spring). The primrose is a spring flower primarily of the northern temperate zone; it (usually) has yellow umbels on stocky stems. Among the Germanic tribes, it was sacred to Freya. —In the Middle Ages it was considered a medicinal and magical plant, thought to be particularly effective in "unlocking" hidden treasures. —It is a symbol of spring, since it ushers in spring as the "first" flower; seeing the primrose drives away melancholy thoughts of winter.

Primrose

Prince The prince occurs in numerous fairy tales as the resplendent hero, as the embodiment of youthful, active, moral action and change, but also as stalwart endurance. —Psychoanalytically he can be understood as the representative of victorious ego powers. See PRINCESS.

Princess In the fairy tales of many peoples, she is the image of a goal and of the highest good that the hero can attain after overcoming various obstacles and dangers. —The princess is interpreted psychoanalytically as the embodiment of the personal unconscious in contrast to the "old King," who represents the collective unconscious. See PRINCE.

Prostitution See SACRED PROSTITUTION.

Prudence See PRUDENTIA.

Prudentia The female personification of *prudence*, one of the four cardinal virtues, she is often represented with the attributes of SERPENT, MIRROR, SIEVE, and TORCH.

Purification See BAPTISM, BATH, HAND AND FOOT WASHING.

Purple It is a color associated symbolically with RED or VIOLET. Genuine purple, derived from the *porphura*, a shellfish yielding purple dye, was reserved for the clothing of kings and priests due to its costliness; hence it was a symbol of power and honor. Later it was generally regarded, especially among the Romans, as a sign of luxury and prosperity.

Quail A symbol in China of spring because it is a migratory bird that returns in spring, it is associated with fire and light, and thus with the yang principle (see YIN AND YANG). Because of its annual migrations, the quail symbolizes the alternating influences of polar powers. See FROG.

Quicksilver See MERCURIUS.

Quince In antiquity it was a symbol of good fortune, love, and fertility and was sacred to Aphrodite (Venus). —In Greece a wife brought a quince into the house of her husband at the time of their wedding as a symbol of a hoped-for happy marriage.

Quintessence See FIVE.

Rabbit See HARE.

Radish In the Middle Ages it was associated symbolically with quarreling and conflict. Like the turnip, it was said to be related to evil spirits, thus radishes and turnips were sometimes blessed (i.e., made harmless).

Rags They are a symbol of material poverty. Especially in fairy tales, rags often conceal inner riches and thus represent the superiority of the essential over mere appearance.

Rain A universal symbol of the effects of heaven (see SKY) on the EARTH, rain is associated with fertility and with the fertilization of the earth by the sky (rain drops represent the sky god's sperm). In this sense it is also a graphic symbol of the gods' spiritual and emotional influence on the earth. See ONE-LEGGED.

Rainbow It is a symbol of the connection between heaven (see SKY) and EARTH. —According to Talmudic tradition, the rainbow was created on the evening of the sixth day of creation. —In Greek mythology the rainbow is the embodiment of the goddess Iris. —According to the Bible, God placed a rainbow in the heavens after the flood as a sign of his compact with humans; for this reason, Christ is enthroned on a rainbow in medieval representations of the Last Judgment. The rainbow also became a symbol of Mary, the mediatrix of reconciliation. —The symbolic interpretation of the colors of the rainbow depends on how many colors are distinguished; in China, for example, FIVE colors are known, the synthesis of which symbolizes the union of YIN AND YANG. —On the basis of the tradition of Aristotelian tripartite division, only the three primary colors are distinguished in Christianity (a symbol of the Trinity): blue (water of the flood or of Christ's heavenly origin); red (the future conflagration of the world, or Christ's passion); and green (the new world, or Christ's acts on earth). See BRIDGE.

Rainbow: Christ seated on the rainbow. Detail from a picture of the Last Judgment, 1543.

Ram A symbol of power and strength, in antiquity it was one of the most common sacrificial animals. —The Egyptian creator god Khnum was represented with a ram's head. —The

Ram: The astrological sign for Aries.

Ram: Sacrifice of a ram to Jupiter Ammon. After a picture in A. Kircher's *Oedipus Aegyptiacus*, 1652.

Greeks and Romans revered the original Egyptian wind god Amun as a manifestation of the highest god in the form of the ram-headed Jupiter (Zeus). —The ram is an attribute of Indra and of Hermes. —In Christianity the image of a ram sometimes refers to Isaac's "sacrifice" as a precursor of Christ's sacrificial death. —The ram, ARIES, is the first sign of the ZODIAC; its element is FIRE.

Rat In Asia it is a propitious symbolic animal; in Japan it accompanies the god of wealth; in China and Siberia the absence of rats in houses and barns is regarded as an ominous sign. —In Indian mythology the rat is the steed of the elephant-headed god Ganesha (see ELEPHANT). —In Europe, however, the rat is regarded in folk belief as the personification of illnesses, witches, demons, and goblins. It is regarded as an ominous sign (usually indicating lack of food reserves or other unusual conditions) when rats desert houses and ships. —The rat is the first sign in the Chinese ZODIAC and corresponds to *Aries* (see RAM).

Raven Because of its (usually) black color, its croaking call, and its obtrusiveness, it has been regarded by many peoples of the Orient and the Occident as an evil omen foretelling illness, war, and death. The Bible counts it among the impure animals. —In the symbolism of the Middle Ages, it sometimes represents the mortal sin of *gluttony*. —In many cultures it was regarded as divine and solar (possibly because of its intelligence). —In Japan it was the messenger of the gods and, especially as the red raven, a sun symbol. According to Chinese ideas, a three-footed raven lives in the sun. —In Persia ravens were sacred to the god of light and of the sun and consequently played a role in the Mithras cult. (Ravens were sculpted on numerous Mithras stones.) —Greeks and Romans saw white ravens in conjunction with Apollo and the sun god Helios. —In Nordic mythology two ravens, Hugin (thought) and Munin (memory), were assigned to the god Odin, the highest of the Old Norse gods. —The intelligent raven also plays a role in various stories of the flood. Noah released the raven to seek land; Babylonian sagas tell a similar story. —Sometimes ravens were regarded as cruel parents who neglected their young (hence today the designation common in German of "raven father" and "raven mother" for cruel parents). —Since the raven likes to live alone, it also signifies self-imposed solitude; thus in Christianity it possibly symbolizes heretics and unbelievers. —The call of the raven was regarded by the Romans as a symbol of hope (in Latin, *cras, cras* means tomorrow).

Rebis: The rebis as dragon slayer.

Rebis In alchemy the rebis (from *res bina*, twofold) is the designation for the HERMAPHRODITE.

Red Red is the color of FIRE and BLOOD, and like these symbolically ambivalent. In a positive sense it is the color of life, love, warmth, inspired passion, and fertility; in a negative sense it is the color of war, the destructive power of fire, loss of blood, and hate. —In antiquity there was a widespread belief that red protected one from dangers. Sometimes, for example, animals, trees, and objects were painted red to protect them from evil influences or to make them fertile. —In Egypt red, the color of the glowing deserts, was regarded as a symbol of evil and destruction; the scribe, for example, used a special red ink for bad words. As the color of the crown of lower Egypt, however, red had a positive significance. —Among the Romans, brides wore a fire-red veil, the *flammeum*, a symbolic reference to love and fertility. For the Romans red, also symbolic of power, was the color of the emperor, the nobility, and the generals. —High-level judicial officers have often made use of the color red (e.g., in the Middle Ages the executioner, as lord over life and death, wore a red garment; in many countries today, red is the color of judges, particularly those of high rank). —The cardinals of the church wear red with reference to the blood of the martyrs. —Satan, the Lord of Hell, and the whore of Babylon are dressed in red; in this context red is the expression of the devouring power of hellfire or of untamed desires and passions. —In alchemy red is regarded as the color of the PHILOSOPHERS' STONE, which is considered the stone that carries the sign of the light of the sun. —As a striking signal color that promises new life and warmth, red is the flag color of revolution, particularly of socialism and communism.

Reed Because it sways easily in the wind, it is a symbol of fickleness and weakness, but it also sometimes represents flexibility. —According to the mythological conceptions of Shintoism, the creation of the world began when reeds sprouted everywhere from the primal waters. —Because the Roman soldiers ridiculed Jesus by giving him a scepter of reeds, reeds are sometimes also an attribute in "ecce homo" representations.

Reindeer It is an animal that appears in prehistoric ROCK PAINTINGS and possibly served cult and ritual ends. —In the northern regions of Eurasia, the reindeer is an important lunar symbolic animal, which, as psychopomp (spirit guide), is closely associated with night and the realm of the dead.

Resin It is a symbol of immortality because of its incorruptibility and because it is extracted from evergreen trees. See INCENSE, MYRRH.

Rhombus Since its form is similar to the female genitalia, it is a female sexual symbol; it therefore sometimes signifies earthy and chthonic powers.

Ribbon Frequently a symbol of sovereign or judicial power, it designates the power to bind and to loose. In other connections it may also be an image of bonds voluntarily accepted or entered into.

Rider: Statuette of Charlemagne as rider. Statuette, 9th century; horse, 16th century.

Rice As the most important source of nourishment in Asian countries, it corresponds to WHEAT in Europe and thus shares essentially the same symbolic meaning. —In Japan rice, especially the rice-filled storehouse, is a symbol of abundance and spiritual riches. —In China red rice, in particular, is a symbol of immortality. —The laborious work of cultivating rice was often viewed as a consequence of the break between heaven (see SKY) and EARTH.

Rider It is a symbol of the control of wild power. (The European statues of mounted regents share this symbolism.) —After the opening of the first four seals in the Apocalypse, four riders appear mounted on a white, a fiery-red, a black, and a dun horse. The rider on the white horse possibly represents Christ as victor; the others suggest the angels of war, famine, and death.

Right and Left In folk belief and in many religions, the right side is regarded as the better and more auspicious. —In antiquity, the right arm (which carried the weapon) and the right side in general symbolized strength and victory. —The place to the right of God, a regent, or a host was regarded as the preferred place of honor. —At the Last Judgment the chosen stood to the right of God, the damned to his left. —Black magic presupposes the conscious reversal of the right-left values scheme (i.e., ritual acts are performed with the left hand, on the left side, etc.). —In China the left side (which in the Christian occidental tradition is seen as passive) is associated with sky and thus with the active, masculine, yang principle; the right with earth, fertility, harvest, and thus with the feminine, yin principle (see YIN AND YANG) In China, for example, one gives with the left hand and receives with the right. —According to Cabalistic tradition, the right hand of God symbolizes mercy, the left justice; the right hand is consequently the hand of blessing and the priesthood, and the left is that of monarchy.

Ring As a form having neither beginning nor end, it represents eternity. It is also a symbol of joining, fidelity, or membership in a community and thus of distinction, office, and dignity (e.g., the official rings of Roman senators; the rings of officials, knights, doctors). —The supposed magical power of the CIRCLE relates to the ring as well, and an apotropaic effect was often ascribed to it (e.g., against the evil eye). Rings were also carried as AMULETS; in folk belief, losing or breaking the ring signifies trouble or calamity.

River Because of its relation to fertility, it was often revered as a deity (e.g., among the Greeks and Romans, a river was frequently associated with the particular local male god). —Generally close in symbolic meaning to

River: The four rivers of paradise. After an Alsatian miniature, 12th century.

WATER, its flowing is a symbol of time and transitoriness but also of perpetual renewal. —The confluence of all rivers in the sea symbolizes the union of the individual and the absolute (e.g., in Buddhism and Hinduism this confluence signifies dissolving in Nirvana). —In Judaism the river flowing down from the mountain represents heavenly grace. The idea of four rivers of paradise occurs in Judaism, Christianity, and in India; in Christian art the four rivers, symbolizing the four gospels, often arise from a hill upon which stands Christ or the Lamb of God.

Rock It is a symbol of solidity and steadfastness. In the Bible the rock represents the strength and fidelity of God who protects. The rock that gives forth water in the desert symbolically anticipates Christ as the source of the water of life. As the cornerstone of the church, Peter (the surname of Simon, from the Greek *petros*, rock) is compared with the rock. —In Chinese landscape painting the rock or cliff appears as firm or solid, corresponding to the yang principle, and is frequently depicted as the opposite of the changeable, constantly moving WATERFALL, which embodies the yin principle (see YIN AND YANG). —According to Greek mythology, the boulder that *Sisyphus* must constantly roll up the mountain, and which at the last moment always rolls down again, represents fruitless efforts; it is also a general symbol of human wishes, which are never conclusively satisfied.

Rock: Sisyphus with the boulder. After a Greek vase painting.

Rock Paintings They are representations of people, animals, objects, and cult signs on rocks and especially on cave walls. European rock paintings all date from prehistoric times to the Paleolithic age; rock paintings are still created by primitive peoples living today. For a long time they were considered to be expressions of magical practices, especially of hunting magic; today they are viewed as symbolic depictions of religious experience or as simplified, symbol-like combinations of pictures, which possibly anticipate pictographs.

Rock Painting: Cave picture with hunt scene. From the cave of los Caballos, Castellon, Spain.

Room (Chamber) In many initiation rites it was common to enclose the initiate in a secret room, chamber, or subterranean space (see CAVE), to represent the maternal womb or the grave; the initiate often spent the night in such a place, and spiritual experiences and knowledge were accorded him or her. —The secret room, which conceals forbidden knowledge and may be entered only on pain of punishment, is a frequent fairy tale motif; it occurs, for example, as the thirteenth room (see THIRTEEN), which, in contrast to the twelve other rooms, is taboo.

Root of Jesse A designation of the family tree of Jesus, which stems from the family of Isai (Greek *Jesse*), the father of David. In art it is usually represented as a TREE growing out of the recumbent Jesse and bearing in its branches the images of Jesus's ancestors.

Root of Jesse:
After a picture of a bronze door, St. Zeno, Verona, ca. 1000.

Rose Because of its fragrance, beauty, and charm (and in spite of its THORNS), the rose is one of the most common symbolic plants. In the West it is analogous to the LOTUS in Asia. —In antiquity the rose was sacred to Aphrodite (Venus). The red rose is supposed to have arisen from the blood of Adonis; it was a symbol of love and affection, fertility, and respect for the dead. Roses served as a crown for Dionysus (Bacchus), as well as for the festival participants at drinking bouts because people ascribed to roses (and to the VIOLET) a cooling effect on the brain. Roses were also supposed to remind the revelers not to blurt out secrets in their intoxication. —In early Christianity the rose was a symbol of secrecy and discretion, often in connection with the cross. Numerous meanings are allotted to it in Christian symbolism. The red rose refers to the shed blood and wounds of Christ and to the bowl that caught the holy blood; because of its relation to the blood of Christ, it is also a symbol of mystic rebirth. Since in the Middle Ages the rose was an attribute of virgins, it is also a symbol of Mary; the red rose, moreover, is generally a symbol of divine love. —The *rose windows* in medieval churches are closely associated symbolically with the CIRCLE, the WHEEL, and the SUN as a Christ symbol. —In alchemy the (usually) seven-petaled rose is a symbol of complex interconnections (e.g., of the seven planets with the corresponding metals, various steps in the alchemical operation, etc.).

Rose: The rose as the rosy cross. From Robert Fludd's *Summum Bonum*.

—Today the red rose is almost exclusively a love symbol.

Rosemary A spicy small shrub of Mediterranean countries, the Romans often burned it during sacrifices for its fragrance. —In folk customs, rosemary was regarded as a protective agent against illnesses and evil spirits, and in this sense it was used particularly at births, weddings, and deaths. —As a hardy, evergreen plant, rosemary is an old symbol of love, fidelity, fertility, and immortality (when associated with the dead); bridal wreaths were often made of rosemary before myrtle was used.

Rose Windows See ROSE, WHEEL.

Ruby Because of its deep red color, it often corresponds symbolically to the color RED. In the Middle Ages it was reputed to have healing powers.

Rush It is a grasslike, perennial plant that is a Christian symbol of God's unremitting love.

Sacred Prostitution Usually practiced in the temple precinct, it was customary in the ancient Orient, Greece, and India (among other places). It was regarded as the symbol of union with the gods and as a fertility ritual.

Sacred Scarabaeus See SCARAB.

Sacrifice As a ritual act it symbolizes (among other things) a renunciation of earthly possessions in favor of a union with God, gods, or ancestors; it is often also a magical act with a certain goal. —A widespread practice consisted of sacrificial meals in which only a part of the offerings were burnt (usually the *sacrificial animals*), and the remainder consumed by the sacrificers as a sign of sacramental community and of union with God, gods, etc. —Jung interpreted certain animal sacrifices (e.g., the Mithraic sacrifice of the bull) as symbolizing the victory of the individual's spirituality over his or her animal nature.

Sage

Sacrificial Animals See SACRIFICE.

Saffron See CROCUS.

Sage It is a half-shrubby mint with aromatic leaves. A versatile healing plant, it is an attribute of Mary in medieval Christian art.

Sagittarius The ninth sign of the ZODIAC, its element is FIRE. See BOW.

Sagittarius: The astrological sign of the archer.

Saints, Attributes of They are objects or symbols that characterize a specific saint or are assigned to a specific category of saints. (General attributes of saints, for example, would be the scroll or book for the apostles or church patriarchs, the palm branch for martyrs.) Attributes of individual saints derive from the life, martyrdom, or legends of the saint.

Attributes of Selected Saints

Anchor
 Nicholas
Angel
 Matthew the Evangelist
Arrow
 Sebastian; Ursula
Axe
 Boniface; Josophat
Baby Jesus
 Antony of Padua; Christopher
Beehive
 Ambrose; Bernard of Clairvaux
Book
 apostles, evangelists, church patriarchs; Teresa of Avila
Bread
 Elizabeth of Thuringen; Nicholas
Cardinal's Hat
 church patriarchs
Chalice
 Barbara; John the Evangelist; Norbert;

Thomas Aquinas
Cloak (being divided)
 Martin of Tours
Cross
 Andreas; Bridget; Helena; John the Baptist
Dove
 Gregory the Great
Dragon
 George; Margaret; Michael
Eagle
 John the Evangelist
Gridiron
 Laurence
Heart
 Augustine; Bridget; Francis de Sales; Teresa of Avila
Lamb
 Agnes; John the Baptist
Lance
 George; Thomas the Apostle

Lion
 Jerome; Mark
Mitre
 bishops and abbots
Organ
 Cecilia
Palm
 martyrs
Ship
 Adelheid; Nicholas; Ursula
Snake
 John the Evangelist
Stag (with cross in antlers)
 Eustachius; Hubert
Steer
 Luke
Sword
 martyrs
Tongs
 Agatha
Tower
 Barbara
Wheel
 Catherine of Alexandria

Salamander According to folk belief of the Middle Ages, it was an elemental spirit that could live unharmed in the fire; hence it symbolizes

Salamander:
The salamander
in the fire. After a
picture by
Charles Pesnot,
Lyon, 1555.

the just person who can preserve equanimity of soul in spite of tribulations.

Saliva Among black African peoples, it is often closely associated with words and sperm, and thus with creative energies.

Salt Highly valued because of its life-sustaining importance and its scarcity in earlier times, it was regarded as symbolizing vital energy and as warding off misfortune. Since it was generally extracted from WATER through evaporation, it also represented a union of water and FIRE. —The grain of salt that dissolves in the ocean symbolizes the merging of individuality in the absolute. —Because of its vital necessity, its seasoning and cleansing power, its incorruptibility and preserving properties, as well as its light, transparent appearance, salt is also a widespread symbol of moral and spiritual powers. In the Sermon on the Mount, Christ compares the disciples to the salt of the earth. Also mentioned in the Bible is the "salt of suffering," through which the apostles and Christians must pass to attain eternal life. —In Japan salt was often used ritually as a symbol of inner cleansing and protectedness; in this sense it was strewn, for example, on thresholds, around wells, and on the ground after burials. Today many Japanese strew salt in the house after an unpleasant person has left it. —Because of its seasoning properties, salt is regarded as a symbol of wit and spirited talk. —Among Semitic peoples and the Greeks, salt, often in conjunction with BREAD, symbolizes friendship and hospitality. Bread and salt are often considered the essence of simple, basic food. —In a negative sense salt is a symbol of destructive power and of sterility and damnation, especially the salty desert (e.g., in the Bible or among the mystics). —In alchemy (where it is usually called by the Latin word *sal*), salt is, along with SULFUR and quicksilver (see MERCURIUS), one of the philosophical elements and world principles; it represents the solid, bodily aspect (the corpus).

Sand It is a symbol of infinity because of the countless number of grains of sand.

Sapphire It is a gem regarded in antiquity and the Middle Ages as having healing properties (it was equated with the LAPIS LAZULI). Because of its (usually) blue color, it is a symbol of heaven, heavenly protection, or—for the alchemists —air. In the Apocalypse the sapphire is one of the four foundation stones of the Heavenly Jerusalem (see JERUSLAEM, HEAVENLY). —Like all blue stones, the sapphire is regarded in the Orient as a protection against the evil eye.

Sator Arepo Formula A magic formula in the form of MAGICAL SQUARES composed of 25 letters, it can be traced to early Christian times but is probably older. It appears in magical papyri and for a long time had widespread use, often as an AMULET (especially against rabies and fires). Various interpretive translations and solutions exist (e.g., literally: "With effort sower Arepo holds the wheels," or, proceeding from the letters arranged around the single *n*, a double Pater Noster; also "alpha and omega," or something similar). It appears certain, however, that it was used with varying meaning as a symbol of totality or wholeness.

S	A	T	O	R
A	R	E	P	O
T	E	N	E	T
O	P	E	R	A
R	O	T	A	S

Sator Arepo Formula

Saturn See LEAD.

Saxifrage A low perennial that usually grows on rocks and penetrates into cracks and crevices (the name derives from the Latin *saxifraga*, rock-breaking), saxifrage occurs as a symbol of Christ resurrected, before whom "the rocks and cliffs burst apart."

Scales: The astrological sign for Libra.

Scales A symbol of tempered equilibrium, justice, and hence of judging and the public administration of justice, scales also represent the judgment of the dead. In the Egyptian *Book of the Dead*, Horus and Anubis, in front of Osiris, weigh the heart of the deceased against a feather (see OSTRICH), a scene frequently encountered in Egyptian art. —In antiquity the scales occur, for example, as a symbol of power and justice in the form of the golden scales of Zeus (in Homer's writings). —The depiction of the Archangel Michael with scales, representing a weigher of souls, is common in Christian art, especially in pictures of the Last Judgment.

Scales: A scene from the creation in which the scales symbolize divine justice. After a picture in the *Cotton Psalter*, 11th century.

Scarab (Dung Beetle, Sacred Scarabaeus)

Scales: Weighing the hearts at the judgment of the dead. Egyptian, Ptolemaic epoch.

—The scales (*Libra*) are the seventh sign of the ZODIAC; their element is AIR.

Scarab (Dung Beetle, Sacred Scarabaeus) It is a beetle that shapes "pills" of dung, which it buries in the earth and in which the female lays eggs. The scarab's supposed origin from these "pills" or balls caused it to be seen in Egypt as a sacred, solar animal (the name corresponds to the word for rising sun) and as a symbol of res-

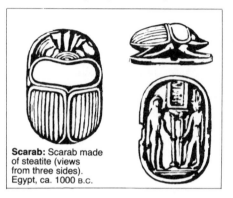

Scarab: Scarab made of steatite (views from three sides). Egypt, ca. 1000 B.C.

Scorpion: The scorpion with the head of the goddess Isis; bronze decoration on a staff. Egypt, late period.

urrection. They were widely used in the form of stone seals or as AMULETS. Larger scarab stones were laid on the hearts of mummies; they bear the text of the *Book of the Dead*, in which the heart is challenged not to speak against the deceased.

Scepter A symbol of the highest power and majesty, it was often regarded as the carrier of divine powers. It was an attribute of deities and developed from the STAFF.

Scorpio See SCORPION.

Scorpion In Egypt it was a dangerous and feared sacred animal to which divine honors were accorded. An Egyptian fertility goddess and protectress of the deceased was depicted with a scorpion on her forehead; representations of scorpions with the head of Isis have been found. —In Africa the scorpion was so feared as the embodiment of dangerous powers that people did not dare to pronounce its name. —In the Bible scorpions appear as punishment from God, as a symbol of the rebellious Israel-

Scythe: Death as a skeleton with scythe and hourglass. Detail after an etching by Anders Trost.

ites, or as a symbol of the Devil. — In medieval art the scorpion symbolizes Satan, the heretic, death, or envy. — The scorpion (SCORPIO), is the eighth sign of the ZODIAC; its element is WATER.

Scythe Like the SICKLE, it is a symbol of time and death, which destroy all. Since the Renaissance it has been an attribute of the SKELETON (which was a personification of death).

Sea It is a symbol of inexhaustible vital energy. — From the psychoanalytic perspective, in so far as it is related to the ambivalent face of the giving and taking, rewarding and punishing Great Mother, it is also a symbol of the abyss, which swallows everything. As a reservoir of countless sunken treasures and forms hidden in darkness, it represents the unconscious. — As an immeasurably great surface, it is symbol of infinity (e.g., for the mystics it symbolized dissolving in God). See WATER.

Sea: Monstrous sea creature. Zillis coverlet, Graubunden, first half of the 12th century.

Seal It is a very common token, particularly in the ancient Orient, of a person's property rights or power. — In the Bible and in Christian literature, the seal, like the coin (see MONEY) is sometimes mentioned as a symbol of belonging to God. Divine secrets are also sealed (e.g., in the Apocalypse, the LAMB opens the book with seven seals).

Seal of Solomon See HEXAGRAM.

Seal: Opening the book with seven seals. After a miniature from the second half of the 13th century.

Seasons The four seasons are frequently represented in art as personifications, especially by female figures or by genies with attributes (such as blossoms, lambs, and kids for spring; sheaves of grain, sickles, or fire-spewing dragons for summer; bunches of grapes, a rabbit, a horn of plenty, or fruits for autumn; game, a salamander, a wild goose, or a fire in the hearth for winter). — In antiquity spring was dedicated to the herald of the gods, Hermes; summer to the sun god Apollo; autumn to Dionysus; and winter to the god of fire, Hephaestus. — In Christian art the seasons sometimes symbolize the phases of life (e.g., childhood, youth, maturity, and death), but because they return each year, they also signify the hope of resurrection.

Seasons: *Allegory of Autumn,* by Francesco Cossa.

Sea Urchin

Sea Urchin It is an echinoderm living principally in the coastal regions of the oceans. To the Celts, petrified sea urchins were symbols of the world. See EGG.

Seed It is a symbol of life and the abundance of possibilities not yet developed. The seed that dies in the earth to let a plant sprout is a symbol of the continual alternation in nature of death and new beginning; it also signifies sacrifice, as well as the spiritual rebirth of humankind.

Sempervivum See LIVE-FOREVER.

Seraph A four- or six-winged being of the upper levels of the spiritual hierarchies, mentioned in the Bible (the name means "the burning one"), it also appears as a burning serpent. It is an embodiment of spiritual power and is close in symbolic meaning to BIRDS, FIRE, and LIGHT.

Seraph: From the Cathedral at Reims, first half of the 13th century.

Serpent Among most peoples it plays an exceptionally important and extremely diverse role as a symbolic animal. Its symbolic character derives from its unique place in the animal world (locomotion without legs, dwelling in holes under the ground, hatching like a bird from eggs); its cold, smooth, shiny exterior; its poisonous bite and its poison, which can be used for healing purposes; its periodic molting. —It occurs as a chthonic creature; as the adversary of humanity (but also as an apotropaic animal); as protector of sacred precincts or of the underworld; as soul animal; as sexual symbol (masculine because of its phallic form, feminine because of its capacity to devour); and as a symbol of the perpetual capacity for renewal (because of its molting). —In Africa the serpent was sometimes worshipped as a spirit or divinity. —In the ancient middle-American cultures, the feathered serpent in particular played a great role. Originally it was a symbol of rain and vegetation. Later it became the "night-sky serpent covered with green quetzal feathers" as opposed to the "turquoise or day-sky serpent"; when united, they symbolized the cosmos. —In China the serpent was connected with WATER and the EARTH and was thus associated with the yin principle (see YIN AND YANG). —Indian mythology speaks of the *nagas*, serpents that func-

Serpent: The uraeus serpent with the sun disk. Bronze.

tion as beneficent or maleficent mediators between gods and humans, and sometimes are associated with the RAINBOW (like other serpents in other cultures). The kundalini serpent, depicted as coiled up at the lower end of the spinal column, is regarded as the seat of cosmic energy and as a symbol of life and (psychoanalytically viewed) libido. —The oldest example of an Asclepius staff (see ASCLEPIUS, STAFF OF), which dates from the end of the third millennium B.C., comes from Mesopotamia. —In Egyptian symbolism the serpent plays an essential and varied role. There were, for example, several serpent goddesses, such as a cobra goddess, that watched over the growth of plants. Also good or evil fate was sometimes revered in the form of a serpent (e.g., as a "spirit of the house"). Moreover, there are numerous mythological serpents (winged, footed, many-headed, etc.). The *uraeus* serpent was regarded as the representative of a many-named goddess; she was the embodiment of the eye of the sun god and, according to mythological conceptions, she rises up on the sun or on the forehead of the sun god and destroys her enemies with her fiery breath. As a protective and royal symbol, the *uraeus* serpent was worn on the forehead of Egyptian kings. Apophis, the archenemy of the son god and of the world order, has the form of a serpent. It is in Egypt, moreover, that the symbol of the UROBOROS, the serpent swallowing its own tail, appeared for the first time. —To the Jews, the serpent was primarily a threatening creature. The Old Testament counts it among the unclean animals, it appears as the prototype of sin and of Satan, and it seduces the original human couple in paradise. It also appears, however, as a symbol of cleverness. When God punished the disobedience of the Israelites with a plague of poisonous, winged serpents, he commanded Moses, who had prayed for help, to make a serpent of bronze; whoever had been bitten by a poisonous serpent and then saw the bronze serpent would remain alive. Hence a bronze serpent of this sort was for a long time a ritual object for the Jews. For the Christians it symbolically anticipated Christ because of its healing character. The serpent forms on the bi-

Serpent: The bronze serpent of Moses on the cross, alchemically interpreted as the *serpens mercurialis*. From Eleazar's *Uraltes Chymisches Werk*, 1760.

Serpent: The kundalini serpent and the major channels of the nadi system, depicted as a serpent-entwined staff.

Serpent:
The serpent in paradise in the tree of knowledge. Detail after a woodcut by H. Baldung (known as Grien), 1505.

Serpent: The serpent as female temptress in the tree of paradise. Woodcut by Steffen Arndes, from *Hortus Sanitatis*, Lubeck, 1492.

shop's staff refer, among other things, to the bronze serpent as well as to the serpent as a symbol of cleverness. — In antiquity numerous mythical and symbolic serpents were common, often in the form of monsters (e.g., CHIMERA, echidna, HYDRA). In the cult of Asclepius, god of healing, the serpent (because of its molting) played an important role as a symbol of perpetual self-renewal (see ASCLEPIUS, STAFF OF). In Roman houses, serpents often symbolized the spirits of the house and of the family. — The Midgard serpent of Old Norse mythology is a gigantic, destructive serpent surrounding the earth (Midgard), which was believed to be a disk. This serpent symbolized the perpetual threat to the order of the universe; in early Christianity it was equated with the LEVIATHAN. — Christian art of the Middle Ages often emphasizes the seductive aspect of the serpent in paradise through its close association with woman (e.g., in representations of serpents with a woman's head and breasts), implying an inner relationship to Eve, who was seduced. — The Hopi Indians in Arizona still use live snakes in their snake dance at the end of the summer season to bring rain. — The serpent is the sixth sign of the Chinese ZODIAC and corresponds to Virgo (see VIRGIN). See also ASPIS.

Sesame It is an ancient, widely cultivated plant with thimblelike blossoms and capsular fruits that contain oil-bearing seeds. In China and the ancient Far East, the seeds were regarded as a food that prolonged life and strengthened the spirit. — The "Open sesame!" formula from *Thousand and One Nights*, which was supposed to cause the treasure cave to open and yield its riches, may be associated with the sesame plant (i.e., one gets to the prized seed only after breaking open the sesame hull).

Seven A number regarded since antiquity as holy, probably because of the four different phases of the moon, each of which measures seven days, seven is a number of completion and fullness. It unites the SKY symbolism of THREE with the terrestrial (see EARTH) symbolism of FOUR. — Buddhism speaks of seven different heavens. — The Chinese see the seven stars of the Great Bear in connection with the seven bodily openings and the seven openings of the human heart. —In antiquity there were seven known planets (including the SUN and MOON; see METALS), which were understood as the divine and visible expression of cosmic order. For the Babylonians there were also the "evil seven," a group of seven demons usually appearing together. —In Greece the number seven played an important role. Seven was sacred to Apollo and others; there were the seven (or three) Hesperides, the seven gates of Thebes, the seven sons of Helios, the seven sons and seven daughters of Niobe, the seven wise men, and the seven against Thebes. There are the "seven wonders of the world," a collection of the most magnificent architectural structures and works of art of antiquity. —In Judaism seven is an especially distinguished number (e.g., the seven-armed CANDLESTICK). In the Bible the number seven occurs many times, in both a positive and a negative sense but always as an expression of totality (e.g., the seven tribes, the book with seven seals, the seven heavens in which the angelic hosts dwell, seven years in which Solomon built the temple, etc.; but also the seven heads of the apocalyptic beast, seven cups of divine wrath, etc.). Evil appears symbolically in the Apocalypse as the half of seven (i.e., three and one-half), a sign of Satan's broken power. —Seven is an important totality number in fairy tales and folk customs: seven brothers, seven ravens, seven kids, seven different foods on special days.

Serpent: The serpent wound about the tree of knowledge. Detail from a picture in the *Codex Vigilanus seu Albeldensis*.

Sesame

Shadow It is the opposite of LIGHT and is an aspect of the yin principle (see YIN AND YANG). It is also a sort of copy of each physical phenomenon and is often interpreted as a specific form of being of earthly creatures. In Africa, for example, the shadow is regarded as the second nature of all things and beings and is related to death. —In several Indian languages the word *shadow* designates both *picture* and *soul*. —In various conceptions of the afterlife, the dead are thought of as shadows. —The soul and the vital essence were often considered to be shadow; correspondingly, spirits that appear in human

Seven: The seven-petaled flower. From Boschius's *Symbolographia*, 1702.

form, or humans who have sold their souls to the Devil, have no shadow. —As a "bloodless" and only apparently living form, the shadow is, in the philosophical view, a symbol of the illusionism of the physical world (as in Buddhism) or of a depth of understanding arrested at the level of mere opinion but not oriented to the realm of eternal images (as in Plato's CAVE parable). —In Jungian terms, shadow represents the totality of the unconscious layers of the personality, which are transformed and integrated consciously, step by step, in the process of individuation.

Sheaf It is a symbol of harvest and plenty. During harvest rites the first or last sheaf bound was often said to have special powers that would manifest negatively if certain rules were not followed (e.g., giving the sheaf away or throwing it onto the neighbor's land). —As something made of many individual parts, the sheaf corresponds symbolically to the BOUQUET.

Shears As a cutting instrument it is a symbol of the active, masculine principle. —In Greek mythology it is an attribute of Atropos (one of the FATES), who cuts the THREAD of life. Shears represent dependence on the powers that guide one's destiny; they also denote sudden death.

Sheep See LAMB.

Shepherd In many cultures the shepherd or herdsman has symbolical significance as a cautiously caring father figure. God and the king were sometimes considered to be herdsmen. —The insignias of the Egyptian rulers came from the world of the herdsman. —God is the herdsman or shepherd of the people of Israel; Jesus Christ is the Good Shepherd. The most typical early Christian depiction of Christ derives from the idea, widespread in Mesopotamia and Greece, of the herdsman who carries a LAMB or a calf on his shoulders.

Shepherd:
Christ as the Good Shepherd, early Christian representation, 3rd century.

Ship It is a symbol of journey and crossing, and thus a symbol of life ("the journey of life"). —With reference to Noah's ARK, the ship in Christianity is often a symbol of the church steering a safe course through the waves of worldly dangers. The architectural form of the church was compared with a ship, often in detail (the term *nave* is from the Latin *navis*, ship); sometimes altars are in the shape of a boat.

Shoe In antiquity the wearing of shoes was a prerogative and symbol of the free person; slaves went barefoot. The shoe (having, so to speak, a "female" form) is related to the phallic symbolism of the FOOT and was a fertility symbol in various harvest and marriage customs.

Shout Commonly expressed in most cultures as the *war cry*, it represented the enthusiasm of attack. The shout also embodies the vigor and joy of life (e.g., at certain festivals in antiquity, usually those associated with fertility rites).

Sickle Often associated with the CRESCENT MOON because of its shape, it is a symbol of the harvest, which is renewed each year, and also of time and death (when depicted with the harvester or reaper). In addition, it signifies hope of renewal and rebirth. See SCYTHE.

Sickle: The Lord with the sickle. After a miniature in the *Bamberg Apocalypse.*

Sieve A symbol of sorting out and of critical separation and differentiation, especially of good and bad or evil. In this sense it is often mentioned in symbolic connection with divine justice or with the Day of Judgment, particularly in metaphors referring to the sifting of grain. — In conjunction with the four CARDINAL VIRTUES, the sieve symbolizes intelligence.

Silver As a shiny white metal, it is a symbol of purity. Among the Sumerians, during antiquity, and through the late Middle Ages (especially in the practice of alchemy), it was associated with the MOON and thus also with the feminine principle (in opposition to the masculine, solar GOLD). — In Egyptian mythology the bones of the gods are of silver, their flesh of gold. — In Christian symbolic usage, silver obtained through refining ore symbolizes the purification of the soul. In the Psalms the word of God is compared with silver; Mary, as the pure virgin, is also associated with it.

Silver Age See AGE.

Sirens In Greek mythology they are demons with birds' bodies and women's heads (and

Siren: Odysseus and the sirens. Stamnos of the painters of the Sirens, ca. 475 B.C.

La morte

Skeleton: Detail from a woodcut in *La Danse Macabre des Femmes*, Paris, 1486.

Skeleton: Skeleton as depicted in "Death and the Merchant" from H. Holbein the Younger's *Dance of Death.*

Skull: St. Hieronymus meditating on a skull. After a pen sketch by Durer.

often appear with breasts). They dwell on cliffs by the sea and are gifted with supernatural knowledge and a power of song that drives men crazy and draws seafarers to them, whom they then kill and devour. The Sirens symbolize the dangers of sea travel or seductive, mortal dangers in general. Psychoanalytically they can also be understood as symbols of compulsively self-destructive tendencies. —Later in antiquity the Sirens were viewed positively as the bards of Elysium who were connected to the harmony of the spheres. Because of this relationship to the world beyond, they were also often sculpted on sarcophagi. —The Sirens are frequently depicted with fish tails in medieval art, where they represent worldly and satanic temptation. —The *Lorelei*, who dwell in the Rhine, can be understood as a German version of the Sirens.

Sisyphus See ROCK, TANTALUS.

Six As the midpoint between TWO and TEN (ONE was not considered a numeral), six was considered by the Pythagoreans to be a perfect number. —In China the number six is associated with the influences of heaven. —In Christian symbolism, six is ambivalent. It is sacred as the number of the six days of creation and significant as the number of the works of charity; in the Apocalypse, however, six appears as the number of evil; 666 is the number of the apocalyptic animal. See HEXAGRAM.

Skeleton The personification of death, it is often depicted in a reflective pose or with a SCYTHE and an HOURGLASS. It began to appear as a symbol in late antiquity (the Greeks still represented death as a youthful brother of sleep or as a genius with a lowered torch). —The late medieval *dance of death* motif shows people of both sexes and of all ages and classes dancing a roundelay with skeletons that snatch them away; in later representations the skeleton also approaches persons as an unexpected threat in the midst of life.

Skiff See BOAT.

Skull (Death's Head) The skull was compared symbolically with the vault of the heavens (an expression of the symbolic similarity between the human and the universal microcosmos). —Especially in occidental art, it is a symbol of transience. —As a material "container" for the spirit or the intellect, the alchemists used the skull as a vessel for transformation processes. The skull cult, documented in various cultures, was probably based on the idea of the skull as the locus or seat of the spirit. —The skull of ADAM is often depicted below Christ's cross.

Sky Frequently seen as a half-sphere arched over the EARTH, it plays a great role in the mythological and religious conceptions of almost all peoples. It is the place from which gods and divine beings are thought to exert their power and to which the soul rises after death. This conception of the sky, which was originally literal rather than symbolic, was probably based on the fact that heaven is "above" (see HEIGHT). It is where the lawfully ordered movement of the stars takes place, where the fertilizing, vitally necessary rain comes from, and where natural phenomena that awaken fear and awe (e.g., storms, LIGHTNING, comets, meteorites, the RAINBOW) occur. —Originally heaven and earth were thought to be united; according to this view, heaven represented only one half of the total world. There was a widespread parallel notion of heaven as masculine/active and earth as feminine/passive; through the fertilization of the earth by the sky, all terrestrial creatures arose. (In Egypt, however, the opposite idea prevailed of the maternal sky goddess, Nut, as the spouse of the earth god, Geb.) —Widespread also was the idea of several heavens or heavenly spheres, one above the other, corresponding to the various hierarchies of spiritual beings or to the various stages of purification of the soul.

Sky: Heaven fertilizes the Earth and brings forth man; after Thenaud, Traité de la Cabale, 16th century.

Sky: The Egyptian sky goddess, Nut, in whose body the sun rises and sets, bends over the earth, represented as a disk. Relief on a sarcophagus, 30th Dynasty.

Sling In some Indian cultures it is an attribute of the storm god, probably because of the sound made when a projectile is hurled from it.

Smith As the subduer of METALS (especially of IRON) and as the powerful, creative agent of transformations, the smith is a cosmogonic symbolic figure. In the religious ideas of many peoples, he is assigned as helper to the major

Smith: Picture from Hortus Sanitatis, 1492.

god (e.g., Hephaestus and Zeus); he frequently works with LIGHTNING and THUNDER. —As a human, the smith often appears as a commander of fire, healer of illnesses, and rainmaker; there is an equally common negative image of the smith dealing with the forces of subterranean fire, black magic, and hell. —Among African peoples, the smith (who, among other things, creates the images for rituals and cults, and the ancestor figures) plays an important, sometimes also feared, role and hence often holds a high social rank; among some tribes, however, he is despised.

Smoke It is a symbol of connection between heaven (see SKY) and EARTH, spirit and matter. The column of smoke is sometimes related symbolically to the WORLD AXIS. See INCENSE, PEACE PIPE.

Snail In many cultures it is a lunar symbol, since it alternately shows or withdraws its feelers and itself; it is thus an image of the perpetually waxing and waning moon and a general symbol of perpetual renewal. —As an expression of their capacity to penetrate into every corner (just as the snail withdraws into its shell), Indian wind gods were often represented in the form of snails. —Like the MUSSEL, the snail was sometimes compared with the female genitals; for this reason, and also because of its protective shell, it was a common symbol in some Indian cultures of conception, pregnancy, and birth. —In Christianity the snail is regarded as a resurrection symbol, since it was thought to burst the confines of its shell in the spring. —Because of the form of its shell, the snail stands in symbolic relation to the SPIRAL. —The porcelainlike shell of the cowrie was prized by various primitive peoples not only as adornment and money but also as an AMULET and fertility symbol.

Snail:
The Mayan wind god arising from the shell of a snail.

Sneeze Some primitive peoples attribute sneezing to the influence of demons who seek to drive the soul out of the body. The Lapps believed that a violent sneeze could cause death. Possibly in reference to these ideas, there is a custom, documented since antiquity, of wishing sneezing persons good health and good fortune.

Snow Because of its color (WHITE), purity, and coldness, it represents chastity and virginal immaculateness; in Christian symbolism it signifies Mary.

Snowdrop As one of the first spring flowers, it is a symbol of hope. In medieval Christian paintings it is an attribute of Mary, since the "birth of hope" was due to Mary.

Snowdrops

Sodom and Gomorrah In the Old Testament, they were Biblical cities destroyed by Yahweh because of their godlessness and corrupt morals. From ancient times to the present day they are proverbial for wickedness and decadence. See FIRE.

Sol Invictus See SUN.

Solstice In Christian symbolism the northern hemisphere's summer solstice (the longest day of the year, after which there is ever diminishing length of daylight for six months) is a symbol of John the Baptist ("He will increase, but I will decrease"); the winter solstice (the shortest day of the year, after which there are increasing hours of daylight for six months) symbolizes Christ or the birth of Christ.

Soma It is the intoxicating sap of a like-named plant from which a ritual sacrificial potion was prepared in India. It was often symbolically identified with the MOON.

Sparrowhawk In Egypt it was the bird of Horus and accordingly a SUN symbol; it was also associated with the sun by the Greeks and Romans. —The fact that the female is larger and stronger than the male sometimes made the sparrowhawk a symbol of woman's dominance in marriage.

Spear See LANCE.

Speech Aside from numerous individual symbolic meanings associated with sounds and characters (see ALPHA, ALPHA AND OMEGA, LETTERS, OMEGA, TAW), language as a whole is generally a symbol of God as creator; in the conceptions of many religions, God's *word* or speech stood at the beginning of the world. Speech is

177

regarded today as the expression of ordered reason immanently underlying all things.

Speedwell (Veronica) In most varieties it is a blue-blossomed herb of the figwort family. The Latin name possibly derives from the Greek word *berenike* (bringer of victory); later the pun *vera unica medicina* was formed and thus symbolically related the plant to Christ as the "single, true medicine." —Since speedwell supposedly drew lightning, people avoided bringing it indoors.

Sphere Close in symbolic meaning to the CIRCLE, it represents the universe, the terrestrial globe, the firmament, and the unity of all mutually exclusive opposites (e.g., it sometimes symbolizes the HERMAPHRODITE). —In architecture (especially Islamic and Christian), the sphere or the half-sphere, like the circle or the arch, usually represents the SKY, whereas the SQUARE or the CUBE signifies the EARTH.

Sphinx: Sphinx depicted on a Greek amphora.

Sphinx An animal/human creature with the body of a lion and the head of a king or (rarely) a queen, it is an ancient symbol of rulership. Among the Egyptians it was usually a representation of the pharaoh, or sometimes of the sun god, as steadfast, powerful protector. Among the Phoenicians, Hittites, and Assyrians, it was depicted as a winged lion or steer with a human head. —Among the Greeks the sphinx, usually female and winged, was originally an enigmatic, often cruel creature (to which current colloquial usage refers). —In recent times (e.g., in the symbolic art of the late nineteenth and early twentieth centuries), the sphinx was frequently used as a symbol of the mysteriousness of woman or of the femme fatale.

Spider A symbolic animal with antithetical meanings. Because of its artful, radially arranged web and its central position in it, the spider is regarded in India as a symbol of the cosmic order and as the "weaver" of the world of the senses. Since it produces the threads for its web from within itself as the SUN produces rays of light, the spider is also a sun symbol; from this viewpoint, the net can also symbolize the emanations of the divine spirit or intellect. Because it climbs up the threads it has spun, the spider is a symbol in the Upanishads of spiritual self-liberation. —In Islam, white spiders are regarded as good, black spiders as evil. —In the Bible the spider occurs as a symbol of things perishable and of vain hopes. —Folk ideas sometimes juxtapose the death-bringing spider and the BEE; in superstition the spider is regarded as promising either good fortune or misfortune, depending on the time of day it appears. —In many Native American myths, Spider Woman is a creative figure whose father is the sun.

Spider: Maya, the eternal spinner of the illusion of the world of the senses, as a spider enclosed by an uroboros. Vignette from the title page of a collection of Brahmanic proverbs.

Spinal Column See WORLD AXIS.

Spindle (Distaff) Because of its regularly turning motion, it is a symbol of unchanging lawfulness, inexorable fate, or the eternal return; it is sometimes also a sexual symbol.

Spiral It is a favorite ornamental motif since prehistoric times, the symbolic content of which is contested by scholars. It probably has to do with a complex of meanings including cyclic development; moon phases and their influence on water, fertility, etc.; and (especially the double spiral) the movement of involution and evolution in the cosmos as a whole, return and renewal, and perhaps also the LABYRINTH.

Spiritual Pride See SUPERBIA.

Spleen In Europe and among the Arabs, it was believed to be the seat of the humors and of laughter; various colloquialisms refer to this meaning.

Spiral: The spiral, probably as a life and fertility symbol. Bacha, Sweden, Neolithic period.

Spring Generally revered as the origin of life-giving powers and as a symbol of purity and fertile abundance, the spring was personified by many peoples (e.g., the Greeks) as a female deity. —In the Bible it is sometimes a symbol of eternal life and rebirth. —Jung considered the spring to be a symbol of inexhaustible spiritual and emotional energy.

Square As one of the most common images, it is a static, nondynamic symbol often seen in reference and in contrast to the CIRCLE. The square is a symbol of the EARTH in contrast to heaven (see SKY), or of the limited in contrast to the infi-

Square: Combination of human figure and the square. From a bowl from West Norway, 9th century.

Squaring the Circle: "All things exist only in threes, in fours they rejoice." After a picture in Jamsthales's *Viatorium Spagyricum*, 1625.

Stab

Staff: Aaron before the greening staff. Bronze door, St. Zeno, Verona, ca. 1100.

nite. It also represents the four directions of the compass. —It is often used for the ground plan of temples, altars, cities, or as an architectural element (e.g., in Roman architecture). —In China the cosmos and the earth were believed to be square. —To the Pythagoreans the square was a symbol of the combined effects of the four ELEMENTS and thus of the powers of Aphrodite, Demeter, Hestia, and Hera, subsumed in the mother of the gods, Rhea. According to Plato the square, along with the circle, embodies absolute beauty. —In Islam the square plays a varied role. The hearts of normal people, for example, were regarded as square because they stood open to four possible sources of inspiration (from God, angels, humans, and the Devil); the hearts of the prophets, however, were considered triangular because they were no longer exposed to the Devil's attacks. —In Christian art the square is sometimes a symbol of the earth in contrast to heaven. The square HALO of persons depicted when living indicated that their form still belonged to the earth. —Jung saw in the square a symbol of matter, life, and earthly reality. See CUBE, FOUR, MAGICAL SQUARES.

Squaring the Circle As an insolvable task, it symbolizes the striving for reconciliation of the symbolic content of the CIRCLE and the SQUARE.

Squirrel In Germanic mythology it is sacred to the god of fire and the god of thunder, and it lived in the world ash tree, Yggdrasil (see TREE). —In antiquity the squirrel was a symbol of Hermes because of its ability to move to many different levels. —In medieval symbolism the red squirrel represents the Devil because of its alacrity and its fire-red color.

Staff A symbol of power and of (magical) knowledge (e.g., the magic staff or wand) often imagined to take effect through contact (thus, e.g., Moses's staff, which in the miracle draws water from the rock). —In Greece the staff of Hermes was considered to be magically effective and beneficent. —Indian deities, specifically the god of death, carry a staff as a sign of their power to judge and punish. —Apotropaic effects were ascribed to the staff. In ancient China, for example, evil powers were driven out with a staff (usually of peach or mulberry wood). —The Bible and the Apocrypha mention a staff that transforms into something living (see green BRANCH, SERPENT), thus expressing divine will (e.g., Aaron's staff, Joseph's staff prior to his betrothal to Mary). —As a sign of their function as messenger, angels (especially in Byzantine art), are often depicted carrying a long messenger's staff. —The crosier (crooked staff) of bishops and abbots developed from the shepherd's staff, which in Christian art is associated with Christ, the prophets, and the saints. —Staffs indicating rulership, such as the marshal's staff or the SCEPTER, are symbols of legal and often judicial power. —Sometimes the WORLD AXIS has been compared to a staff. —Breaking the staff was an ancient Franconian custom signaling the break in the community of law; it was also customary at executions. See ASCLEPIUS, STAFF OF, CADUCEUS.

Stag In Paleolithic caves there are representations of stags and of people garbed as stags, which probably served cult purposes. —The stag was an animal revered worldwide. Because of its annually renewed large antlers, it was compared in many cultures and epochs to the TREE of life. It was also a symbol of fertility and of waxing and waning. Moreover, because of their form and the blood-red color of the cuticle sloughed off in the spring, the antlers were a symbol to many people of rays of light and of fire; the stag was therefore viewed as a solar animal or as an intermediary between heaven (see SKY) and EARTH. —In Buddhism the golden stag (along with the gazelle) symbolizes wisdom and asceticism. —The solar aspect of the stag was sometimes interpreted in China in a negative sense, that is, as a symbol of drought and sterility. —In antiquity, the stag and the DOE were animals sacred to Artemis; the battle between the stag and other animals symbolized the battle between light and darkness. The stag occurs in antiquity and among the Celts as psychopomp (spirit guide). —The stag was also seen in antiquity as the enemy and slayer of SER-

Stag: St. Eustachius with the flag on which is depicted the stag with the crucified Christ. Detail from Dürer's *Paumgartner Altar*.

PENTS. This idea, mediated by PHYSIOLOGUS, also appeared in medieval Christian art. The identification of the stag with Christ (who treads on the serpent's, i.e., Satan's, head) is based on this and other associations. The legends of St. Eustachius and of St. Hubert, for example, report the appearance of a stag who bore the crucified Christ between his antlers. In Christian art the stag is also depicted in association with the water of life (with reference to Psalm 42). —Occasionally the stag is a symbol of melancholy, since it loves solitude. —Because of its striking behavior when in heat, it also functions as a symbol of masculine sexual passion.

Stairs A symbol of emotional and spiritual development and of incremental gains in wisdom and knowledge, it has essentially the same symbolic meaning as the LADDER. However, in contrast to the ladder, which was generally understood to lead from the bottom up (and thus in the direction of the SKY or of heaven), the stairs sometimes also descend under the earth and into dark realms. Thus they can symbolize either descent into the realm of the dead or the

Stairs: The steps toward the heavenly city. Woodcut from Raymundus Lullus's *Liber de Ascensu*, Valencia, 1512.

approach to occult knowledge or to the unconscious. —White stairs point symbolically to clarity and wisdom; black stairs to black magic. —In the Egyptian solar religion, stepped pyramids represented the stairs on which the soul ascends to heaven; there are also pictures of boats in the middle of which stairs are erected on which the soul ascends toward the light. The Babylonian *ziggurat* probably can be understood in a similar sense. —The spiral stairs share the symbolism of the SPIRAL.

Starfish In Christian imagery it symbolizes Mary radiating guidance through the waves and storms of the world and granting comfort to the faithful.

Star of David See HEXAGRAM.

Stars As lights in the dark night sky, they signify spiritual light penetrating the darkness. They also represent higher or excessively high ideals ("reaching for the stars"). —The movement of the stars in regular courses symbolizes the harmoniously coordinated workings of divine forces. —In the mythological conceptions of many peoples, the stars in general or specific stars are interpreted as the deceased who have been transported to and set in the sky; some Indian cultures assume a corresponding star in the sky for every living being on earth. —According to late Jewish ideas, every star was protected by an angel; a star (Star of Bethlehem) or an angel also accompanied the three wise men from the East to Bethlehem. —In the Old Testament the starry sky symbolizes the promised, numerous progeny of Abraham, who, according to interpretations by medieval theologians, represent various peoples and races bound together spiritually in the church. —Mary, as the Immaculate Virgin, is sometimes represented with a crown of stars on her head. See COMET, EVENING STAR, MORNING STAR, POLESTAR.

Steer A symbol of strength, masculine (fighting) courage, and wildness, it is associated with the SUN because of its activity and with the MOON because of its fertility; the horns of the steer and the COW are also moon symbols because they look like the CRESCENT MOON. —Among many

Star: The blessed Virgin with the halo of stars. From *Speculum Humanae Salvationis*, 14th century.

Star: The creation of the sun, moon, and stars. After the depiction of the creation in Genesis, mosaic in the Palatine Chapel, Palermo, second half of the 12th century.

Steer: The astrological sign for Taurus.

Steer: The steer and the bullfighter. After F. de Goya.

Steer: Before Isis a lotus is offered to Apis, the steer sacred to the Egyptians. Small bronze sculpture.

peoples the steer was an especially valuable sacrificial animal. —In Neolithic rock paintings in North Africa, steers are represented with the sun between their horns. —In Egypt the fertility god Apis was revered in the form of a steer, often with the sun disk between his horns; since he was also equated with Osiris, he was likewise a god of death. The death and burial of the sacred Apis steer were always celebrated solemnly and led to a "resurrection" (i.e., the selection of a new steer calf). —The steer played a particularly important role in the Minoan culture as a symbol of power and fertility. —In Iranian mythology the embodiment of cosmic fertility is in the form of a primeval steer that was slain by Mithras, whereupon all plants and animals grew out of its body. In the Mithras cult, the steer SACRIFICE and the baptism with steer's blood, from which women were excluded, represented the continually repeated struggle to come to terms with the steer's powers of fertility, death, and resurrection. —In India the god Shiva is associated with a white steer, the symbol of subdued or restrained powers of fertility. —Among various peoples the steer is associated with thunderstorms, RAIN, and WATER because of its fertility. —From the psychoanalytic viewpoint, the steer corresponds to the animal powers and sexuality in humanity (e.g., bullfights represent the continually renewed attempt to anticipate in visible enactments the inner victory over these powers). —The steer (TAURUS) is the second sign of the ZODIAC; its element is EARTH. See MINOTAUR, OX.

Steering Wheel It is a symbol of responsibility, authority, and higher wisdom.

Stepladder See LADDER.

Stilts In China the use of stilts (e.g., in ritual dances) served to identify the wearer with the CRANE, a symbol of immortality.

Stone It plays a significant symbolic role in most cultures. *Meteorites*, as "stones fallen from heaven," have been universally worshiped as a symbolic connection between heaven (see SKY) and EARTH. —Because of its hardness and unchangeability, the stone has frequently been associated with eternal, immutable, divine powers and often understood as an expression of concentrated force. In spite of its hardness, however, the stone has generally not been seen as something rigid and dead but as life giving; in Greek myth, for example, humans arise after a flood from the stones that Deucalion had sown. Many stones, especially meteorites, were regarded as bringing fertility and causing rain. They were touched by infertile women who wanted children; in the spring or during times of drought, people made sacrifices to them to get rain and rich harvests. —In early antiquity prior to the representation of the gods in human form, an unhewn stone was regarded as a symbol of Hermes or Apollo. —Upright stones as *grave stones* signified the protection of the dead from hostile powers; sometimes they were also considered to be the place in which the power or the soul of the deceased lived on. Sacred black stone belonged to the cult of the mother goddess Cybele. —The central element in the ritual life of Islam is a black meteorite, the *hadjar alaswad*, in the Kaaba in Mecca. —In the Bible the ROCK and the stone are symbols of God's protective strength. See FLINT, GEMS, MENHIR, NAVEL, PHILOSOPHERS' STONE.

Stork It is counted among the unclean animals in the Bible, but is otherwise generally revered as a symbol of good fortune. In the Far East it is a symbol of long life, since it was assumed that the stork lived to an old age. Often (e.g., in Egypt, in antiquity, and among the church patriarchs) it was regarded as a symbol of childlike gratitude because young storks that could fly were said to feed their parents. —As a hunter and killer of SERPENTS, it was regarded in Christian belief as an enemy of the Devil and hence as a symbol of Christ. —Since it fed on animals that live in the ground (which supposedly bear the souls of the deceased), it was sometimes also seen as a carrier of souls. —As an annually returning migratory bird, it is a symbol of resurrection; it is also regarded as the deliverer of babies, perhaps because it returns at the time nature reawakens from winter. —Standing on one leg, it presented an image of calmness and reflection; the marabu stork in particular came to symbolize philosophical contemplation.

Storm In the religious imagery of many peoples it is a symbol or a real expression of the acts of divine powers. Temporal turning points (e.g., new seasons, centuries, epochs) are often visualized as storms or natural catastrophies. See LIGHTNING, THUNDER.

Strawberry The strawberry was known in the Middle Ages only in its small-fruited form. Because of its threefold leaf, it was a symbol of the Trinity; because of its lowly growth habit and its virtues, it symbolized noble humility and modesty. The blood-red, pendant fruit was sometimes considered a symbol of the shed blood of Christ or the martyrs, and the five-petaled blossom symbolized the five wounds of Christ. —The ripe fruit could also indicate the readiness of a young woman for marriage and motherhood; it sometimes signified desire for worldly pleasures.

String Like the CHAIN, it represents joining, especially of heaven (see SKY) and EARTH (also understood in the sense of heaven fertilizing the earth; hence it sometimes symbolizes RAIN). —According to Buddhist, Hindu, Neoplatonic, and other world views, the human spirit is connected to the soul or the body by a golden astral string or cord. —For the Freemasons, a knotted string symbolizes the community of all Freemasons.

Sulfur In alchemy it, like SALT and mercury (see MERCURIUS), is one of the philosophical elements and universal principles. It represents the "fiery" element or the energy and the soul (anima) of nature; it was sometimes also compared to the SUN. —Medieval folk belief associated sulfur with the infernal and saw it, its flames, and its odor as attributes of the Devil.

Sun In most traditions it is one of the most important symbols. Many primitive peoples and early advanced civilizations revered it as god; often it is represented as the visible embodiment of LIGHT and of the highest cosmic intelligence, of warmth, of FIRE, and of the life-giving

Sulfur: Detail from a picture in *Musaeum Hermeticum*, Frankfurt, 1677.

Sun: Symbol of the sun or of God. From the Jakobuskirche, Tubingen.

Sun: The sun depicted as Helios. On a coin from Rhodes, 3rd century.

principle. Its daily renewed ascent and descent made it a symbolic precursor of resurrection as well as generally of every new beginning. Since the sun casts its light equally on all things and thereby makes them visible, it is also a symbol of justice. —The sun was especially revered in Egypt, where it was regarded as the embodiment of the sun god Ra (at times also in association or identified with other gods); Ra had two sun boats in which he traversed the heavens. Frequently the SCARAB is represented with the sun or the (often winged) sun DISK with the uraeus SERPENT. —Additional sun gods include the baboon Shamash, the Greek Helios (with HORSES and the chariot of the sun), and the Roman *sol* or the late Roman *sol invictus* (the "invincible sun"). Among the Incas, in Egypt, and in Japan, the sun cult was closely connected to the cult of the king or emperor. Other gods, not strictly sun gods, are also associated with the sun (e.g., Osiris and Apollo). —The Indian Veda compares Brahma, the absolute, with the spiritual sun. —In China the sun, in contrast to the MOON, was regarded as an expression of the yang principle (see YIN AND YANG). —Plato considered the sun to be the visible representation of the good. —In Christianity, Christ is compared with the sun (e.g., as the "sun of justice"; in early Christian times Christ was also associated with the late Roman *sol invictus*). —The sun-moon opposition corresponds for most peoples to the male-female pair of opposites, but there are numerous examples (e.g., in central Asia and among Germanic-speaking peoples) with reversed meanings, where the sun is known as the warming, nourishing, maternal principle. —In alchemy the sun corresponds to GOLD, which is also called the "sun of the earth". —Particularly in hot regions, the sun appears negatively as the principle of dryness and drought, and hence as the opponent of the fertilizing RAIN. —In some Indian cultures the idea of a *black sun* exists (i.e., the sun that leaves this world during the night to shine in another world). It is a symbol of death and disaster; it appears in pictures (e.g., on the back of the god of death), sometimes in the shape of a JAGUÁR. In alchemy the black sun is a symbol of

Sun: The falcon-headed Ra-Harachte with the rising sun. From the tomb of Sennudjem, 20th Dynasty.

Sun: The king sacrifices to the sun. Egyptian picture, 18th Dynasty.

Sun: The sun as a symbol of strength and fertility. Val Camonica.

Swan: The Swan as a symbol of the spirit. Detail from Mylius's *Philosophia Reformata*, 1622.

the *prima materia*. In contemporary art and literature a black sun usually represents metaphysical angst or melancholy.

Sunflower Because of its radially arranged petals, its yellow color, and its heliotropic habit, it is a symbol in various cultures of the sun and of majesty. —In Christianity it is a symbol of God's love and of the soul, which incessantly directs its thoughts and feelings toward God; accordingly it is also a symbol of prayer.

Superbia The female personification of *(spiritual) pride*, one of the seven mortal sins, she rides on a lion or a horse. The attributes of pride include the CENTAUR, the EAGLE, and the PEACOCK.

Swallow As a regularly returning migratory bird, it often symbolizes spring, light, and fertility. Its nesting on houses was regarded as propitious. —In the Middle Ages it was a resurrection symbol because it returns after the passing of winter and because it could supposedly impart sight to its young by using the sap of the CELANDINE (just as God could make the dead see again on the Day of Judgment). —Among black African peoples the swallow is symbolic of purity because it does not sit on the earth and hence does not come in contact with dirt.

Swamp In Asia it is sometimes a symbol of rest and contentment. —For the Sumerians it was a sign of undifferentiated material substance, of passivity, and of woman. —In ancient Greece the symbolic meaning of the swamp was close to that of the LABYRINTH. —In psychoanalytic dream interpretation the swamp is sometimes an image of the unconscious.

Swan In Asia Minor and in Europe the white swan symbolizes light, purity, and grace. The black swan, on the other hand, sometimes appears in occult contexts, as does the black SUN. This symbolism, in turn, is partly divided into female and male subgroups. Especially among Slavic and Scandinavian peoples and in Asia Minor, the female aspect predominates: the swan is a symbol of beauty and of the heavenly virgin (fertilized by WATER or by the EARTH). In India, China, Japan, Scandinavia, and among the

Arabs and Persians, the figure of the swan maiden appears, a fairy-tale personage from the beyond. In antiquity, however, the male aspect predominated: white swans draw Apollo's chariot, Zeus approaches Leda in the form of a swan, Aphrodite and Artemis are also sometimes accompanied by swans. —According to Greek beliefs, the swan possessed the ability to prophesy and announce death. —In the Far East the swan is a symbol both of grace and of distinction and courage. —Among the Celts the swan was regarded as an embodiment of supernatural beings; as in Hinduism, they did not always distinguish between the symbolic meaning of swan and GOOSE. In many other cultures, however, the goose is understood as a negative counterpart to the swan. —In alchemy the swan is assigned to MERCURIUS; it symbolizes the spirit and serves as the mediator between water and FIRE. —The swan's egg sometimes appears as the world EGG. —The trumpeter swan, which supposedly sounds its plaintive song before its death (especially if it is frozen in the ice), became a symbol of a person's last works or words; in this sense it also symbolizes Christ and his last words on the cross.

Swastika A CROSS with four arms of equal length, the ends of which are extended at right angles or in a curve, giving the impression of circular motion. It is also called *crux gammata* because it appears to be made of four (usually reversed) Greek letters for *gamma*. It appears extensively as a symbol in Asia and Europe, less often in Africa and Central America. It is usually interpreted as a sun wheel, as crossing flashes of lightning, or (in northern countries) as Thor's HAMMER. It is also considered to be a symbol of good fortune and of healing; among the Buddhists it symbolizes the "key of paradise." In Romanesque art of the Middle Ages, it probably had apotropaic significance.

Swastika: Detail from a stone relief showing symbols promising good fortune. North India, 1st-2nd century.

Sweat In folk belief it was sometimes regarded as the vehicle of the powers of the person sweating and was thus used for purposes of magical healing and harming. —In some Indian cultures sweat of the body was interpreted as a sacrifice to the sun god and thus as penance and purification.

Swine It is an animal with various symbolic meanings. Because of its many offspring, the sow is above all a fertility symbol (e.g., among the Egyptians, Greeks, and Celts) and was used in pictures as an AMULET to bring good fortune and fertility. —The German expression "to have a swine" (meaning "to have undeserved good fortune") was probably originally meant scornfully; it derives from medieval games of chance in which the "unearned" prize was often a swine. —In Greek and Roman antiquity the swine was among the preferred sacrificial animals. —The swine was also despised by many peoples. For the Jews, Mohammedans, and others, it was regarded as an unclean animal because of its voracity. Its habit of miring in mud and filth commonly signifies baseness and coarseness; in medieval art it represents immoderate behavior, especially GLUTTONY and unbridled passion, as well as ignorance. —The *boar* was revered (e.g., among the Greeks and the Japanese) as a symbol of power and of the fighting spirit. Among the Celts the wild swine was a symbolic animal of the warrior and priestly castes and was consumed at sacred feasts. —In medieval art it symbolizes the demonic. In medieval Christian art of Germanic-speaking peoples, the wild boar sometimes appears as a Christ symbol (probably because of the erroneous derivation of *Eber*, the German name for wild boar, from the Hebrew *ibri*, the ancestor of the Hebrews). —The swine is the 12th and last sign of the Chinese ZODIAC and corresponds to *Pisces* (see FISH).

Swing In Southeast Asia (and to some extent in Greece and Spain), the swing is associated with fertility rites. The motion of swinging is related to the ebb and flow of natural growth and possibly to the earth-fertilizing wind (which can arise from swinging). Especially in India it symbolizes the setting and rising of the SUN, the rhythm of the seasons, and the eternal cycle of death and birth; it sometimes also represents the harmonious union of heaven (see SKY) and EARTH and

Swine: Sacrifice of a swine to the fertility goddess, Demeter. After a picture on an Attic bowl.

xpulit cos ir padilo gladio ignito

Sword: Expulsion from paradise with the flaming sword. From *Speculum Humanae Salvationis*, 14th century.

thereby occasionally the union of the RAINBOW and the RAIN.

Sword It is often a symbol of military virtues, especially of manly strength and bravery; thus it also occurs as a symbol of power and the SUN (with reference to the active, masculine principle as well to the sun's flashing, swordlike rays). In a negative sense, it symbolizes the horrors of war; many war and storm gods have the sword as their attribute. It is sometimes also a phallic symbol. —As a sharp, cutting instrument, it is a symbol of decision, separation into good and evil, and justice; in many representations of the Day of Judgment a sword, often double-edged, comes from Christ's MOUTH. —According to the medieval two-swords theory, which formulated the ecclesiastical (primacy of church over state) and the imperial (equality of both church and state) conceptions of power, one sword symbolized the mundane and the other sword the spiritual power. —The *flaming sword* that drives ADAM AND EVE out of paradise symbolizes both power and justice. —The sword can also be regarded as a symbol of LIGHTNING, as in Japan and India (where the sword of the Vedic sacrificial priest is called the "lightning of Indra"). —A sword in its scabbard symbolizes the cardinal virtue of moderation or prudence (see PRUDENTIA).

Sword: Christ as judge of the world with a sword in his mouth. After a miniature ca. 1260.

Sycamore The designation includes various deciduous trees. In Egypt it refers to the sycamore fig (*Ficus sycomorus*), which was regarded as a manifestation of the sky goddess. Its foliage and shade signify rest and peace in the life beyond; sometimes the souls of the deceased were thought to be BIRDS that lived in its branches.

Sycamore: The Egyptian sky goddess Nut in the sycamore. Middle of the 2nd millennium B.C.

Table As the center about which people can gather, it is a symbol of communal eating but also of a chosen group (e.g., King Arthur's round table). —In Islamic belief there is a great table in which God has inscribed the fate of each person.

Tail The tail sometimes occurs as a veiled sexual symbol. In Roman art the lion's tail is often associated with ornamental forms.

Talisman Sometimes considered identical to the AMULET, it is differentiated from the amulet (to which principally apotropaic effects are ascribed) because it is supposedly an active agent in bringing good fortune. Astrologically the talisman was interpreted as a link to astral energies, which it was supposed to accumulate.

Tamarisk

Tamarisk It is a shrub or tree having narrow leaves and (frequently) spikelike clustered blossoms. In China it was regarded as an immortality symbol, hence its resin was seen as a drug that prolonged life.

Tansy Any of a genus of plants of the aster family, it has spicy, fragrant, volatile oil and was an ancient medicinal and magical plant. It appears in medieval art as an attribute of Mary. Tansy consecrated on Assumption Day is supposed to grant protection against magicians, witches, and the Devil.

Tansy

Tantalus In Greek mythology he was the king who offered the flesh of his slain son, Pelops, to the gods as food in order to test their omniscience. As punishment he was cast into the underworld and there suffered eternal hunger and thirst. Above him hung the branches of fruit trees that withdrew when he reached for the fruit; he stood in a pool of water that vanished when he wanted to drink. Along with Sisyphus (see ROCK), Tantalus and others are regarded as personifications of the impossibility of fulfilling human wishes.

Tarot Begun in France in the Middle Ages, it is a common card game consisting of 78 cards that repeatedly give rise to speculative, symbolic interpretations. The sequence of the trump cards (major arcana) in particular were thought to symbolize the path of initiation.

Taurus See STEER.

Taw It is the last letter of the Hebrew alphabet. Like the Greek OMEGA, it was regarded as a symbol of the end or of completion.

Teeth They are a symbol of strength, vitality, and aggressiveness. —In psychoanalytic dream interpretation, the loss of teeth is primarily connected with the male sexual organ and is a sign of frustration, weakness, or castration anxiety. The idea of the *vagina dentata* (the toothed vagina) rests on a nondifferentiation or lack of differentiation of the oral and genital spheres and is usually understood to be a projection of a male castration anxiety.

Temperance See TEMPERANTIA.

Temperantia The female personification of *temperance* or moderation, one of the four cardinal virtues, she is often represented with the CAMEL, DOVE, ELEPHANT, HOURGLASS, LION, SKULL, SICKLE, or a sheathed SWORD.

Temple See HOUSE.

Ten As the sum of the first four numbers, and the number of fingers on both hands, 10 is a holy number and a symbol of totality. For intellectual systems based on the decimal system, it is a symbol of return to unity on a higher level and of the CIRCLE closing on itself. The number 10 played an important role for the Pythagoreans (see TETRACTYS). —In China, the number 10 was associated with the totality and midpoint symbol FIVE and with the duality principle TWO. —In the Bible, the number 10 occurs often as the number of a closed totality: Ten Commandments, 10 Egyptian plagues, 10 virgins, 10 lepers.

Tetractys:
Geometric
representation as
the equilateral
triangle.

Tetramorph:
Tetramorph on
two wheels,
symbolizing the
Old and the New
Testaments.
From the cloister
at Athos, 1213.

Tetractys For the Pythagoreans it was a sacred number, the sum (10) of the numbers 1, 2, 3, and 4, signifying the essence of perfection. The sum was regarded as the source of all things and was personified as the god of harmony.

Tetramorph It is a form or shape of four parts. Until the late Middle Ages, it was a collective designation for the four cherubim (see CHERUB) and for the symbol of the four Evangelists (in one shape having four faces and four or six wings; see EVANGELISTS, SYMBOLS OF). The image derives from the Book of Revelation and from Ezekiel's vision of the four winged creatures, one of whose faces resembled a HUMAN BEING, one a LION, one a STEER, and one an EAGLE. Originally it probably had to do with a symbol of the spiritual omnipresence of God.

Third Eye See EYE.

Thirteen Since antiquity it has been considered a number foreboding ill, particularly because in the duodecimal system it follows the number TWELVE, which is thought to bring good fortune; hence for the Babylonians it was the number of the underworld and of the destruction of perfection. —The Cabala mentions 13 evil spirits. —In the Old Testament 13 occurs as the number indicating salvation. However, the 13th chapter of the APOCALYPSE involves the Antichrist and the beast. —In certain contexts (e.g., in antiquity), 13 was a symbol of strength and sublimity (e.g., Zeus was sometimes described as the 13th in the circle of the 12 chief gods). —In some Indian cultures 13 is a holy number.

Thirty-Six As a dividend it contains the symbolic number FOUR (often associated with the EARTH) and NINE (which in turn contains the treble of the sacred number THREE). Thirty-six and its multiples are thus sometimes symbols of cosmic relationships among heaven (see SKY), earth, and humans (e.g., 36 is the number of heaven, 72 is number of the earth, 108 is the number of humans). Thirty-six is also a totality symbol because it represents the sum of the first four even numbers $(2 + 4 + 6 + 8 = 20)$ and the first four odd numbers $(1 + 3 + 5 + 7 = 16)$ (in which 1 is considered to be the first odd number); in this regard it was of significance to the Pythagoreans.

Thistle Like many prickly plants, it is a symbol of difficulty and suffering. In Christian art it signifies the sufferings of Christ and the martyrs, and thus it is also a symbol of salvation (as is the BROOM). —The prickles, which turn away enemies, are symbols of protection. —In China the thistle symbolizes long life, possibly because it retains its form even when it has been cut and dried.

Thistle: 1. Common (or Scotch) thistle. 2. Ruffled thistle.

Thorn It is a symbol of difficulty, obstacles, and suffering. —The thorn of the agave was for some Indian cultures an instrument of mortification. The priests tore open their flesh with agave thorns to sacrifice their blood to the gods. —In Christian graphic and plastic art, a thorn branch wound about a skull symbolizes eternal damnation. —Christ's *crown of thorns* is both a symbol of suffering and of ridicule; the monk's circular tonsure refers, among other things, to the crown of thorns. —The thorn bush in the story of Isaac's sacrifice was sometimes seen as symbolically anticipating the cross and Christ's crown of thorns. See THORN BUSH, BURNING.

Thorn: The Man of Suffering with crown of thorns. Detail from the title page of *The Great Passion* by Durer, 1511.

Thornbush, Burning God appeared to Moses in a thornbush that burned but was not consumed. The burning thornbush is a symbol of the indestructible power of the spiritual FIRE. In Christian art and literature it also symbolizes Mary, who became a mother but remained a virgin (i.e., "burned" yet remained "undamaged").

Thousand See HUNDRED.

Thread It generally symbolizes joining and connecting. The Upanishad, for example, speaks of a thread that connects this world with the next, and all beings with one another. Also time and life are often compared with a thread (see ERINYES). —The thread of Ariadne in Greek mythology is a ball of yarn that Ariadne, daughter of King Minos, gave to Theseus, by means of which he found his way out of the LABYRINTH. It is a proverbial symbol of the principle that guides learning and knowledge.

Thornbush: Moses at the burning bush. After a glass painting from the Stiftskirche at Wimpfen im Tal, first half of 14th century.

Thread of Life See FATES.

195

Three: After a representation of the Trinity. From Hrabanus Maurus's *De Origine Rerum*.

Three A particularly significant number for many peoples, it is the synthesis of ONE and TWO, the symbol of the principle that embraces all, the image of mediation, and the number of heaven (see SKY) in contrast to that of EARTH (i.e., FOUR). The universal symbolic meaning of three probably relates to the elementary experience of productive fulfillment in the trinity of man, woman, and child. Three also forms the basis of numerous systems and ideas of order. For example, in Christianity there are the three virtues of faith, love, and hope; in alchemy there are three basic philosophical elements and universal principles, represented by SULFER, SALT, and MERCURIUS (quicksilver). Divine trinities are known in many religions (e.g., as Isis, Osiris, and Horus in Egypt; as Brahma, Vishnu, and Shiva in Hinduism); divine trinities of this sort are often related to heaven, earth, and the AIR that unites them. In Christianity, however, the triune God is often graphically represented as the unity of three persons (the Trinity). —As the number indicat-

Three: Representation of the Trinity as a unity of three persons. Woodcut, Paris, 1524.

Three: The trinity as unity, the quaternity resting on duality. From Valentinus's *Duodecim Claves*, 1678.

ing fulfillment or completion in a closed totality, three often occurs in fairy tales as the number of tests to be passed or riddles to be solved. —In philosophy the triad plays an important role as the principle of mediation between thinking and being or, as in Hegelian philosophy, as the principle of dialectical progress (thesis, antithesis, synthesis). See TRIANGLE, TRIDENT.

Three Leafed See LEAF.

Three: Window with three joined hares. Cathedral at Paderborn.

Threshold Like the DOOR, it is a symbol of transition from one place or condition to another, and of the separation between places, conditions, etc. —Not letting a person cross the threshold means not wanting to have anything to do with that person, whereas "camping on someone's doorstep" (or threshold) means persistently seeking contact with that person. —The threshold of the temple is regarded in many cultures as holy, and thus a special sort of cleaning or purification is often required before crossing it (e.g., removal of the shoes at the threshold of the mosque). Among various peoples the threshold itself must not be stepped on.

Throne A symbol of rulership and fame in the profane and sacred realms, it is often elevated on a base and furnished with a BALDACHIN. The form and material of the throne are usually symbolically significant. In Buddhist belief, for example, there is Buddha's DIAMOND throne, which is supposed to stand at the foot of the Bodhi tree (see FIG TREE). —Possibly the Egyptian goddess Isis was originally understood to be an embodiment of the ruler's throne, which people thought of as a divine being; Isis often bears on her head the glyphs designating "throne." —The throne of God or of individual gods is regarded in various religions as borne by angels or by sacred symbolic animals. —The Koran often refers to Allah with the name "Lord of the Throne" or "Master of the Throne." The throne in this context symbolizes the sum of divine wisdom; it is described as made of shining, green metal that is incomprehensibly bright, and provided with 70,000 tongues, which praise God in all languages. It is supposed to change color 70,000 times each day and to contain in itself the primordial images of all existing things; the distance between the supporting pillars equals the distance that a rapidly flying bird can cover in 80,000 years. —In Judaism the king's throne, or the entire city of Jerusalem, symbolically represents Yahweh's throne and rulership over his people. In the Old Testament the throne appears above all as a symbol of God's power as judge. —The early Christian church adopted the cathedra, a chair with an arched back, upon which high-placed persons sat while others stood. The church made this into a symbol of the office of spiritual teacher and imparted litur-

Throne: Throne of the monarch. From the Viviano Bible, 840.

gical significance to it as the seat of the founder of the church or of the bishop. —Early Christian art developed the motif of the symbolic preparation of the throne for Christ's return on the Day of Judgment (see ETIMASIE).

Thumb As the finger that gives the hand its full grasping capacity (because it opposes the others), it is often interpreted as masculine and creative and is thus also a phallic symbol. See FINGER.

Thunder Like LIGHTNING, it is in many cultures the expression and symbol of divine power and hence is also an attribute of the highest divinities. —For ancient Germanic tribes, thunder arose when Donar threw his hammer. —In the Bible it is the voice, especially the angry voice, of God. —The Celts interpreted thunder as the expression of a cosmic disturbance that evoked the anger of the elements; additionally they saw in it a punishment of the gods. —In Siberia and North America there is an idea of a mythic bird that produces thunder with the beating of its wings; it may appear as a wild GOOSE or DUCK, as an iron BIRD, or as an EAGLE. —For the Chinese, thunder arose when a heavenly DRAGON moved. —Sometimes (e.g., in some Indian cultures) a ONE-LEGGED thunder god occurs. Thunder gods frequently have SMITHS as helpers who forge such things as LIGHTNING, HAMMERS, and clubs for them.

Thyrsus Common especially in antiquity, it is a staff with PINE branches, crowned with a pine cone and entwined with IVY and grape leaves (see GRAPEVINE, WINE). It is a symbol of fertility and immortality and was used in celebrations of mother goddesses, in honor of Hermes (Mercury), and in the Dionysian mysteries in Eleusis. It is also an attribute of Dionysus and of the maenads. —In Christian art the thyrsus is a symbol of vegetative vital energy or of heathendom.

Tiger It is a positive and negative symbol of strength and wildness. —In China the tiger was originally the protective spirit of the hunt and later of agriculture. Sometimes the tiger, which lives in the dark thicket and is informed espe-

Tiger: Chinese picture, Ming period.

198

cially by the yin principle (see YIN AND YANG), occurs as a good or evil opponent of the DRAGON. The white tiger is a symbol of royal virtues. — In Buddhism the tiger, which finds its path through the jungle, represents spiritual exertion. Since it can orient itself even in darkness and at the time of the new moon, the tiger also represents the inner light, the increase of light, or the life after dark and difficult times. — As a predatory animal the tiger symbolizes the dangerous power of uncontrolled drives. — The tiger is the third sign of the Chinese ZODIAC and corresponds to *Gemini* (see TWINS).

Tin It was equated in medieval alchemy with Jupiter, which was described as a beneficent planet. It was considered to be a mediator between heat and cold and between Mars (see IRON) and Saturn (see LEAD), and induced cleverness and liveliness. See METALS.

Toad As an animal loving dark and moist places, it was connected in China to the yin principle (see YIN AND YANG), the MOON, fertility, and riches. — Like the FROG, it was associated in many cultures with RAIN and rain magic. — In the Occident the toad may have been associated in earlier times with solar symbolism and later was interpreted ambivalently. It was seen as the protector of treasures, as a good domestic spirit, and above all as the assistant at births (since in antiquity the womb was imagined in the form of a toad), but it was also seen as a poisonous witches' companion. — In Egypt the toad was considered to be an animal of the dead (perhaps because of its preference for dwelling in the earth) and, like the frog, symbolized resurrection (probably because of the striking transformation of its form from tadpole to mature animal). — In medieval art the toad appears in pictures of death and in connection with the vices of lust and greed.

Toad: Two toads dancing in honor of Satan. After a picture in Collin de Plancy's *Dictionnaire Infernal*, 1845.

Tomato Because of its red juice and its many seeds, it is associated among black African peoples with blood and fertility. — In Europe it, like the red APPLE, was a love symbol.

Tongue Because of its form and rapid movement, it is equated symbolically with the FLAME.

—Among some black African peoples, the tongue is associated with fertility because it is the organ that "generates" the word and hence is associated with rain, blood, and sperm.

Torch: The eye of Horus holding a torch. After a mural in an Egyptian grave.

Torch As a concentrated form of FIRE, the torch has the same meaning as fire. It is a common symbol of purification and enlightenment in rites of initiation. In antiquity the downward-pointed torch held in the hand of a youth or a genius was a graphic symbol of death as the extinguishing of life. —In medieval representations of the mortal sins, the torch sometimes symbolizes anger. —In folk usage the torch was associated with fertility, particularly in winter and spring.

Tortoise It is an important animal in the mythologies of India, China, and Japan. The markings on its carapace were interpreted as the patterns of the structure of the cosmos. Sometimes the tortoise itself or its feet are depicted as the supports of the universe, the throne of heaven, the primal waters, or the islands of the immortals. In Mongolian myths a golden tortoise carries the central MOUNTAIN of the universe. The arched carapace of the tortoise was sometimes regarded as a copy of the heavens, a sort of belly armor, raised above the disk of the earth previously believed to be flat. The tortoise itself was considered to be the mediator between heaven (see SKY) and EARTH, or a symbol of the entire universe. —Since it lives to a great age, it is also a symbol of immortality (e.g., on Chinese graves); from its shell and its brain, supposedly life-prolonging elixirs were prepared. In Japan, where the tortoise was reputed to live to an age of 12,000 years, it was often depicted along with the PINE and the CRANE, two other immortality symbols. —Its great age as well as the mysterious markings on its back, interpreted as writings, also made it a symbol of wisdom. In Africa, where it is sometimes represented with a back like a chess board, it symbolizes wisdom, adroitness, and power; its carapace represents the vault of heaven. —Since it can withdraw into its shell as into another world, it is a symbol of concentration and meditation particularly in India. —In China the tortoise is the embodiment of winter, the north, and water. —Because of its

Tortoise: Detail from a picture of the creation of the world in which the primeval sea of milk is changed into butter through periodic turning of the world axis, which rests on a tortoise. After a Hindu painting.

numerous progeny, it was regarded in antiquity as a fertility symbol and was sacred to Aphrodite (Venus); because of the phallic form of its head, it was also sacred to Pan. Its ability to withdraw into its shell made it a symbol of domestic virtues as well. —Especially in the Orient and in that part of the Occident influenced by the Orient, the tortoise was regarded as a demonic animal in league with dark powers. For example, depictions of the tortoise (as darkness) warring with the cock (as LIGHT) derive from this idea. —For the church patriarchs the (swamp) tortoise living in the mud was a symbol of baseness and mere sensual pleasure. Since in antiquity its shell was used to make the sounding board of the lyre, the tortoise is also mentioned in Christian literature as a symbol of the moral transformation of sinful flesh by the power of the spirit. —"Turtle Island" is an American Indian term for North America. The Ojibway creation story contains details of how the turtle created the earth.

Touch-Me-Not See MIMOSA.

Tower It is a symbol of power or of transcending the everyday level. Because of its form it is a phallic symbol; however, when windowless and closed, it can be a symbol of virginity (thus Mary is compared with a tower of ivory). —As a fortified space isolated from the world, the tower can also be a symbol of philosophical thought and meditation (although IVORY TOWER has negative connotations). —In medieval Christian art, the tower represents vigilance. In early Christian times, a tower often symbolized the entire "sacred city"; a *lighthouse*—actually a tower with a light—was a symbol of the eternal goal toward which the SHIP of life steered across the waves of this existence. —The Babylonian stepped tower, the *ziggurat*, was probably a symbol of the world MOUNTAIN; the individual steps symbolized the incremental ascent of humans toward heaven. The Tower of Babel (see BABEL, TOWER OF) was a ziggurat.

Tower: The biblical images in the Song of Songs, as symbols of Mary, surrounding the Blessed Virgin (among them the tower of David). Picture in P. Canisius's *De Maria Virgine*, Ingolstadt, 1577.

Transmutation See V.I.T.R.I.O.L.

Treasure It appears in the mythological imagery of many peoples, especially as a hidden treasure, often guarded by MONSTERS. It is sometimes understood as the symbol of esoteric knowledge and, in the psychoanalytic view, as a symbol of the sought-after goal of individual development.

Tree It is a symbol having one of the widest ranges of meanings and the most extensive geographical distribution. As a powerful representation of the plant kingdom, the tree has been ritually revered as the image of divine essence or as the residence of numinous powers. The *deciduous tree*, with its annual renewal of foliage, is above all a symbol of the rebirth of life, victorious over death; the evergreen CONIFER is a symbol of immortality. The form of the tree—with its roots imprisoned in the earth, its powerful, vertically ascending trunk, and its crown that seems to strive toward heaven—has symbolized the union of the cosmic realms of the subterranean-chthonic, of terrestrial life, and of heaven. These aspects contribute to the idea of the world tree, which has been viewed as either supporting the world or, more often, as the embodiment of the WORLD AXIS (e.g., the ever verdant world ash, Yggdrasil, in Nordic mythology). The leaves and branches of such world trees are frequently inhabited by mythic animals, by the souls of the deceased or the unborn (often in the form of BIRDS), or by the rising and setting sun and moon. With probable symbolic reference to the ZODIAC, 12 sun birds that inhabit the branches of the world tree occur in many mythical world views (e.g., in India and China). Birds that live in the crown of the world tree represent higher levels of spiritual being and development. —Anthropomorphic interpretations of the tree (which stands erect like a human and which, humanlike, grows and passes away) are widespread; hence the tree appears as the mythical ancestor of humans among various peoples (e.g., in central Asia, Japan, Korea, Australia). The tree is further identified symbolically with the human being through the custom of wedding the bride with a tree before marriage; this custom is common in many regions in India, where its aim is to strengthen fertility.

Tree: Adam, Eve, and the serpent under the tree of knowledge. After a picture in the *Codex Vigilanus seu Albeldensis*.

Tree: Round dance around a tree idol. Clay figurine from Cypress, ca. 1000 B.C.

Similar to this custom are symbolic marriages between two trees, whose vital energy is supposed to transfer to a specific human couple. —The tree bearing fruit and granting shade and protection has been understood by many peoples as a feminine or maternal symbol, although the erect trunk is usually a phallic symbol. —The association of the tree and FIRE is also widespread and probably has to do with attributing life force to the tree. In the wood of certain trees, fire is supposedly concealed and is drawn out by rubbing. —In the Indian tradition, the image of a tree growing upside down, the roots anchored in heaven and its branches spread out under the earth, possibly signifies the life-giving power of the sun in the physical realm and the spiritual LIGHT in the spiritual realm (see DEPTH, HEIGHT). The *Bhagavad Gita* interprets the inverted tree as a symbol of the unfolding of all being out of a primal ground. The roots represent the principle of all manifestation; the branches, the concrete and detailed actualization of this principle. The inverted tree also occurs in other contexts (e.g., in the Cabala as the tree of life or in Islam as the tree of happiness or fortune). —In the Bible the tree appears in double form as the tree of life and the tree of knowledge of good and evil. The tree of life represents the primordial fullness of paradise and is a symbol of the hoped-for fulfillment of the end of time; the tree of knowledge, with its seductive fruits, represents the attraction of acting contrary to divine commandments. Christian art and literature create a close symbolic relationship between the tree of paradise and Christ's cross, which "has restored paradise to us" (see TREE CROSS) and is "the true tree of life." —Psychoanalysis sees in the tree a symbolic reference to the mother, to spiritual and intellectual development, or to death and rebirth. —Certain psychological procedures attempt to evaluate drawings of trees as symbolic expressions of the whole personality. See APPLE, ARBOR PHILOSOPHICA, ASH, CEDAR, CHRISTMAS TREE, CYPRESS, FIG TREE, LIME TREE, OAK, OLIVE TREE, PEACH TREE, PEAR TREE, PLUM TREE, ROOT OF JESSE, TREE CROSS, TREE OF LIFE.

Tree: The tree of knowledge in paradise, depicted as the tree of death. Woodcut by Jost Amman.

Tree: Trees of life. On Egyptian glass jar (the oldest in the world), 1500 B.C.

Tree cross: The personified Church with the verdant cross. Book illustration, ca. 1180.

Triangle: The eye in the triangle as symbol of God. Figure surmounting an altar.

Trident: Trident as attribute of Neptune.

Tree Cross Especially in Germany and Italy, it is a form of the cross of Christ with leaves, blossoms, and fruits, symbolizing victory over death (see TREE). —Occasionally a fruiting, leafed tree bearing a crucified figure refers to the tree of knowledge in paradise and thus to the victory over original sin through Christ.

Triangle Symbolically associated with the number THREE, in antiquity it was variously understood as a light symbol. With the apex pointing upward it is a common symbol of fire and masculine virility; with the apex pointing downward it is a symbol of water and the female sex. —The equilateral triangle is often used as a sign of God or harmony. In Christianity it is a Trinity symbol (often, especially since the seventeenth century, in conjunction with the hand, head, eye, or the Hebrew name of God, Yahweh). —In folk usage, the three was an apotropaic sign among magicians and mages. —For the Freemasons (among others), the three symbolizes the strength, beauty, and wisdom of God; the cornerstone of the Freemasons' temple; the realm of minerals, plants, and animals; the levels of spiritual development (*separatio, fermentatio, putrefactio*); right speech, right thought, right action; birth, maturity, and death; etc.

Trident A staff with three prongs used for spearing fish, it is an attribute of sea gods, particularly Poseidon, and also symbolizes the teeth of sea monsters, the rays of the sun, and lightning. —In India the trident is an attribute of the god Shiva and symbolizes threefold time (past, present, and future) or the three fundamental stages or qualities of the empirical world (becoming, being, and passing away).

T-Square An instrument used in drawing right angles (see SQUARE), it is a common symbol of the EARTH (with reference to the number FOUR). Since only right angles can be drawn using the T-square, it is also a symbol of uprightness, sincerity, and lawfulness. It plays a special role in the symbolic thought of the Freemasons. It is also associated symbolically with the COMPASS.

Tumulus See GRAVE.

Twenty-Four

Turban The Hindu and Moslem headdress made of strips of cloth wound about the head, it is part of various (sometimes quite magnificent) outfits and is often a symbol of dignity and power. The Muslims distinguish themselves from the unbelievers by wearing the turban.

Turkey For the Indians of North and Central America, it is a symbol of female fertility and masculine virility; it is frequently used as a sacrificial animal in fertility ceremonies.

Turquoise It is a decorative blue to blue-green stone symbolically associated in many Indian cultures with the SUN and with FIRE. It is used in the Orient as an AMULET.

Turban: After a picture of Sultan Selim III.

Twelve The fundamental number of the duodecimal system (used by the Babylonians) and of the sexagesimal system, it was thus a sacred, lucky number and a symbol of spacio-temporal fulfillment or wholeness. It is still significant in astronomy and in the measurement of time (e.g., twelve is the number of the months of the year, the hours of the day and the night, the signs of the zodiac). In China and central Asia there was also a time measurement of periods lasting twelve years. —In alchemy, twelve is a symbolically significant number because, among other reasons, it contains as factors the number of the four ELEMENTS and the three alchemical basic principles (SALT, SULFUR, and mercury [see MERCURIUS]). —In the Bible and in Christian symbolism, twelve plays a major role as the symbol of completeness and perfection. It is the number of the sons of Jacob and hence of the tribes of Israel; of the gems on the breastplate of the Jewish high priest; of the apostles; of the gates of the Heavenly Jerusalem (see JERUSALEM, HEAVENLY); the woman of the Apocalypse wears a crown with twelve stars; and the number of the elect is 12 × 12,000, a figure which symbolizes the totality of all saints.

Twenty-Four It is the total number of the hours of day and night, and the double of the perfect number TWELVE. It therefore represents the number of harmonious equilibrium. In the Apocalypse it is the number of old men.

Twenty-One As the product of THREE times SEVEN, it is a holy number in the Bible and a symbol of divine wisdom.

Twins: The astrological sign for Gemini.

Twins They occur in various forms: identical in color and shape; one light and the other dark; one red and the other blue; one with the head toward the sky, the other with the head toward the earth; etc. Because of their dual identity, twins represent the inner opposites in the human being or the duality of DAY and NIGHT, LIGHT and SHADOW, equilibrium and imbalance, harmony and discord. —The cosmogonic beliefs of various peoples (e.g., the American Indians) feature twins, one of whom is good, the other evil; the one helpful for civilization, the other destructive. —*Gemini*, the twins, is the third sign of the ZODIAC; the corresponding element is AIR.

Twins: Personifications of the astrological signs. After a relief by Agostino di Duccio, Rimini, Tempio Mala-testiano, 15th century.

Two Among the Pythagoreans it was regarded as the first true number because it represented the first plurality. Two "gives birth" to multiplicity. Two is the symbol of doubling, separation, discord, opposition, and conflict, but also equilibrium. It symbolizes the movement that initiates all development. —Numerous phenomena support a dualistic view of the world, such as the opposites of creator and created, LIGHT and SHADOW, male and female, spirit and matter, good and evil, life and death, DAY and NIGHT, heaven (see SKY) and EARTH, land and WATER, active and passive, RIGHT AND LEFT. Pronounced dualistic world views are represented in the concepts of YIN AND YANG in Chinese philosophy, and the principles of good (Ahura Mazda) and evil (Ahriman) in Persian Zoroastrianism.

Tyche Also known as the Roman FORTUNA, she is the Greek goddess of fate.

Udjat eye See EYE.

Umbilical Cord It is a symbol of the tie maintained with the mother and early childhood.

Umbrella See PARASOL.

Unicorn It is a fabulous animal, usually white, in the form of a GOAT, ass, rhinoceros, STEER, or (particularly later) HORSE with *one* horn. Known to many peoples, it was popularized in folk belief in the Christian Orient by PHYSIOLOGUS. The single horn can be considered a phallic symbol (see ONAGER), but since it is located on the forehead, the "seat" of the intellect, it is also a symbol of the sublimation of sexual powers and could thus be regarded as signifying virginal purity. —The straight and pointed (and sometimes spiral shaped) horn, moreover, is also a symbol of the sun ray (see SUN). —In Zoroastrianism the unicorn symbolized the pure power through which Ahriman was vanquished. —In China it represented the virtues of rulership. —The unicorn is a Christian symbol of strength and purity. According to saga it can be caught and tamed only by a pure virgin to whose lap it flees when it is pursued. Hence in Christian art there are depictions of Mary with the unicorn in her lap, a reference to the Immaculate Conception (*Maria immaculata*). —Unicorn powder (from the ground horn) was supposed to heal wounds, and medicinal powers were ascribed to unicorn's heart; for these reasons the unicorn was sometimes chosen as the mark of apothecaries.

Unicorn: Virgin with a unicorn. From *Defensorum Virginitatis*.

Unleavened Bread See LEAVEN.

Unveiling See VEIL.

Uraeus See SERPENT.

Urn See GRAVE.

Uroboros It is a SERPENT depicted as biting or swallowing its own tail (sometimes also shown as one or two dragons or, less often, as one or two long-necked birds). It is a symbol of infinity,

Uroboros: From Horapollo's *Selecta Hieroglyphica*, 1597.

eternal return, or the descent of spirit into the physical world and its return. In alchemy it represents mutable matter.

Valerian It is any of a genus of perennial herbs, many of which were used in antiquity as medicinal plants. From the Indian nard of the valerian family came the famous "nard oil" with which Jesus was anointed in Bethany; in this connection the plant sometimes appears in tableaux of the Middle Ages. —In medieval folk belief valerian was used to "smoke out" the Devil and drive away witches.

Valley In contrast to the MOUNTAIN, the valley is a symbol of descent and depth. In a negative sense it represents spiritual and emotional loss; in a positive sense it represents a deepening of experience and knowledge. In contrast to the "masculine" mountain, which rises up, the valley is a symbol of the womb. —In Islam it signifies the path of spiritual development. —The symbolic valley is often encountered in Taoist literature. The broad, open valley symbolizes openness vis-a-vis heavenly influences; as a place where all the waters streaming from the mountains collect, it represents spiritual concentration. —Among various peoples the green, fertile valley is a symbol of plenty and prosperity in contrast to the sterile mountains.

Vegetation Rites They are ritual, symbolic actions through which the growth of plants is supposed to be influenced. The desired height of grain, for example, was symbolized by equally high leaps; the fertility or fertilization of the earth was represented by the ritual watering of a virgin, etc.

Veil: The veil falling from the countenance of the Ancient of Days. After a miniature in the Tours Bible.

Veil It is a symbol of disguise and secrecy. *Unveiling*, however, symbolizes revelation, recognition, and initiation. Sometimes access to spiritual secrets is expressed in the unveiling of the human body. The ritual unveiling of the Egyptian goddess Isis, for example, was a symbol of the appearance of divine light. In this respect, Christ's nakedness on the cross is sometimes

interpreted as a sign of the manifestation of esoteric secrets. — In Indian philosophy, *Maya*, the
condition of the possibility of all transient appearances, is compared with a veil; like the veil,
Maya simultaneously reveals and hides. Because it conceals the true ground of all being, it
can impart to the world of appearances a seemingly objective character. — In Islam, the countenance of God is believed to be concealed in
70,000 veils of light and shadow; they mute the
divine radiance, making it bearable for humans.
According to many interpreters, however, they
do not actually surround God, but envelop his
creatures; only the saints are able to raise these
veils to some extent. — The Koran speaks of a
veil separating the damned from the elect. — In
cult and folk usage, the veil often serves as protection from hostile demons. — As a sign of reverence or fear of the sacred, sacrificers often
wear a veil before their faces. — The veil of
mourning symbolizes the mourner's withdrawal;
the bride's veil or the Moslem woman's veil symbolizes modesty and is a sign of marriage. The
veils of nuns, who consider themselves to be
the brides of Christ, have a similar meaning.

Venus See COPPER.

Veronica See SPEEDWELL.

Vetch It was a symbol in ancient Egypt of the
delicacy of young girls. — In medieval Christian
art it is a symbol of Mary.

Vetch

Vineyard See GRAPEVINE.

Viola Tricolor See PANSY.

1 Violet It is a fragrant, low-growing, usually
blue-blossomed spring flower. At festivals in antiquity, THYRSUS staffs and the participants in the
festivals were crowned with violets, primarily because these flowers were believed to protect a
person from intoxication and headaches. — In
the Middle Ages, the violet signified modest vir-
tuousness and humility and thus was a symbol
of Mary. Because of its color, it is also a symbol
of Christ's passion.

2 Violet A hue combining RED and BLUE, it often
symbolizes mediation; balance between heaven

Violet

(see SKY) and EARTH, spirit and body, love and wisdom; and moderation. —In Christian art, violet is often the color of Christ's passion (as symbolic reference to God's complete union with humans through Christ's life and death); in the Catholic liturgy, violet symbolizes seriousness and mindfulness of penitence and is consequently the color of Advent and Easter. —In folk imagery and custom, violet sometimes symbolizes fidelity.

Virgin: The astrological sign for Virgo.

Virgin A virgin is a symbol of innocence and the abundance of possibilities not yet developed. The Christian mystics also compared a virgin to the soul ready to receive God. —*Virgo*, the virgin, is the sixth sign of the ZODIAC; its element is the EARTH.

Virgo See VIRGIN.

V.I.T.R.I.O.L. As a symbolic formula of the alchemists, it had many meanings. It was often used for the process of *transmutation*, the transformation of base metals into precious metals, especially GOLD. The letters were usually understood to be the initial letters of the formula *Visita inferiora terrae rectificando invenies occultum lapidem* ("Seek out the lower realms of the earth, perfect them, and thou wilt find the hidden stone," i.e., the PHILOSOPHERS' STONE). As an esoteric initiation formula, V.I.T.R.I.O.L. probably must be understood in connection with deep introspection into one's own soul and the search for one's innermost essence.

Vulture A symbolic animal associated in several American Indian cultures with the purifying and vivifying power of FIRE and the SUN; for the Mayans it was also a death symbol. —Since it

Vulture: The vulture as protector of the Egyptian kings.

eats carrion and transforms it into vital energy, the vulture is sometimes considered by Africans to be the being who knows the secret of the transformation of worthless material into GOLD. —In Egypt the vulture was a protector of the pharaohs; the Egyptian queens frequently wore the protective vulture-shaped headdress, the wings of which covered the sides of the head while the vulture's head extended above the brow. —In antiquity the vulture was regarded as a bird whose flight augured fate; it was sacred to Apollo. —Since according to ancient natural science the eggs of the female vulture are fertilized by the east wind, it is a Christian symbol of the virginity of Mary.

Wagon See CHARIOT.

Walnut See NUT.

Warcry See SHOUT.

Water It is a symbol with a very complex range of meanings. As an unformed, undifferentiated mass, it symbolizes the abundance of possibilities or the primal origin of all being, the *prima materia*. In this sense it occurs in numerous creation myths. In Indian mythology, for example, the world EGG floats on it; Genesis speaks of the spirit of God, which at the beginning hovered over the face of the deep. In the mythologies of the most diverse peoples there is the symbolic act of an animal diving into the depths to retrieve a piece of earth from the waters. —In Islam, Hinduism, Buddhism, and Christianity, water is a symbol of bodily, emotional, and spiritual cleansing and the power of renewal (see BAPTISM, BATH, HAND AND FOOT WASHING); the FOUNTAIN of youth shares this symbolism. —In China, water is assigned to the yin principle (see YIN AND YANG); similarly, in other cultures water is usually associated with the feminine, the dark depths, and the MOON. —Water is a universal symbol of fertility and life (see RAIN, SEA); for this reason it is sometimes juxtaposed to the DESERT. Likewise spiritual fertility and spiritual life are often represented by water (see FOUNTAIN); for

Water: The water pourer, Aquarius. From the zodiac of Dendera.

example, the Bible speaks of the water of life in the spiritual sense. —Water that cannot be contained within any boundaries appears in various contexts as an eternity symbol (e.g., the water of eternal life). —Water can also have negative symbolic meaning as a destructive force (e.g., the flood). —Psychoanalysis regards water primarily as a symbol of the feminine and of the powers of the unconscious. —In alchemy water is designated by an inverted triangle. —In the ZODIAC water is associated with the astrological signs of *Cancer, Scorpio*, and *Pisces*.

Waterfall It is an important motif in Chinese landscape painting. Its plunging downward is viewed as the opposite of the upward-striving cliff (see ROCK); its dynamism is considered to represent the opposite of the cliff's immobility. The waterfall and the cliff are associated with the YIN AND YANG pair of opposites. Its seemingly constant form, which endures the continual change of the flowing water, is regarded in Buddhism as a symbol of the transitoriness and the insubstantiality of everything worldly.

Water:
Water as the element uniting the opposites. After a picture in *Tresor des Tresors*, 17th century.

Waves While they are generally associated with the symbolism of WATER, waves in the form of *billows* assume an impersonal, threatening character. Waves and billows are consequently symbols not only of movement and liveliness, but also of uncontrolled powers.

Waves: Storm at sea. After a miniature in a pericope, ca. 1040.

Weapon A symbol of power and an attribute of heroes and warrior gods, the weapon has many symbolic meanings, since it serves for attack as well as for defense and protection. In the symbolic language of the Bible, both Yahweh and Satan have armor and weapons. —Other symbols can serve as spiritual weapons (e.g., a cross held out before oneself).

Weasel See ERMINE.

Weathercock See COCK.

Weaving It is frequently a symbol of the workings of the powers of fate. In Islam, for example, the structure and the movements of the entire universe are compared to a woven cloth or fabric. The SPIDER weaving its web is sometimes seen in this context.

Weeping Willow See WILLOW.

Whale It is a symbol of the abysmal, multivocal dark. It appears, for example, in the Bible story of the prophet Jonah, who evaded the divine charge to preach in Nineveh, was cast overboard, swallowed by a huge fish (usually represented as a whale), and cast up on land 3 days later (symbolically interpreted as Christ's death, entombment, and resurrection). The whale, like other animals such as the CROCODILE, elephant, and TORTOISE, is seen in the mythologies of many peoples as carrying the universe.

Whale: Jonah emerges from the jaws of the whale. After a picture in the *Speculum Humanae Salvationis,* 14th century.

Wheat The sowing, growth, and harvesting of grain, specifically of wheat, have represented birth and death as well as death and rebirth. In ancient Greece, the head of grain, as the fruit of the maternal womb of the earth, symbolized the fruit of the human body; it was a symbol of Demeter and played a central role in the Eleusinian mysteries. —In Egypt the growing wheat was regarded as a symbol of Osiris rising from the dead. —In the Middle Ages the grain of wheat signified Christ descending to and resurrected from the underworld. To the present day, the Eucharist is symbolically alluded to on altar furnishings by the images of the ear of grain and the grape. The stalk of wheat, moreover, is a symbol of Mary, for she contained the grains from which came the flour for the host. Mary, depicted in a dress showing ears of grain, is also compared to the field on which Christ, as wheat, could grow.

Wheat: Ancient coin showing a sheaf of wheat, here probably symbolizing fertility and prosperity.

Wheel It combines the symbolic content of the CIRCLE with the idea of movement, becoming, and passing away. The radiating spokes also play an important symbolic role. In most cultures the wheel appears as a sun symbol; it is still a common symbol in many places at the time of the winter solstice. The four-spoked wheel was a symbol in many prehistoric cultures in Europe (it appeared in central Germany for the first time in the Neolithic age) and was probably considered a solar symbol. The many rosettes found in architectural decoration in the Mideast may also be associated with the solar symbolism of the wheel. —The wheel is a major symbol of Bud-

Wheat: Madonna in dress with wheat motif. Woodcut, 15th century.

Wheel: Representation from the Temple of the Sun in Konarak, India.

Wheels: The wheels of Ezekiel. Detail after a miniature in the Gospel Book of the library in Aschaffenburg, 13th century.

Wheel: Rose window as a wheel.

Wheel of Fortune: Picture after Petrarch's *Concerning the Medicine of Both Kinds of Fortune*, 1532.

dhism, representing the various forms of existence that stand in need of redemption (the "Wheel of Life"), as well as the teachings of the Buddha (the "Wheel of Doctrine"). —The wheel can also symbolize the entire cosmos (with reference to constant cycles of renewal in the cosmos, e.g., the "rota mundi" of the Rosicrucians). —On early Christian grave stones, the wheel symbol represents God and eternity. The Book of Daniel reports the vision of flaming wheels around the head of God, and Ezekiel writes of wheels with eyes that simultaneously turn and remain still, thus expressing God's omnipotence. —The ZODIAC (the "circle of animals") is often compared with a wheel. —According to Jung, the central rose window of medieval cathedrals is equivalent to a wheel symbol, a special form of the MANDALA signifying unity in multiplicity. See WHEEL OF FORTUNE.

Wheel of Fortune It is a special form of the WHEEL symbol, emphasizing transitoriness and perpetual change. In antiquity a nude youth was represented standing on two winged wheels, which symbolized not only passing fortune but also the propitious moment, the *kairos*. TYCHE, (FORTUNA), the goddess of fortune and fate, stands on a wheel. —In the art of the Middle Ages, the wheel of fortune was often depicted being turned by Fortuna and with people or allegorical figures clinging to it; it symbolizes the change of fortune, the perpetual transformation of all beings, and occasionally the Last Judgment.

Whip It is a symbol of power and judicial authority. —Sometimes LIGHTNING is compared to the blow of a whip. —In the Vedas, whip lashes transform the primal milky ocean (see MILK) into BUTTER, the first food of living creatures.

White The color of LIGHT, purity, and perfection. Like its opposite, BLACK, white has a special place among the colors of the spectrum (which combined yield white). It is closely associated with the absolute (both the beginning and the end, as well as their union) and consequently is used at marriages, initiations, and death rites. It is the color of mourning in Slavic lands and in

Asia, for example, and occasionally at the French court. —White was the preferred color of specially selected sacrificial animals. —Priests often wear white garments to symbolize spirit and light, and the angels and the blessed in Christianity are often clothed in white for the same reason. Newly baptized Christians wear white clothing; at Christ's transfiguration his garments became "white as snow"; the white ceremonial dress of brides, postulants, and those making first communion signify innocence and virginity. —In contrast to the vital color RED, white is also the color of ghosts and specters. Sometimes the color red is associated with man and white with woman.

Wickerwork In early medieval ornamental art, it was probably a symbol of the movements of growth.

Wickerwork: From a Romanesque chapel.

Willow It is a tree or bush that was regarded in antiquity as sterile and that was consequently associated with chastity (as late as the Middle Ages). —Since one can endlessly cut new shoots from it, it was compared in the Bible to an infinite source of wisdom. —In folk belief the willow can, through magic, vicariously absorb illnesses. It is supposed to be a favorite dwelling place for spirits and witches. Willow branches blessed on Palm Sunday were believed to protect against lightning, storms, and evil influences. —Because its form is likened to streams of tears falling to the ground, the *weeping willow* is often a symbol of the wake for the dead.

Willow: The weeping willow.

Wind Because it is intangible and often changes direction quickly, it is a symbol of transitoriness, inconstancy, and nothingness. As STORM, it is also a symbol of divine powers or human passions; as *breath*, it is a symbol of the effects or the expression of divine spirit. Consequently, winds, like angels, can also be regarded as messengers of God. —In Persia the wind was believed to support the world and be the guarantor of cosmic and moral equilibrium. —In Islam the wind carries the primal waters which, for their part, support the divine THRONE.

Window It sometimes represents receptivity and openness to outside influences. —The stained glass windows of Gothic churches often symbolize the colorful abundance of the Heavenly Jerusalem (see JERUSALEM, HEAVENLY). —In the art of the Middle Ages, the window, which itself does not give forth light but lets the light of the sun shine through, often signifies Mary the Mother of God, who in purity and humility bore the Son of God.

Wine Because of its color and the fact that it is made of the "vital sap" of the grapevine, it is often a symbol of blood (for the Greeks it was the blood of Dionysus). —It is frequently regarded as an elixir of life and a potion of immortality (as, e.g., among Semitic peoples, the Greeks, and Taoists). In Greece, wine sacrifices to underworld gods were forbidden, since wine was the drink of the living. —Because of its intoxicating effect, it was sometimes regarded as a means of attaining esoteric knowledge. —In Islam wine is, among other things, a beverage of divine love and a symbol of spiritual knowledge and the fullness of being in eternity; hence in Sufism the soul was imagined to be surrounded by the wine of immortality before the creation of the world. —According to biblical tradition, wine is a symbol of the joy and abundance of God's gifts. In the transformation of the Eucharist in Christianity, wine has its most sacred and deepest significance as the blood of Christ.

Wing See BIRDS.

Witch's Foot See PENTAGRAM.

Wolf It is an animal that symbolizes the wild and diabolical, as well as positive, spiritual aspects. Since it sees well in darkness, it was regarded as a symbol associated with light, particularly in northern Europe and in Greece; thus it appears as a companion to Apollo (Apollo Lykios). —The Mongolians regarded a heavenly wolf as the ancestor of Genghis Khan; the Chinese saw it as the guardian of the heavenly palace. —There is also the legendary female wolf that suckled the abandoned twins, Romulus and Remus, and that became the emblem of Rome. She is a symbol of the helpful animal or of chthonic powers. —Like the DOG, the wolf also

Wolf: The Capitoline wolf.

occasionally appears as psychopomp (spirit guide). —The ravenous, all-devouring wolf occurs in Germanic mythology as a dangerous demon that announces the end of the world with its howling. —In Hinduism the wolf is a companion of horrific deities. —Among many peoples it is a symbol of war or aggression. —In antiquity the wolf was associated with the underworld (e.g., Hades wears a cloak of wolf pelt). —Christian symbolism refers principally to the relationship between the wolf and the lamb, in which the LAMB symbolizes the faithful and the wolf the powers threatening the faithful. A wolf biting a lamb in the throat is also a symbol of Christ's death. Among the seven mortal sins the wolf symbolizes gluttony (see GULA) as well as avarice (see AVARITIA). —Medieval folk belief regarded the wolf as a threatening, demonic animal; sorcerers and witches or the Devil appeared in the form of wolves. In many sagas and fairy tales the wolf also appears in a similarly negative sense. —The proverbial wolf in sheep's clothing is a symbol of feigned harmlessness.

Womb It is a symbol of fertility and of containment and protection, as well as of mysterious, hidden powers. The alchemical oven, in which physically, mystically, and morally significant transformations took place, was often compared with the womb. See INITIATION, YONI.

Wood As one of the oldest and most important raw materials, wood was originally equated with matter in general or with the *prima materia*. Wood is thus closely associated symbolically with the complex of meanings embracing "vital energy," "mother," and "carrying, containing, protecting." —In China wood, one of the five ELEMENTS, corresponds symbolically to spring.

Woodpecker The *green woodpecker* is regarded by many peoples as bringing protection and good fortune, and sometimes is seen as prophetic and weatherwise. Among the Germanic tribes it was also considered a symbol of LIGHTNING (possibly because with its long, pointed beak it could penetrate the bark of trees) and of thunder (because of its pecking).

—In Christianity the woodpecker is a symbol of incessant prayer because of its continual hammering. Since it destroys WORMS, it was also regarded as an enemy of the Devil, and hence is a symbol of Christ.

Word See SPEECH.

World Axis Many peoples believed that an axis unites heaven (see SKY) and EARTH, or the underworld, earth, and heaven. Such an axis symbolizes the interrelationship of all levels or realms of the cosmos known to humans, and represents the center around which they are organized. The world axis has been imagined in many forms, among the most common of which are the COLUMN, pillar, ascending column of smoke, TREE, high MOUNTAIN, STAFF, LANCE, and Indian LINGA. —The world axis has been linked with symbolism of LIGHT; thus, according to Plato, it consists of radiant diamonds. —Christian literature also compares Christ's cross with the world axis. —Tantrism sees in the *spinal column* a symbol of the world axis.

World Egg See EGG.

Worm As an animal that primarily lives under the earth, it is a symbol for some peoples of life awakening from darkness and death. —In the Middle Ages it was occasionally identified with the SERPENT and the Devil.

Wormwood A variety of mugwort that grows to a height of one meter and is found in the warmer regions of Eurasia, it is generally used for spice and medicine. It symbolizes pain and bitterness because of its bitter taste.

Wrapping In China, since ancient times, the wrapping of objects has followed definite rules having not to do with the object to be wrapped, but rather with the symbolism of the number five, which the Chinese consider sacred. The object, flanked by the four corners and sides of the paper, cloth, etc., represents the number five and thus is analogous to the center of the world.

Wreath Differentiated from the CROWN primarily by the material of which it is made (usually foliage and flowers), it served in antiquity as ornament, decoration, and a sign of being chosen by the gods in contests, festivals, and sacrifices (sacrificial animals were also crowned with wreaths). It was believed that wearing a wreath (initially of ivy, later often of herbs) could protect one from drunkenness. —The Bible speaks of wreaths of honor, joy, and victory (largely synonymous with the concept of the crown). —In Christianity the antique wreath of victory was a sign of having achieved salvation; in this context it appears on gravestones and sometimes in conjunction with the CHRIST MONOGRAM or with the DOVE and the LAMB. —In antiquity, the Middle Ages, and in modern times, regents and victors have been depicted with laurel WREATHS. Since the Age of Humanism, the laurel wreath has also been a favorite mark of distinction for outstanding artists, poets, and scholars. —The advent wreath, consisting of four candles in evergreen boughs, appeared after World War I as a symbol of preparation and hope; it is a common symbol among Germanic-speaking peoples. See MYRTLE.

Yantra In Hinduism it is the customary graphic visualization of a deity or divine force, especially of the goddess Shri as Shakti. The yantra is also a symbolic visualization of the originally undifferentiated unity with Brahma, which unfolds as the multiplicity of the empirical world; it is commonly used as an image upon which to meditate and also as an AMULET.

Yellow It is associated with the symbolism of GOLD, LIGHT, and the SUN; like gold, it is symbolic of eternity and transfiguration. —As the color of autumn, yellow is considered to be the color of ripeness or maturity. —In China it was contrasted to BLACK but was also its complement; the close connection between yellow and black corresponds to the manifold relationships of the yang (yellow) and yin (black) (see YIN AND YANG). Hence, for example, yellow arises out of black as the earth arises out of the primal waters. Since yellow designates the center of the uni-

Yantra

verse, it was also the color of the emperor.
—Sometimes a distinction is made in the meaning ascribed to various nuances of yellow. For example, golden yellow represents goodness and light; sulfur yellow, evil or devilishness. In Islam, for example, golden yellow designates wisdom and good advice; pale yellow, betrayal and deception. —In ancient Egypt and during the Middle Ages, negative interpretations predominated. Yellow was the color of envy or disgrace (e.g., in the clothing of Jews, heretics, prostitutes). In a positive sense, it occurs in medieval murals primarily as a substitute for gold.

Yew Tree As an evergreen and because of its longevity, it is an immortality symbol. Since its needles and seeds are poisonous, it was also seen as deadly and hence as symbolizing both death and resurrection. —In the Middle Ages it was thought to be a remedy against enchantment.

Yin and Yang They are the two complementary, fundamental cosmological principles of Chinese philosophy to which all things, beings, events, and periods of time are assigned. The yin principle corresponds to the negative, the earth, femininity, darkness, passivity, moistness, and the broken line; the yang principle corresponds to the positive, the sky, masculinity, brightness, activity, dryness, and the unbroken line. The two principles represent a polarization into which the unity of the primal, original condition fell. They are graphically represented as a circle symmetrically divided by an S-shaped curved line. One half of the circle is dark, the other half light, yet in the center of each is a point of the other color, signifying the interdependence of the two principles. The influences of yin and yang are never fundamentally hostile to each other; rather, they are constantly influencing each other, and the intensity of influence periodically increases or decreases in specific time periods.

Yin and Yang: Adapted as trademarks for macrobiotic foods.

Yoke It is a symbol of suppression, heavily imposed burdens, and the unhappy union of two individuals or matters (e.g., the "yoke of marriage"). —In the religions of India, however, the yoke (the English word derives from the Indo-European root *yug*, as does the word *yoga*) symbolizes, in the positive sense, subordination to spiritual principles, self-discipline that embraces body and spirit.

Yoni As the female correspondent to the LINGA, it symbolizes the maternal womb and the capacity to give birth. The yoni is usually depicted as the base of the linga. The graphic sign for the yoni is a TRIANGLE standing on its apex.

Yoni

Zedrat Lemon Known in the Far East as the "Hand of Buddha," it is a symbol of long life. Because of its numerous seeds, the zedrat lemon is also a fertility symbol.

Ziggurat See STAIRS, TOWER.

Zodiac As the zone that is apparently traversed by the sun once each year, it lies on either side of the ecliptic. It is approximately 18 degrees wide and embraces the courses of the sun, the planets, and the moon. It is divided into 12 constellations of stars or corresponding signs. From all locations on earth it appears the same; however, various peoples have either seen different (although usually 12) images in the constellations or have named them differently (although they are the same constellations of stars for all peoples). For example, what we know as *Cancer*, the CRAB, the Chinese call the cat. Because

Zodiac: Representation of the relationships between humans and the astrological signs. Woodcut from a calendar, Augsburg, 1490.

Zodiac:
Astrological signs and their associated planets. (An asterisk indicates "day houses" of the planets; the remaining are "night houses".)

Spring signs:
Aries (Mars)
Taurus (Venus)
Gemini (Mercury)

Summer signs:
Cancer (Moon)
Leo* (Sun)
Virgo* (Mercury)

Autumn signs:
Libra* (Venus)
Scorpio* (Mars)
Sagittarius* (Jupiter)

Winter signs:
Capricorn* (Saturn)
Aquarius (Saturn or Uranus)
Pisces (Jupiter or Neptune)

of the precession of the equinoxes, the zero or starting point of the zodiac is continually shifting; thus the constellation and the astrological sign must be distinguished (e.g., on February 2, 1978, the sun entered the constellation Aquarius, but on February 19, 1978, the sun entered the astrological sign Pisces). In astrology, the individual signs of the zodiac correspond to various forms of life. There are countless speculations concerning why signs are assigned to specific character types (as, e.g., Virgo type, Aquarian type). For example, it is assumed that the character of a person born at a certain time of year is influenced by a specific astrological sign, and that human experience is symbolically connected to the character of the sign for which the constellation was named. —The astrological signs form a connecting link between many symbolic details of astrology and alchemy. In medieval medicine, and into the eighteenth century, the cosmic astrological signs were seen to have corresponding expression in the human organism. —The idea of the cosmic WHEEL links the zodiac with the symbol of the wheel. —In Christian art of the Middle Ages, the zodiac (often associated with monthly labors) symbolizes passing time, but also the divine immutability beyond all change. The astrological signs are also depicted as symbols of the heavenly spheres. Individually, the various signs of the zodiac referred to the 12 apostles or to various Christian subjects, frequently with varying meanings. For example, the RAM, *Aries*, was interpreted as a symbol of Christ the Lamb; the TWINS, *Gemini*, as the Old Testament and the New Testament; the *lion*, LEO, as a symbol of resurrection and of victory over the SCORPION, *Scorpio*, symbolizing the serpent; the FISH, *Pisces*, as the Jews and the heathen saved by the water of baptism, which, in turn, is poured by the water bearer, *Aquarius*.